Happy 40t

" The Rising o
is the Risin

It wont take another forty
before I see you on the
barricades.

Lots of love
Tim
xxx

We will Smash This Prison!

Gail Omvedt

We Will Smash This Prison!

Indian Women in Struggle

Gail Omvedt

Zed Press, 57 Caledonian Road, London N1 9DN.

We Will Smash This Prison! was first
published by Zed Press, 57 Caledonian Road,
London N1 9DN in January 1980.

Copyright © Gail Omvedt, 1980

ISBN Hb   0   905762 44   4
       Pb   0   905762 45   2

Designed by Mayblin/Shaw
Typeset by Kathy Munro
Proofread by Beverley Brown
Printed by Maple Vail, USA
Cover photo courtesy of A. Nadeschdin

Published and distributed in the Republic of
India by Orient Longman Ltd., 3/5 Asaf
Ali Road, New Delhi 110002.

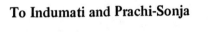
To Indumati and Prachi-Sonja

Contents

Acknowledgements

The research project which made possible my involvement
with Indian women in 1975-76 was financed by a grant
from the American Association of University Women and
a supplementary grant from the Academic Senate of the
University of California, San Diego. I owe thanks to all
those mentioned in the book and to many more besides,
and especially to my husband Bharat Patankar, for his
continuing help and stimulus to my work, and to my
mother-in-law Indumati Patankar for making its completion
possible.

Introduction

The first time I ever gave a speech on women's liberation was to a group of illiterate, ex-Untouchable agricultural labourers in India.

The time was February 1971. The place was a big capitalist farm in the state of Maharashtra in western India, an area just entering into the throes of what was to be a three-year drought. I was there because I had been invited by the local communist organizers of an agricultural labourers union in that area, and I had made my acquaintance with them in the process of doing PhD research on a peasant-based movement in the state which had challenged Brahman dominance and called for the abolition of the caste system. Coming out of Berkeley (in the US) in the 'big years' of student unrest, I had no compunctions about meeting left-wing leaders and was interested in the current struggles of the ex-Untouchables, now called Dalits or 'downtrodden'. And when I found both were interested in American struggles – in the anti-War movement, the Black movement, the women's movement – we found common ground. I wrote articles for local newspapers, I gave talks, I attended rallies and sat and watched red flags flying while leaders spoke of revolutionary upheavals around the world. And, finally, I found myself there in Ahmednagar, talking in a tumultuous hall thronged with women field labourers and a few of the lower middle class wives of government clerks who were members of a local 'women's club'. I discussed my talk beforehand with a district union leader; his suggestions ('talk about double exploitation – they're exploited both as workers and as women') were not so different from what I was going to say anyway. I gave my talk in English, and it was translated into Marathi and later printed in a special issue of their newspaper, *Village Toiler*.

Why were communist organizers in western India interested in women's

1

liberation? The reason was simple.

'Women were the most militant,' they said. It was not only these particular leaders of the local Lal Nishan (Red Flag) Party who said it, but other organizers also, other communists, independents, young men of new Marxist groups. They were all men, but they gave their testimony: 'Women are the most ready to fight, the first to break through police lines, the last to go home.' The peasant leader who mobilized his entire village to stage demonstrations and refuse to pay taxes until a road was built, was asked who gave the firmest support. 'The women first . . . '

In these beginning years of famine in Maharashtra, there were demonstrations throughout the rural areas — marches, sit-downs, *gheraos* (encirclements) of officials — demanding that the government set up relief works because there were no crops and no jobs in the fields. Women were prominent among agricultural labourers in the area, and they made up nearly half the workers on the relief projects. Not only lower caste women, but also women from peasant families who had never worked outside their own homes or plots of land before, came to the projects. And these women had to confront not only rising prices and the drastic lack of food to feed their families, but also the cheating and petty oppression of supervisors on the job. Naturally they were angry — and determined. It was the women in Ahmednagar district, I was told later, who invented the technique of 'road-closing', blocking off traffic on roads to get the attention of the government. One young activist told me, 'Sometimes it was the women who suggested actions and carried them out. For instance in Shrigonda, when one government official didn't get their pay to them in time, they tied him to a tree and kept him until evening! That was never suggested before by any political party . . . '

It was the militancy of women, the realization that women were a *force* in movements for change, that impelled these male left-wing leaders to deal with women's own oppression. In the face of all the traditional stereotypes of the submissive home-bound women, these women were workers, they were working for less wages than men, and they were struggling in addition with burdens of child care and housework. They were coming to the forefront in the general class movement, and with this they were voicing some of their own demands, the minimum ones of the right to work and equal wages. And the organizers were finding that taking these up, giving some attention to the special oppression of women, was heightening the power of their movement.

But why were the organizers all men? Why not women organizers?

Many answers could be given to this question. (There were of course some women leaders in the left parties, but they were generally middle class, working in the cities, not at the lower levels in the villages.) But the most simple answer came in my 1971 discussion with those agricultural labourers of Ahmednagar. When one of the leaders told them, 'It's not enough just to be militant, you should come forward and be leaders as well, come to study groups,' one of the most outspoken women replied, 'What can I do? I don't have time. I have six children.'

And this was my introduction to the problems of working women in India. It heightened my interest in the issue of women's oppression and how to fight it. When I returned for two months in the summer of 1973 to work on a pilot study of peasant organizing and the role of caste and sex, I not only heard the same stories about the militancy of poor peasant women, but I also found many young educated women stirring with new ideas. Themes of women's liberation from the movements in the West were beginning to reach India and, in spite of distortions in the magazine and newspaper accounts, were interacting with the awareness already growing inside India that women were not only unjustly treated, but were also a huge potential force for change.

College students were becoming increasingly restless with the old barriers of traditional marriage arrangements. They lamented the continued existence of the dowry, the price which the girl's parents had to pay to a boy's family to get a husband for her. The dowry was not declining in 'modern' India; it was apparently rising. A young sociology researcher lamented her fate: 'I have to work to earn money for my own dowry because my parents can't afford it. But the longer I work, the older I get, so the more it will cost!' This was slavery, they agreed, this was 'marriage as a marketplace', and they were ready to demand that it should be changed.

New ideas were having a hearing in India in those days. Young women students, working in slums or on famine relief projects in villages, were appalled at the poverty they found and the weary endless toil that women had to endure. They were impatient, also, with restrictions their own families tried to put on their movements, and they were reading at the same time about events in China, Vietnam, and the US. One young leftist had been reading about lesbianism. 'Do they really mean *physical* sex?' she asked. I said yes. But her response was somewhat surprising, for it bypassed the ideological debates on this issue in Western leftist circles. It wasn't clear from the literature she had been reading, she told me, that they were talking about physical sex, because all the arguments for lesbianism were in terms of the value of developing warm, close relations with other women. 'We have that here,' she said. Women in India were not brought up to compete with other women for men since their marriages were normally arranged for them; and in a context where close friendships with the other sex tended to be excluded, women had always formed their closest relationships with other women. The other side of the arranged marriage system!

Women in India obviously had different problems from women in the United States, but exactly how different were they? And what about class and caste differences? The upper middle class college students of Bombay were almost as much in the dark about village life as I was, just as likely as any Westerner to be appalled at village poverty and backwardness. Many of them were at that time beginning a kind of voyage into the depths of their own society, trying to make contact with poor peasant culture in the process of seeking peasant militancy. We talked about the position of lower class women. I was ready to argue that because such women, especially poor peasant and agricultural labourer women, tended to work outside the home, they had more social independence than women in the middle levels of society, who stayed at home with their children while their husbands went out to factories and offices. Statistics of divorce and remarriage tended to fit this: low caste women had traditional customary rights to divorce their husbands and remarry while the orthodox norm of no divorce weighed down on middle-class Hindus. But it was easy, on the other hand, for my friends (and me) to be overwhelmed by the sheer physical burdens these women bore in everyday life; they seemed to be facing the very height of oppression. More important, what did the poor peasant women and the slum women themselves think about their position?

How do lower class women in India really feel about being women? Here my inquiring radical friends were asking questions which the academic scholars of India had never really thought about before. There are countless anthropological and sociological studies of village life. I had read many of them; they gave fine accounts of the forms of the traditional family and its variations, the domination of the mother-in-law, the position of women as a pawn in status-seeking marriage games, her cultural subordination at all levels. But all saw women as passive victims; all tended to assume that the women simply accepted their position and their definition as inferior. Thus the anthropologist David Mandelbaum, in his *Society in India* (Vol. 1, p. 82), writes, 'Formally and manifestly the birth of a daughter is a much less auspicious event than the birth of a son. When a choice must be made between the needs of a young son and a young daughter, the son is far more likely to get the better food, clothes and care . . . ' This, incidentally, is why the sex ratio in India is 931 women for every 1,000 men: girls die at every age at a higher rate than boys. ' . . . *And yet,*' he goes on, '*the girls themselves do not seem resentful of any discrimination* . . . Similar favouring of sons is common elsewhere in India as is a similar lack of strong resentment by daughters either as children or in their later recollections.'

Is this really true? Don't the girls care? Who did Mandelbaum ask, anyway, and why would they tell him? What kind of life did these village women lead, what kind of self-expression did they have? Were they ready to protest their condition at all? Was it only my middle class college friends who were brooding about their fate as women in what they described as a still 'feudal' culture, or did my translated speech on women's liberation also mean something to the agricultural labourers who barged through police lines and came forth on marches with their children on their hips?

Questions like these led to a research project on 'Women's Movements in India' which I carried out during 1975 and part of 1976. Coincidentally, 1975 was declared by the UN to be International Women's Year, but perhaps it was not so coincidental if women all over the world were stirring in the way that the Ahmednagar labourers and the Bombay students were. International Women's Year not only lent my own study legitimacy, it also helped the arguments of the women (and men) who were beginning in that period to mobilize the working class women in the villages and city slums of India. They could say, 'The leaders of all countries have agreed that women all over the world are oppressed and that they should have equal rights. Women must struggle to win those rights!' Finally, International Women's Year brought, for me, a wealth of encounters with Indian women of all classes, and turned my research into an experience with Indian women beginning to organize and fight for their rights.

The following pages give an account of ten months in 1975, beginning with a meeting with women agricultural labourers in a remote village in central India and leading up to a 'United Women's Liberation Struggle Conference' held in the industrial city of Pune. In part, they tell the story of how that Conference came about, and this story itself is inextricably interwoven with the political convulsions of contemporary India. Thus readers will come across representatives of an apparently bewildering variety of Communist and Socialist parties and will find themselves immersed in union organizing, peasant uprisings, marches, demonstrations, all coming up in the end solidly in confrontation with that most famous Indian woman, Indira Gandhi. I did not originally intend to include the politics of the Emergency in this account; but it was there.

More than the politics, though, I hope that readers will find a vital and living portrait of the variety of Indian women I was privileged to meet — agricultural labourers, urban workers, college girls, bank employees, ex-Untouchables and Brahmans, young and old women organizers. When I talk about my experiences of those days, I am invariably asked, with some amazement, 'But was your experience typical? Were these women typical?' No, of course not. Why should they be? First, readers should remember that the events described here took place mainly in one part of India, the state of Maharashtra, which has a relatively high rate of women's work participation and a strong tradition of social-cultural revolt, both factors leading to a relatively vigorous expression of women's militancy. Second, the women I met for the most part (though not always) were in some way or another involved in organization and protest activity. They were not 'typical' in the sense of being randomly chosen to represent a numerical average. But they are authentic. However much they are involved in fighting their society's traditional bondage, they are part and parcel of that society, their experiences and their concerns are those of all the women of the society.

I have not tried to include my own analysis of the roots of women's oppression or of the origin of women's movements or of the way in which they can be united with movements of other oppressed groups to build a revolutionary challenge to the very system of exploitation. Such issues do come up in the book as they were discussed and dealt with by Indian women (and men) organizers themselves, and I have included as Appendices the analyses made by three Indian organizations mentioned in the text. I have also given as 'Bibliographical Notes' some more theoretical material (including my own) that deals with such questions. But I do not really feel ready at this point to give my own answers to issues which are still being debated in India, partly because the practical experience which makes it possible to answer such questions (particularly the question of strategy) is barely beginning. Instead, I have written an Afterword on the unfinished problems raised by the United Women's Liberation Struggle Conference and the budding movement it expressed, which brings the story up to date in terms of the people involved. It also attempts some answer to the real question that usually lies behind the awkward 'but was your experience typical?' — that is: Are there really enough women like that to make a difference? Is there really a women's movement in India?

I should add, finally, that not only were the women described here not 'typical', they also include only a few of those involved in the 1975 organizing process itself. For various reasons, many quite important people are omitted. This is not intended to be the 'full story'. Rather, it is an attempt to give women in other parts of the world some understanding of the lives and struggles of their sisters in one part of the huge subcontinent of India.

Gail Omvedt
Kasegaon, India
April 1979

1. 'Women have to do double work'

Encounter with an Agricultural Labourer

Questions of a Woman Agricultural Labourer

Chorus
All our life is on fire, all the prices
    rising,
Give us an answer,
O rulers of the country!

A handful of American wheat,
A kilo of *milo* mixed with chaff,
Doesn't our country grow crops
Or do we have only mud-mixed grain?
Give us an answer . . .

We have forgotten the colour of milk,
Coconuts and fruit have gone underground,
Our children have only *jaggery* tea to feed on,
Give us an answer . . .

Sweet oil for cooking is the price of gold,
Coconut oil for our hair cannot be found,
Without rock oil for lamps we have grown familiar
    with darkness,
Give us an answer . . .

We burn in the summer, we are drenched in the rains,
We bear the rigour of winter without any clothes,
Why don't we yet have any shelter?
Give us an answer . . .

We toil night and day and sleep half-starved
While the parasites fill their bellies with butter —
Why does the thief get food while the owner is
    cheated?
Give us an answer . . .

There are pastures for the cattle of the rich,
For forest development land is preserved,
Why is there no land to support living men?
Give us an answer . . .

Tall buildings rise before our eyes,
The roads cannot contain their motorcycles and cars,
On whose labour has such development been built?
Give us an answer . . .

We filled the jails for independence,
We hurled bombs into the cars of the white men,
Did we do it to fatten the sacred cow?
Give us an answer . . .

When we ask for a rise in wages, for work for the
    unemployed
When we demand land for cultivation,
Why are we met with jail, beatings and bullets?
Give us an answer . . .

Now you have taken a new disguise
And appear in the colours of socialism,
But we no longer want for today the promises of
    tomorrow!
Give us an answer . . .

Now we will stand on our own feet
We will throw caste and religious differences to
    the winds,
We call for the brotherhood and sisterhood of all
    toilers!
We vow today to fight with our lives,
We will bury capitalism in the grave
And sound the drums of our own state!

All our life is on fire, all the prices rising,
Give us an answer, O rulers of the country!

by Bhaskar Jadhav, Lal Nishan organizer
Song written during the
famine period to a women's
traditional grinding tune

Bori Arab: village on the sun-baked plateau of central India, with little to distinguish it from hundreds of thousands of other Indian villages except that I have decided to visit it for my first encounter with agricultural labourers. Bhimrao, a young union organizer friend, whose home it is, tells me about Bori Arab during our bus ride.

'There are about 4,000 people. They grow corn, millet, vegetables, some cotton. It's mostly dry land, like the rest of the area. There are seven big landlords who own about 500 acres each, they are Marwaris, the merchant caste. Yes, they live in the village, though some own land in other villages too. Two of them have cars, one owns a factory. It's a cotton ginning factory with about 300 workers, both men and women, who have to work twelve hours a day for three and a half rupees. There are a few middle peasants, including one Dalit, who have about fifty acres. That's not very much when it's dry land . . . '

He pauses as the jolting bus swings aside to pass a bullock cart. Outside, in the early morning air with the indefinable smell of cowdung fires still mingling with other odors, I can see men and women at work in the fields, bicycles moving down the road, an occasional stunted tree on the rolling land. Inside people jostle us, women in faded saris, peasants with turbans wrapped around their heads carrying tins of grain or bundles of goods tied up in dirty cotton cloth.

'About half the village people are landless. They include all sorts of castes and communities − tribal people, Muslims, Banjaris, Mahars or Dalits, Telis, Kunbis, Marathas. Before, many of them were tenants, but after land reform the big landlords managed to keep most of the land and throw out the tenants, and now all of them work as wage labourers.'

Mahars are the biggest ex-Untouchable caste in the area, and have almost always been village servants and agricultural labourers. But they have been well organized as a group, and converted en masse to Buddhism many years ago in disgust with the Hindu religion which ostracized them. Now many of their angry young educated people call themselves *Dalits* or 'downtrodden', much as young Negroes in America began to use the term 'Black'. My friend Bhimrao is a Dalit, from an agricultural labourer family of this village. *Banjaris* are another low caste of the area, traditionally casual labourers. *Telis* were traditionally oil-pressers; now most are peasants. *Kunbis* and *Marathas* have been the main landholding peasant caste of the state, and in most villages many of them are among the richer peasants who have benefited from land reform and the technological developments known as the 'Green Revolution'. In Bori Arab, however, they seem to have been victims of the growing impoverishment and class polarization of the last decade.

This is the Indian caste system, so complicated in its ramifications and so much a source of fascination for foreigners. But I have come to search the depths of an even older form of social inequality: the position of women.

'Every landlord has about seven *saldars*, labourers hired on a yearly basis who are almost bound serfs. They are at his beck and call every hour of the

day; their wives serve the landlord's family too. The rest work on
daily wages. No, they're not much in debt, they're not tied to the
landlords, they're casual labourers, with men and women both getting
whatever work they can in the fields. Their wages are low because there's
no other work available. They have to take what they can get.'

I am going to Bori Arab because I want to meet rural women. In the two
months since coming to India in December 1974, I have met and interviewed
housewives, students, women factory workers and middle class employees —
but always with the feeling that I have to get away from the towns to get at
the heart of things. The old cliche is true: the villages are the source. After
150 years of colonial rule and three decades of independence, the fate of
Indian women is still tied to the land.

I know the statistics practically by heart. Most Indian women do not get
jobs outside the home, but of those counted as 'workers' by census takers,
50% are agricultural labourers, which means they work for wages in cash or
kind, and 30% are cultivators, which means they work on family-owned land.
Of the rest, most are employed in what is called the 'unorganized sector',
which means they are casual labourers doing unskilled work at inadequate
wages on roads or construction projects, or working as domestic servants.
Only 6% of all working women are in white collar or factory jobs which
employ large numbers of people and are likely to be unionized.

And there is so much variation in this as in other things in India! In the
north, very few women work outside the home, even in agriculture. Elsewhere, in the hilly 'tribal' states and in the south and west, work participation is higher and women make up nearly half the agricultural labour force, a
major portion of the work force in the rural areas.

What is the reality behind these figures? Part of it, I feel, is that where
women do get work outside the home they are likely to have more social
independence and near equality with the men of their class. Where they do
not, where they are bound to the home, they are at the mercy of the traditional barriers, of servitude in the home, of dependence on men, of customs
like dowry and arranged marriages, of the vows and fasting and particular
religious observances assigned to women. Among the middle sections in
India, from white collar families to factory workers, women may have
overwhelming work burdens, managing the home, dealing with continually
rising prices and the tedious tasks of preparing food where nothing comes
'ready-made' — but it is not the kind of work that gives them independence.

But among the lowest classes, especially in the rural areas where women do
contribute to agricultural production and have land or work of their own,
their toiling life seems to mean more social freedom. I know that low caste
women have customary rights to divorce husbands and remarry whereas
upper caste and middle caste women can hardly dream of this even today,
that they move around more freely, that they talk to their husbands and
brothers more on a level of equality . . .

If they have land and work of their own, that's the problem. Both land
and work are vanishing in India. Landlessness is rising, and job opportunities

are declining, so that where 33% of all workers were women in 1901, only 20% are women today. Correspondingly, where the very lowest caste and tribal women may have more traditional freedoms, the subordination of women seems to extend far into the society. And I know other figures (as I noted in passing in the Introduction): that the sex ratio in India is now 107 men for every 100 women, and that this gap is increasing, and that it means simply that girls die at every age more than boys, and that the simple cause is that girls do not get as much food and medical care as boys. And in a country where food and medical care are in absolute shortage among the poor, this difference is a matter of life and death.

I know of stories which dramatize the fate of women very much like those I can see through the bus window stooping in the fields or carrying burdens of grass. In Bihar in the north, where feudal traditions are stronger, Mary Tyler has told the stories of poor women she has met in prison, women in jail for defying their families and trying to marry men outside their caste, women forced to sell their meagre oil and soap rations in the jail to save money so they can give a feast for village elders after being released in order to regain their caste status which has been degraded by sharing a jail cell with who-knows-who. Mary writes of an old woman who had killed a daughter made pregnant by the village headman's son simply because she could not face the total ostracism of the village (and was ever after haunted by it), of another woman jailed for aborting the child of a man who had forced himself on her. And I know the story of the ex-Untouchable women of the district of Uttarkarshi in the state of Uttar Pradesh, where researchers found that families who were tied in debt-bondage to high caste landlords would have their daughters — treated as slaves by these landlords — sold into the prostitution network in Bombay. Such women, when interviewed, were cynical about legal or social work solutions: 'Buy freedom for our men, give them land and only land. It is these green fields which will contain our girls. Nothing else can.'

Land. From the rich rice-growing district of Thanjavur in the southern state of Tamilnadu comes a different kind of story. Here the land is worked by agricultural labourers who are also ex-Untouchables or Dalits, but through years of organizing under communist leadership they have freed themselves from serfdom and fought for higher wages. Women, nearly half the wage workers in the state, were prominent in the struggles and strikes. Then, in 1968, in the village of Kilvenmani, in the midst of one such struggle, the landlords collected a gang of 200 thugs and marched on the Dalit settlement at night. The men ran, the women and children who couldn't fled into one of the huts. And the landlords and their men burned this hut down with the rest, barricading the doors and forcing those who tried to escape back inside. In the morning it was discovered that 42 people, mostly women and children, had been burned to death in Kilvenmani, one of the most notorious atrocity stories of recent India.

But the story did not end in 1968. The labourers continued to fly the red flag and cling to their union. And the women in subsequent years became

11

involved in a women's association where, according to Mythily Shivaraman, one of its organizers, 'their capacity for leadership was really developing; they saw this as their own.' And in December 1974, about the time of my arrival in Bombay, the Democratic Women's Federation held its first state conference twelve miles from Kilvenmani. Of its 27,000 members, nearly half were the women agricultural labourers of Thanjavur, and it was the women of Kilvenmani who marched the miles to plant the flag that open-ed the conference.

The poor rural women of Uttar Pradesh and Bihar in the north appear as victims of a brutal social order, the agricultural labourers of Thanjavur as fighters against such oppression. Were the women of Bori Arab victims only or fighters too? In this state of Maharashtra I know that rural low class women almost always do field work, and the upright, often confident, and sometimes fierce, bearing of such women seems to testify to their vigour. They don't have the look of people beaten down by hopelessness. But Bori Arab itself has had no history of organization at all, no attempts at labour unionizing in the ginning factory or the fields, no 'communist' propaganda of militant equality. Waves of change have rolled over India, but Bori Arab seems to be one of those villages barely touched by the storm of the national movement or Gandhism. Yet there has been the militant Dalit liberation movement led by Dr. B. R. Ambedkar, who was the most famous Untouch-able leader of modern India, the one my friend Bhimrao is named after. And there have been new cars bought by the rich, a single small factory, and the new schools which, after all, have produced from agricultural labourer families children like Bhimrao. who went to college and got thrown out for taking part in a student agitation.

But how much has this touched the women of Bori Arab? What will they have to say?

When the bus finally pulls into the village, it is nearly 11a.m. We step out into one of the dusty, nondescript villages that seem so typical of India, with people hanging around the bus stand and nearby tea stalls. Merchants sit in their shops and stare as we walk past; off to the right is a school and what is probably a village council building set back from the road in a compound flanked with trees and a few flowering shrubs. We head off into a side street, down winding stony lanes, past small baked-mud houses with children squatting or playing in the dust, an occasional goat tethered to a stick, a chicken squawking across the road, one or two mangy dogs slinking around. This is the Untouchable quarter, still called by its age-old caste name, Maharwada. 'Where there's a village, there's a Maharwada,' is the Marathi equivalent of saying, 'Where there's a city, there's a slum.'

About twenty-five women are gathered already in the small yard surround-ing Bhimrao's hut. They are mostly middle-aged, wearing faded red or green saris, some made of two or more pieces stitched together, a few younger women, children hanging around the outskirts, and one or two young men.

All are people who did not get work today or who chose not to go to the
out of the excitement of a proposed meeting with a foreigner. In some ways
these women seem as different from the different from the middle class
women of the cities as they are from me. Even their saris are different from
the smooth, unwrinkled synthetics of the cities. They wear them differently,
with the end pulled over their heads – some would say out of traditionalism,
but it protects them from the burning sun – and with the longer bottom
part pulled between their legs so they can move freely in the fields. These
women call the shorter sari of the middle classes a 'round sari', and say that
they can't work in it.

What is your life like? What do you think about your country? These are
the things I want to know. But we begin concretely: what time do you get
up in the morning and what do you do? And it doesn't take them long to
get over whatever hesitancy or shyness in speaking may be there. One woman,
Kaminibai, a strong, independent-looking woman of indefinable middle age,
emerges as the main speaker.

What is their work day like? They get up at 5 a.m., get water from the
well, collect cow-pats for fuel, cook, clean the floor, take their baths, wash
clothes and then go to the fields at 8 or 10 a.m. They work until 6 p.m. –
on the days when they can get work – and then return for cooking and
household duties until they finally go to sleep at 9 or 10 p.m. Sixteen hours of
work a day – we add it up together – and for this the landowners pay them
1¼ to 1½ rupees.

'What do men get?'

'Two and a half rupees for light work, three for heavier work.'

What is the difference in work? Kaminibai tells me: men's work is plough-
ing, cutting ears of corn, collecting the crop, carrying it away, collecting left-
overs for cattle. Women's work is winnowing grain from chaff, weeding, pick-
ing cotton and removing the seeds, sowing. This is the normal division of
labour in India; it only has to be added that women generally apply fertilizer
where this is used and do the work of rice-transplanting in rice areas.

'What do you eat?'

'*Bhakri – jawari bhakri* or *lal bhakri.*' This means a coarse, tortilla-like
bread made of millet and sometimes of American *milo* (sorghum) which is
often imported and sold or given to the poor.

'And vegetables?'

'Vegetables – what shall we tell you?' says Kaminibai. 'If we have
vegetables we can have spices but no salt, or salt but no spices, such is our
poverty! There is no work. Some collect twigs, some collect wood and sell it,
or use it for fuel. What can we do? We are poor . . . '

They complain of the lack of work. Sometimes they get it, sometimes not,
about two or three days of work a week. If they don't get work, they often
just lie around and try to sleep because there is no food and they have no
strength to do more. They can't eat, they say; all have become beggars these
days because prices keep rising while wages remain stagnant.

Why do men get more pay? 'Do men work sixteen hours a day?' I ask.

'No, women have to do different work from men, with a *leave*' (Kaminibai uses an English word here to mean 'work break'; many such words have crept into the language even of these rural women) 'between 4 a.m. and 9 a.m., just to go to the fields and come back at 6.'

'This year is International Women's Year — do you know that?'

'They don't know anything of that,' says Bhimrao, and we try to explain, saying that the leaders of all countries have agreed that women are oppressed and should have equal rights, that women all over the world are organizing to win these rights, that women in the cities of India have had huge marches against rising prices.

'We know nothing, *bai*,' replies Kaminibai. 'We can't read, we can't write, we can't do anything. If you say to sit someplace we sit there, if you say sleep someplace we sleep there, such is our work. We are *jungli* people.' *Jungli* means 'rural', uncivilized'. There is a bitter awareness of deprivation in this.

'There should be demands for *jungli* women too,' I say.

'Yes, there should be demands. You make an attempt — we will follow you.' Bhimrao and I explain that one person can do nothing, that there must be a united effort. He gives an enthusiastic pep talk about a 'union'; he has been working for the last several months as a union organizer.

'Unity? How can we have unity? There is no united opinion among us. If I don't go to work, someone else will go, and I will lose. There is no unity among us! The farmers, though, they have unity.' And the discussion of unity that follows excites them and illustrates again the awareness born of desperation, the sense that the poor have for the importance of unity, and their initial feeling that it is impossible.

I return again to the issue of the particular problems of women. So far they have not picked up on this too much; economic issues seem primary. But what follows shows that ideas have been germinating.

'Another question. About divorce. If your husband goes, can you take another husband?'

'Oh yes,' says Kaminibai immediately. 'We can take another. Two, three, no matter. We can take out a licence if we want, or not.'

'Ask Rukmini,' says someone else. So I ask Rukmini, a young and vigorously beautiful woman, to tell her story. Yes, she says, her husband left her several months ago and since then she has lived with her sister and worked alone. Is that all? 'Can't you take another husband?' I urge.

'No,' she says, then pauses, giggles. 'There is a guest . . . ' The women all laugh. There seems an ambivalence about the high caste standards which define such liaisons as immoral. They recognize the standards, but seem to want me to know that they take them lightly, that they are not really helpless. I press the point: 'You go out, you earn, so if one man goes it doesn't matter, you're independent.' Rukmini grins and agrees. Neighbours may talk, she says, but it doesn't bother her.

'It seems that in your agricultural labourer community there is more equality between men and women than in the higher communities!'

'Yes, yes,' they say.

'But is there male supremacy?' I ask. I use the Marathi term *purush pradhan* which I have heard from others, but it seems too literate and 'sanskritized'. I wonder if they understand.

At this point Bhimrao feels the need to intervene and goes back to the issue of wages. 'Yes, there is male supremacy. Still, during the days of government relief work during the famine, they got equal pay. But in the work they do in the fields, men get more daily wages and they get less, and the reason for that is that men's work is heavier, more toilsome. Women's work is different — '

' — but women — ' I begin.

And then Kaminibai bursts in:

' — have to do *double* work!' (And again an English word!) 'We have to do the housework and when the housework is finished we have to do the field work and when the field work is finished we have to take care of the children, we have to do all the work! Suppose someone is thinking like this, some reader-and-writer, let him sit down and write an account: what sort of work has to be done, what sort of work the men do, what work we do. I am ready to tell you. What do men do? They get up, they take a bath, they eat some bread and go to the fields. But understand what their duty is: they only do the work that is allotted to them in the fields. They only do one sort of work — '

She pauses for breath and I say that, in the US also, women who work outside the home get less pay than men and also have to work in the house without pay.

'Oho! That is the case here too. We remain without pay. If it would have been paid we would get *double* pay! If housework were paid it would go to the women! Are you men listening? Admit it! If there is competition about housework we would defeat them completely.'

The second shift, the unpaid shift, the double burden of women. And wages for housework! Did anyone say there weren't some universal issues of the women's movement?

We go on. What about dowry? 'Is there dowry among you?' I know that in some low castes there has been instead the custom of a small brideprice (where the husband's family pays money to the bride's family), though many have been switching over to dowry in recent years under the impact of the prestige of high caste customs and the lesser importance of women as workers.

'Dowry, yes,' says Kaminibai. 'Gold chains, horses, cycles, money, wristwatches . . . '

'You know,' I say, 'that in the Indian constitution dowry is supposed to be illegal. Untouchability is illegal, dowry is illegal, there are rights but in reality — '

'There are no rights. Yes, that is correct.' Kaminibai is the perfect lower class cynic about democracy on paper.

'It's written in the constitution,' says Bhimrao. And in fact, in legal terms, India has full equality and more guaranteed rights for women than most countries, including equal pay, maternity benefits and so on for women workers.

'It's written, but it's not like that.'

These women, as Kaminibai shows throughout our talk, have a tremendous ambivalence towards education, towards what is 'written' and towards 'readers-and-writers' who have control over this magic. It is something that represents the aspirations and promises of a better life, but it also represents the continuing betrayal of those promises and the departure of the educated elites who leave their people behind in the villages.

'When you go to work, do these other people — Kunbis, Marathas, Telis — practise casteism against you?' This is from Bhimrao, who is as preoccupied with the horrors of caste as I am with the oppression of women.

'They do, but we don't have to bother about that. We have our own pots and drink from them, we don't bother. We are not going to drink water from their hands. Now they don't do it much.'

Water is the ultimate symbol of casteism. For these village women, the idea of eating together and marrying with other castes is beyond the realm of possibility; the concrete reality of caste in daily life is the refusal of caste Hindus to share water with Untouchables. In most of India's villages there are still separate wells. Kaminibai isn't bothered by the difference too much; but there have been cases of drought when caste Hindu denial of the use of the common well to Untouchables has resulted in death.

What about the effects of caste on general class unity? 'What do you think, with Kunbis and Telis and all other agricultural labourers, is unity possible?'

'No. We need unity, but it won't be. If we Buddhists don't go to work, others will go and then we will fall. What can we do? If our own leaders go ahead, of course we'll follow them, but they stay behind, they sit in their houses, so where can we go? And if there's some money the big people eat it up. They eat up the votes. They take the money, we give votes, but we remain starving . . . ' The bitterness of a corrupt democracy, at its worst, is the bitterness that the poor themselves see none of the benefits of corruption.

'New leaders are needed,' I venture.

'Yes, leaders of pure metal!'

'Like Ambedkar?' throws in Bhimrao.

'Yes, he was great, but there's none like that now. Now they want *dhotis* of 50 rupees and their wives want saris and we have to endure rags.'

What about Indira Gandhi? Has having a woman prime minister made any difference to India's poor? 'Some people feel that women in India must have more rights, that you must have made some progress.'

'Not at all, not at all, not even one anna in a rupee (i.e. about 6%). She's doing politics and it's all right, it's not for us, our life has not changed.'

'You're being sarcastic,' says Bhimrao.

'You can take it that way. I'm talking out of anger. But it's not false. They've done nothing for us, there's no happiness for us.'

'In the time of the English — was that government better than this one, or not?' asks Bhimrao.

There is a chorus: yes, yes. Kaminibai elaborates: 'We were small then, *bai,* but we were getting everything, grain, food, everything. Money was less but our stomachs were full. Tell me, if there is no grain, if there is nothing for our stomachs, what have we to do with the state? Nothing at all. We condemn it. Because we are miserable, we say the state is miserable. Isn't our life miserable? Then, whatever it does it does for them, it does nothing for the poor. So tell us . . . we are expressing our sorrows to you, but up to this day no one has come to ask us about our sorrows.'

'But, in the time of the English, wasn't there more casteism?'

'Now it's better, about 4 annas in a rupee' (about 25%).

Bhimrao tries to ask if India really does have independence, to talk about economic dependence, foreign ownership of factories, neo-colonialism.

'What can we understand of that? We don't know how to read and write, we have no information at all about the country, about who runs the factories. We have no information. Only that we don't get anything, that our wages are less, that our food and clothing are insufficient, that everything we get falls short, only *that* we know and try to discuss. If I had been educated I would have been a leader. But, as it is, I am only a bull for a festival.' What Kaminibai means is that she may be ceremoniously honoured on one day out of the year, as bullocks are covered with bright blankets and paraded around, but must slave as a lowly drudge the rest of the time.

Women like Kaminibai have, after all, been touched by the waves of social change that have swept unevenly but tumultuously over India. They are not the poorest of the poor. There are people worse off, men and women driven out of their villages completely for lack of even the most meagre work, labouring elsewhere on construction projects for a pittance and tied down to the contractor by endless debt, camping under trees or in open-air small town markets as their only 'home' for years on end, with no question of educating their children, no question of dowry because they have no money at all. Women like Kaminibai are only near the bottom, they have some kind of village home, occasional work, perhaps a tiny piece of land and a living community around them.

More than this, they have a long experience of promises, promises from the government of better lives, promises from the leaders of their own caste of human dignity and achievement. And many of these promises have centred around the dream of education. Children of these agricultural labourer families do go to school in the village and some go on to high school and even college. Some of these graduates are returning to work in the fields because no other employment is available. One young girl in this group is a high school graduate and still working in the fields, though for her it seems all the school has done is to give her a middle class shyness to replace the fierceness of the illiterate women. Women like Kaminibai are the ones passed over by education and mobility. Their field work has not changed, they have not seen the new products of the factories in their houses, but they know that there are things that they don't have, and they know that there are things that they don't know, and they are angry about it.

They are even ready to by cynical about me. For when someone raises a question about why an American woman should come to talk to them, Kaminibai replies, 'Now she has come, so she'll do something for us, perhaps for one anna in a rupee, forget about the other fifteen.'

Bhimrao takes my side. 'She's going to study the conditions of women here and whatever obstacles there are to building an organization, how to overcome them, in what way to build it, she'll write something – '

'Yes, but will she write to us? She'll write something worth reading and writing, but it will be in thin small letters and we won't be able to read it, not at all, there will be no profit or loss to us.' (General laughter.) 'Is this true or false, *bai,* what I am saying to you? Understand, we will show our difficulties to you, you send from there some paper, and some educated person, some children, will read it to us, and we know nothing, whatever they tell us or explain to us we will understand. If we even have the time.'

We are called into Bhimrao's house for lunch. There is little difference in the organization of the kitchen area of this poor labourer's hut and the homes of richer peasants in the village, or of the slum and working classes and even most of the lower middle classes in the cities. There is a cleared corner area, the *mori,* where dishes are washed, and if there is running water, it is here. But few homes in the villages and only about half of those in the cities actually have water. Otherwise women carry it from village wells, several trips a morning in large brass vessels, or stand in line in the slums to make use of public taps. There is the hearth, or *cul,* where women cook squatting down. Only the upper middle classes in the cities and a few of the most modern village homes have stand-up counters for cooking; in other cases the women spend much of their day on the floor doing the tedious tasks of food preparation. The slightly better off families have tiny kerosene stoves; the middle class above have gas in containers which they get after an application and a wait of several years, or sooner by bribery; poor women like Bhimrao's mother fuel their hearths with wood kindling or cowdung. *Mul ani cul,* 'child and hearth', this is the woman's place according to the common Marathi saying, and all women share this fate. The difference between the poorest kitchens and those of the better off peasant and working class families is in the amount of food grains stored in the kitchen, the number of vessels for cooking and storage, whether they are tin or brass or stainless steel. Bhimrao's mother has almost nothing, and the food she serves us is the heavy unleavened bread or *bhakri* of the poor, a small curry of hotly spiced vegetables, and some thin goat milk spread over it to ease it down. Flies buzz around us as we eat, constantly settling on the food, and I have to keep waving my free hand to ward them off. The flies, universally present, universally tormenting us as we eat, are everywhere in the quarters of the poor, in city or country.

And worse is the sullenness of Bhimrao's mother. 'She wanted me to get a job, she was very upset when I got thrown out of school,' he explains. This poor family, toiling as underpaid wage labourers for years, had put all their hopes in an educated son who, they had thought, would at least get some kind of settled white-collar employment and be able to give them a better life in their old age – and his mother cannot understand his decision to give up a career and go into the underpaid, insecure and possibly dangerous work of being a communist union organizer. To her it is a kind of betrayal, and Bhimrao's hard fury against social injustice and his idealism are beyond her.

I think of a poem, 'So That My Mother May Be Convinced' (Appendix 3 in this volume) written by one of the most famous poets of Bhimrao's militant generation of educated Dalits. It is a bitter and anguished poem of a revolution-minded son addressed to the illiterate mother who has suffered and worked continuously but who has been able to give him nothing of the sense of world turmoil and revolutionary hope and who wants him only to take a wife and settle down safely. He accuses her of being a mute barrier in his path and warns, 'I have become Satan . . . don't stand in my way!' Like this woman, like every sociologist's image of the tradition-bound female, Bhimrao's mother resists his transformation into an organizer. But Kaminibai, bitter and militant herself, asking for and almost demanding the kind of leadership the young radicals might provide, is another type entirely.

After lunch we wander outside again, and almost everyone is still there, the women and children listening to some of the worker and peasant songs recorded on my tape recorder. We return to more discussion of the same themes, problems of poverty, caste issues, the possibility of united action. We discuss the idea of a women's organization. When could they get time? Where could they find leadership? These are the questions raised, the questions to which I have no immediate answer. Kaminibai says again that she would follow, that she is ready to do something, but she must have help. When will I return to Bori Arab? That I don't know . . . And Bhimrao himself cannot organize in Bori Arab at the moment; he is needed elsewhere and there are too many small towns and villages in India.

Just before I rise to go, one final topic comes up that had not occurred to me to ask about: the issue of family planning. As I glance around the dusty yard, seeing a little beyond it the dry fields in this area where the landlords are content to live off their income rather than invest in irrigation and agricultural improvement, where population densities are among the lowest in India but soil productivity is even lower, where men and women cannot get employment to do the work that might raise its productivity, one of the women says, 'The farmers tell us that the reason we are poor is because we have too many children.'

It is the ultimate in family planning as ideology, justifying the power of the rich at the village level. And before I leave the village, I have to deal with its higher levels of power where such ideas are generated and maintained: I visit the village council office and the village school, and sit around and drink tea and exchange pleasantries with the principal and teachers.

The school itself symbolizes rural contradictions. The village cannot produce crops to feed its people, cannot produce enough literacy to keep ahead of the numbers of the poor — but it continues to produce graduates from among the lower castes with growing aspirations and readiness to fight for them, and it produces an increasing sense of deprivation among others. The school produces contradictions. I face a class of young girls and boys, many from poor peasant and agricultural labourer and Dalit families. The questions they ask show their underlying concerns. Is there inflation in America? What about racism? Finally, a boy from the back of the room who was one of those sitting around the edge of the women's meeting, rises to plead, 'Play the songs.'

He means the revolutionary music I have on my tapes. I try to catch Bhimrao's eye: is it all right, here in the school? He nods, he seems to think it's a good idea. And so, with some trepidation, in the schoolroom of a village dominated by seven rich landlords where the poor have not yet found any strength of organization but only 'endless sorrows', I play a song of revolt, written by a male agricultural labourer from another district and sung by another woman labourer:

> The blazing torch in our hands,
> The red sun in the east,
> With the gleaming scythe of unity
> We will cut the throats of the rich!

2. 'The union is our mother!'

Story of a Woman Worker

Working Women's Song

Chorus
We are wives of peasants,
We are wives of workers,
We are working women.
We will no longer remain
Helpless as the cows,
We are working women!

Let us go tell the government,
Let us go tell the moneylender
Our children need food to fill their stomachs!

Until this day we have been beaten and kicked—
Now we will hold our heads high
And the world of looters will fall before us.

The hot sun met us in the fields,
Hunger met us in the house,
We have to make revolution
To get a little shade and rest!

We will not stay ignorant,
We will become educated,
We need knowledge to make poverty and flee.

> We'll take our children on our hips
> And go to join the revolution.
> We'll face police batons and guns,
> We'll become dark in the sun.
>
> We are wives of peasants,
> We are wives of workers,
> We are working women.

Women's song of the
national movement
from the 1940s

Returning to Pune after Bori Arab is like coming to another world. Originally an old political-educational capital that is now a major industrial centre, the city of Pune seems full of cosmopolitan turmoil and modern conveniences in contrast to the dusty barrenness and sleepiness of the countryside. At its heart the houses and palaces that represent the centuries-old heritage of grey-eyed Brahman aristocrats surrounded by the maze of streets of merchants, carpenters, brassmakers and all the artisan servants; beyond that the wide expanse of the newer upper classes with their tree-shaded bungalows and broader, straighter streets; beyond these the three- and four-storeyed apartment blocks of the bank, insurance company, lower-level clerical class, interspersed with the hutments of the poor. Beyond these, again, the deceptively sleepy reaches of the military cantonment, home of Christians, Parsis and majors on one side; and on the other, in green fenced-off compounds, Vulcan Laval, David Brown, Sandvik, Traub-India, SKF, Kirloskar-Cummins — British-, German-, Swedish-, American-, Japanese-collaboration factories, surrounded by the huts and hovels of workers, in-adequate housing on the cleared land of former villages. Old elites, new elites, soldiers, workers; and interspersed with all the tiny shops, roadside stands, hutments, vegetable and fruit sellers, shoe repairmen, bicycle tyre pumpers, the Indian paraphernalia that fills what in more settled countries would be sidewalks; and on the roads the buses, handcarts, trucks, bicycles, motorscooters, motorcycles, motor rickshaws, and pedestrians who walk on the street because there is no room on the sidewalks.

Pune has all the appearance of a booming industrial city. Yet women have very little place in this development. They are to a small degree in the banks, the offices and the universities and colleges (but these are part of old Pune), and they are to be found in large numbers in the streets: middle class women shopping, visiting temples, strolling with their husbands in the evening; students going in clusters to coffee houses and queueing for buses; working class women striding through the streets with babies on their hips; construction workers carrying their pans and tools on their heads; house-wives and servants carrying bags or large tin cans filled with grain on heads or hips. But women are not to be found in the new factories. With perhaps the minor exception of electronics assembly plants where young girls squint over delicate parts, industrial jobs are a male preserve in India.

Who are women workers, then? They are casual labourers and domestic servants; they are construction workers toiling under the hot sun on the new apartment buildings rising for the middle classes; they are workers who roll *bidis,* the small native cigarettes, for twelve hours a day in stuffy, crowded fume-filled rooms with babies on their laps. And, they are the street cleaners: the largest group of employed women in Pune — and the largest single organized work-force of women that I meet during my stay — are the municipal workers, the sweepers.

In Pune, when the streets are filling early in the morning with women bustling to buy early food, when the milk sellers make their deliveries, when windows are thrown open in the middle class apartments and the poor wander from their huts to nearby open places that serve as public latrines, the sweepers can be seen in the streets, stirring up the dirt and dust and scattered refuse of the day, shoving it to the side of the road, gathering it into round baskets, brooms whisking as they walk bent over, brooms flying . . .

'We make the city clean: then why should we be considered unclean?' is the age-old cry of street sweepers in India. For these women and men who clean up the dust and dirt and excrement of towns and villages are Dalits or Untouchables, performing an updated version of their traditional caste service. In earlier days (and still in many small towns of India) their job included clearing out the 'night soil', pulling basins out from under latrines, carrying it on their heads, dumping it in stinking garbage carts. Now, with modern plumbing universal in Pune, this is not a major part of their job, though one group of city workers does take care of public toilets and nearly all those employed to clean apartment toilets are still Dalits. The majority of city employees simply clean the streets. Yet they are still all Dalits by caste, and the majority of them are women. Only the truck driving and hauling is done by men; the women are the sweepers.

These women are militant unionists. Municipal street sweepers were among the first workers in India to organize themselves; their attempts began in the nineteenth century. The Pune workers formed a union in 1930, first under the leadership of men of their own caste, then switching to a communist-led union that was more militant and less corrupt. They have won steady pay rises and a fair amount of permanent status, as well as benefits that include maternity leave, sick leave, two saris a year and city-provided housing. Consequently, where sweeper families once found it difficult to find husbands or wives for their children — because even other Untouchables tended to consider those who performed the traditional duty as degraded — now their children are desirable mates indeed. In these days of stagnating employment, their well unionized positions are considered good jobs, and sons and daughters-in-law will inherit them. So the sweepers are women with some status, some financial independence, often the main support for their families; women who walk the streets they sweep with the oddly lilting yet dignified gait of the lower class workers of Pune.

But what does this economic independence really mean to the women? I am interested in learning about the sweepers, and my friends in the union want to find new ways to involve and mobilize the women. And so a meeting in the union hall is arranged.

I come with a student helper and Leela Bhosle, wife of union leader A.D. Bhosle, an activist herself and a friend of some of the workers. As the women in colourful red, green and blue saris crowd into the hall, the union activists preface the discussion with an ideological talk in which they — not I — throw out the new ideas about women's place, women's rights, the injustice of women having to do double work. It is a new and somewhat amazing experience for me to hear such whole-hearted espousal of *stri-mukti*, 'women's liberation', from male leaders, but it is a pattern that will be repeated later. The initial reaction of the Left to this concept, especially among those close to the masses and concerned about real organizing, is by no means the unbelieving ridicule often seen in the West; the resistance is there in more subtle ways, but this is now beside the point in this first 'meeting on behalf of women's year'.

We start the questions. What is their work like? Do they get the same pay as men? Yes, they say, due to the union: and also, due to the union, the supervisors don't dare to trouble them much. (This contrasts with the common tendency for women workers to be harassed sexually.) How many hours a day do they work? The count begins at 5.30am, when they rise, dress, and, after a cup of tea on the way to work (a proud right: to buy tea independently), gather at the work site for the morning 'sign-in', to 9.30 or 10 at night when they are finally able to sleep. In between are all the usual tasks of child care, shopping, cooking. And do men help at all?

Here there is general laughter. This is hardly the *dharma* (hereditary religious duty) of the male race! 'We may be tired, worn out, sick, still we have to drag ourselves up to do these things!' At this point Leela throws out a challenge — 'And when you come home dragging your feet to find not only your husband but even your children sitting around and tossing out orders for a glass of water — don't you get infuriated?' They laugh again, responding but sceptical.

What about child care? 'Where do you leave your children when you go to work?'

'Under a tree, in a basket, or some little girl takes care of them. Then anything can happen — some get burned by the fire, some fall and break their heads, something or other goes wrong. Don't we also feel love for our children? But we don't have time for love. There are no facilities.' So they complain, and the fact is that whatever promises and programmes there are for child care facilities, nursery schools and day care centres reach only a minority. The vast work of child care in India is done by relatives, but there are not enough grandmothers to go around, and no provision at work sites.

(And Leela comments: Such is the life of the poor who make things comfortable for the upper classes. Those rich women and men who sing the praises of 'family life' build their own daily comforts on the sacrifices of millions of ruined families!)

The big question I want to ask has to do with the attitudes of the women toward their work. But it is not adequate to simply ask 'Why do you work?' or 'Do you work for money or status or what?' This would only lead to incomprehension. Instead, taking my cue from a Bombay sociology graduate, I ask: 'Suppose your husband or son could get a job that paid 1,000 rupees, enough so you wouldn't have to work. Would you want to stay at home?'

And this provokes a tumultuous discussion. A woman says immediately, 'What do you think! Of course, why would we keep going exhausted to work? To do everything at home and then have to go to work is a hell of a life!'

There is some murmuring, then another voice rises from the back, 'Shut your mouth, woman, we aren't going to leave our jobs! It may be true our husband can get more money. We need our own life. Whether it's tobacco or betel nut or tea, it may be any little thing we want, will he give it freely? And without raising his hand against us? If he doesn't behave well tomorrow, are we going to shut up beneath his blows?' And most seem to agree. 'Independence', 'respect', 'status' are abstract terms that only middle class women might relate to, but for the sweepers they have a concrete embodiment: the ability to be able to buy something of their own, even if only a cup of tea on the way to work or a small tin of chewing tobacco, the security of being able to get along alone. It is not something they want to give up.

And I want to ask about the union: Is there any neglect of women's issues? 'If you had some suggestions to make to union leaders about what kind of women's problems they might take up, what would you suggest?' But even this mild phrasing gets nowhere, for at least some of the women sense some implied insult to the union, and from the side of the room the old activist Sitabai, rising up like a gaunt wraith, strides over to shake her fist at me and close the discussion: 'The union is our mother!'

And in truth such extravagance seems to be shared. The sweepers are demonstrably loyal to their union, giving 100% participation in strikes, turning out for sit-ins, fasts or demonstrations, and coming out in numbers of 300 to 400 for the major marches of May Day and the union's anniversary. In broader strikes involving other categories of workers, who may be less ready to join the strike, many are ready to charge in, ignoring the police, and pull the recalcitrant scabs bodily out into the streets. Later, when I begin a survey of these women, I find that the union is practically the only political force in their lives. The national movement hardly touched them; they know little of contemporary political leaders. The only thing comparable to the union, for those who are Buddhists, is the movement led by Dr Ambedkar which resulted in the conversion to Buddhism; and these women will sometimes say, 'The Buddhist movement gave us self-respect, the union helps us fill our stomachs!' In any case, the sweepers are a vibrant example of the kind of union militancy of which women are capable if they are in a position to organize.

But what the union has concretely meant has to be seen in terms of individual lives, the history of personal struggles and the slow winning of dignity. The story of Tarabai, a 35-year-old divorcee with one child, may or may not be 'typical', but it shows the process of change.

Tarabai lives in Pandavnagar, one of several city-provided housing colonies for the workers. To reach it, you walk down one of the larger roads in the upper middle class section of Pune, turn past a small temple on a corner and walk down alongside a wall covered with mostly religious and a few political slogans, past fruit and vegetable sellers and construction workers coming home from work laden with tools, grass, provisions, babies, and pass a slum settlement of low clay huts with their musty smells and cowdung fires and open drains — this is Wadarwadi, home of the Wadar caste who provide so many of the construction workers of Pune. And then you come to Pandavnagar, with its rows of three-storeyed grey buildings, the paint peeling off except where some of the better-off workers have raised the funds to paint their section in bright new colours, lined up beside a central dusty yard where children play. In the evening when we come, the children shout and yell at us, women sit beside their doors gossiping and sorting rice or pulling lice out of each other's hair as they stare at us, and young boys giggle and point.

This is Pandavnagar, by working class standards high quality housing. For a minimal monthly rent, each family gets two rooms, and a bathroom and a toilet shared with the next apartment. This is almost luxurious; in Bombay equivalently paid workers are lucky to get one room with a partitioned-off bath area and a toilet at the end of the whole floor, while in the industrial suburbs of Pune workers may have to pay one-third of their salary for a single room. But — and here is the rub — not all of the 800 regular municipal workers live in their own city-provided apartment. Many, an uncounted number, sublease their flat and live in nearby slums like Wadarwadi, which may also house women who are temporary employees of the city. The reason the regular workers do this, though it is illegal, is usually to pay off debts. Practically every worker is in debt in India, and regular employees like the municipal workers have deductions owing to credit unions taken out of their pay cheques every month. Debts are incurred for a wide variety of reasons, weddings, illnesses, for any number of special expenditures, and simply for consumption, trying to support too many people on one person's salary.

For it turns out that the fate of these working women like Tarabai is highly linked to their family position. Working may give them some economic independence, but socially male domination still prevails. They are married young (from 12 to 15 or 16) and normally the husband and children they are stuck with become the determinants of their fate. If they have a working husband or son contributing to an overall family income, if somehow they don't have to support three or four adult non-workers, they can manage fairly well. But if not, if husbands and other adults are unemployed and particularly if they drink, their situation can be miserable indeed. And drink, the male's refuge from the miseries of daily life, unemployment and poverty, ravages the slums and villages of contemporary India.

Tarabai, for instance, a divorcee with no one to support but one daughter who is studying in a boarding school which gives concessional rates to low caste girls, can manage to have a cot, a radio, chairs, a cupboard to keep clothes in, a good set of kitchen utensils, and a goat tethered on a walkway outside to provide occasional milk; she is planning to buy a kitchen table-and-chair set — an aspiration to almost middle class consumption levels. Or, down the way, Sonabai, who has a large family but one that includes a working husband and a working son, can have a kitchen filled with brass vessels and cupboards and a certain amount of stored grain and two goats, and can be secure in the knowledge that her daughter-in-law, now living with her and taking care of most of the housework, will one day inherit her sweeper's job and be able to maintain her in her old age.

But Hirabai, a young woman downstairs from Tarabai, has no one to help her, only a single unemployed husband who is constantly drunk and beats her. If you enter Hirabai's apartment there is nothing to be seen, not a single piece of furniture, not a cot or a cupboard, only a piece of matting on which she sits nursing a scrawny baby. A few utensils in the kitchen; a bit of coarse millet; her existence is a struggle to survive from day to day just as much as that of the casual daily labourers in the countryside. It is very likely that soon, if she gets an offer, Hirabai will sublet her flat, the only thing she has left that she can get any money from.

So the family situation remains determinant for the sweepers; work only helps them manoeuvre a bit. Yet there are points when this manoeuvring becomes transformed into something more, into a real leap for independence. And this is why I want to hear the story of Tarabai's life, in fact why Leela and I have come to Pandavnagar.

'My name is Tarabai Namdev Sonavane,' she tells us, having passed around the tea and sitting now before the tape-recorder, a bit self-consciously but ever ready to move into the drama of a tale. 'Before that, it was Tarabai Laxman Kshirsikar — my husband's name.' Which means that she is using her maiden name, unusual even for a divorced Indian woman.

Tarabai was born in a village in Pune district, married when she was seven, and went to live with her husband 'when I came of age' nine years later. After some time she had a daughter, but no son, 'and this began to have an effect on my mother-in-law, father-in-law and all. They began to harass me and say, "She can't have a son, let's marry our son to a different woman." And they were really troubling me . . .'

By this time she was working for the city council, through her mother-in-law who was a sweeper. Tarabai worked as a kind of apprentice, 'doing my mother-in-law's work' first and then started to do the same for another woman worker, who paid her privately. In effect she was doing a major part of two women's jobs, without any official employment, and getting paid almost nothing; such arrangements are common in job-scarce India. But the second woman encouraged her to petition the city for official work, and as a result she was hired to do road repair, first for only four to five days a month, then by 1969 on a full-time basis. It was at this point, when her daughter Lata was five, that the real trouble started.

'I began devoting time to my father, who was very old. My mother and father began to come and stay with me, for a few days at a time. I was giving them grain too. Then my older brother's second marriage was arranged, and the next day I was thrown out of the house! I'll tell you how it happened. My in-laws said that it was because I was having an affair with the man next door, but really they didn't like me helping my parents.' What infuriated her in-laws was that Tarabai, already disgraced for not having produced a son, was defying the marriage bond which compels a young wife to forget the family of her birth and give all her attention, toil and earnings to her husband's family. 'A woman when young should be under the control of her father, when adult under the control of her husband, and when old under the control of her son,' wrote Manu, the Hindu 'lawgiver'. The break that comes with marriage is sharp and traumatic. A woman is considered to have no rights or responsibilities to her blood relations after that, and 'under the control of her husband' means normally under the control of her mother-in-law. But Tarabai, standing on the strength of her new earnings, was defying custom by giving money to her father and brother.

'I remember how it happened,' she says. 'We went to work in the morning, my husband and I, then my guests came and my husband and I and all of them sat and drank tea in a restaurant. My brother's new in-laws told me, "You are responsible for them now".' (That is, since her brother was at that time unemployed, Tarabai was being viewed as the family earner.) 'Then my husband said, "Tara, give me a rupee." I said "Why?" He said, "I need it." So he took the rupee, and went somewhere on his cycle, and after an hour came back, and I, my mother, father, brother were still sitting talking and drinking tea, and then we all went to the house . . . '

What is abnormal in this situation? From a traditional point of view, many things. Indian women should not be expected to 'take responsibility' for their brother's family. Nor should they really be sitting in teashops in the first place entertaining guests. Nor should husbands ask, *have* to ask, their wives for money. Nor, going beyond this, should wives presume to ask why. But Tarabai was now the main earner in a job-scarce society. And taking tea out, normally in a shop on the way to work in the morning, has now become one of the small but valued luxuries of life of the municipal workers. And, standing on the strength of these small collective gains and her own financial independence, Tarabai, already defiant in the face of her in-laws' harassment and insinuations, provokes her husband . . .

'Then we went home, and my people, my husband and the people of the house, about eight to ten of us, were sitting to eat when my mother-in-law started swearing at my father, swearing in the language of our community and saying, "You're living like a pimp off your daughter's earnings!" So I said, "Look here, if you want to say anything, say it to me, but there's no reason to talk like that to my father." Then my mother-in-law said, "Live with your father; if not, live with your brother".' (What she was implying was sexual relations in both cases.) 'On hearing this I started to cry. So I said, "We'll take this to court," but my father said, "No, your brother's marriage was illegal, and if you go to court who knows what complications there will be." And at that point my mother-in-law took all my things and threw them outside and locked the door on us.'

So they went to the bus station, where Tarabai, her brother, father, mother and daughter sat until evening, 'And no one came, not my husband nor even my mother-in-law,' she says, crying, 'I felt very bad.' But though her father urged her, she refused to go home.

Instead she slept in the bus station with her daughter and went to work alone the next morning. Then began her period of trial, working, without a home, enduring the threats of her husband who would come drunken to harass her at work, staying for a time with a fellow working woman but forced to leave that house because of the continual visits and threats of her in-laws, often taking baths with her daughter at street pumps. 'I had to wear one sari for seven days once, seven days,' says Tarabai, her indignation showing the real consciousness of cleanliness among these lower caste workers who clean the streets and latrines. During this time Tarabai didn't go to the union, of which she had as yet little experience; rather she appealed for help several times to her supervisors (the 'sahibs') but with little result. In fact, it was women who helped her — her fellow worker, and a middle class woman living in the area of her work who allowed her use of a water tap for bathing . . .

Finally, after three months, Tarabai's divorce came through. 'They asked my husband, "Do you want to live with your wife?" and he said no. Then they asked me, "Will you live with your husband?" and I said no; and he was saying that I had run away with another man, and I said, "At least leave me my honour!" '

But the divorce was by no means the end of her troubles. Her angered in-laws levied a court case against her and the man next door, accusing him of kidnapping her, and Tarabai was again dragged to court, where she related her whole story and added with great indignation, 'Even people who are going to be hanged are allowed one dinner in peace, but my in-laws didn't even let my parents eat!' After this case failed, Tarabai then found she had to fight for her very job:

'After that, my husband, mother-in-law, his brother and all sent a notice to the municipality saying, "She got this job through my influence and she is no longer my wife; she's run away with another man, so she shouldn't have the job," ' and Tarabai had to deal with this. What was involved here was the custom of 'inheritance rights' found in many organized working class jobs: a son has first claim to his father's position on retirement, and a daughter-*in-law* 'inherits' her mother-*in-law*'s position. What such a right does, in a way, is to provide a substitute for the pensions of white-collar employment, and the nature of the inheritance, of course, is a faithful reflection of the Indian family system, for it is the son and daughter-in-law who care for the old on retirement, not a daughter who is married off to another family.

But Tarabai, who was defying all these customs and attempting to stand on her own feet, won this fight too. All this she had done on her own, but she was developing contacts with the union, and went to A.D., the union leader, for her own next minor initiative, saying 'I want to change my name, I don't want to keep my husband's name, I want my father's name back.' And after accomplishing that, 'I've been in the union, in marches, meetings, strikes up to the present. I've been carrying on with the union as my support. Let me die under the red flag, there is no other support.'

The union, she says, is her *sansar*, her 'daily life'. But what does it all mean to her? Tarabai still can't read, and has no knowledge of the Marxist ideology that motivates union leaders like A.D. and Leela. What is the ultimate aim of all their movement and strike activity, I ask, and she replies with enthusiasm, after a period of puzzlement and a bit of prompting from Leela, that 'union rule' should come. Months later, when I meet Tarabai during a strike — the workers all sitting on an initial one day fast in demand for a bonus — she is more specific:

'How many days will you stay on strike?'

'Until we get our bonus. We will fast first, then go on strike, then face the police blows or whatever, but we will go ahead.' By now this is almost old stuff to Tarabai.

'And if the city refuses to negotiate?' I ask.

'If the city refuses! Who will do the work? Their round-sari'd house-bound wives? If they refuse, the garbage will rot on the city streets. We do the work!'

'And if the police come . . . ?'

'We don't care if the police come, we are fighting for our class rights!' And I ask again about their ultimate goal, and one of the more politicized workers says, the establishment of a toilers' state. What is a toilers' state? I ask Tarabai.

'Capitalists, moneylenders, all those Marwaris must go and the peasants' and workers' state must come!'

'But yesterday in the meeting you talked about women's liberation — so what is the connection between women's liberation and the toilers' state?'

'When the workers' state comes, then women's liberation will also come. It will come a little, why not? The exploitation of women will become a little less. Now who rules? — the big people, the moneylenders, the bosses, the landlords, the parasites. In this situation women's liberation is difficult!'

But if this all sounds still somewhat abstract, then compare Tarabai's vivid depictions of the arrogant ways of supervisors and the defiance by herself and other workers, the dirty drudging toil of the job of sweeping, and — above all, and increasingly — the innate superiority of women who, she is convinced, are stronger than men, coping with two jobs and various male harassments. These are not at all abstract. And my most striking memory, finally, is sitting with Tarabai and Leela in a small railway worker's house, grumbling about the ways of husbands, joking over tea until Tarabai almost spontaneously bursts into a mocking song about her husband, a satirical version of the custom in which husbands and wives use each other's name in a rhymed couplet, and then at the end, when everyone is helpless with laughter, turns to me and says, 'Gail-*bai,* don't marry. Don't marry.'

3. 'Women don't have the right to decide about anything!'

College Students and Cultural Bondage

This is the Challenge of Women's Liberation

Chorus
This challenge of women's liberation
Reaches the sky —
Reactionaries, exploiters,
Take note, your time has come!

Father, husband and son force
Their wishes on women;
When she demands her rights
They laugh at her audacity.

Whether she is a clerk or an agricultural
    labourer,
A philosopher, scientist or technician,
Her daily life is a struggle
In the house and on the job.

She may be prime minister of the country,
An official or a ruler,
A woman is still called helpless
And bound to daily life.

Come on, sisters, let's build our unity,
Let's hold high the flag of equality,

Let's build up the power of the toilers
To win our liberation!

*by Madhav Chavan, for the Women's
Liberation Struggle Conference, 1975*

Bimzani College, Nagpur: A women's college in this large but sprawling, amorphous, non-industrial city in almost the exact geographical centre of India. Except in the bazaar heart of town, its streets seem much emptier than those of Pune, with only a few textile mills and some other un-distinguished small factories, far fewer cars and motorcycles, and, instead of motorized rickshaws, the bicycle-pulled type worked by thin-legged sweating men. But Nagpur is an old provincial political capital; its university is one of the five major universities of Maharashtra state; and the young students (Indian college students are always a year or two younger than Western ones) of Bimzani College come mainly from the middle classes of the city. I have been asked to give a talk here on the occasion of International Women's Year.

I wonder what to say. What can 'women's liberation' mean in colleges like Bimzani, one of the countless small town and city colleges that seem to have sprung up all over India? Those of my friends who are interested come from the elite colleges and cosmpolitan social groups of cities like Bombay, Pune and Delhi, and they complain about the lack of response from other students to their radical ideas about women and society. 'They think I'm crazy,' says a Pune philosophy graduate. 'They're not really interested; they say they probably won't be able to get jobs after graduation but they don't really care — they expect their husbands to provide for them.' Another says, 'The students in Ferguson College just aren't interested. We tried. They only care about romance, the cinema . . . ' Is it real lack of interest or just the difficulty of communicating new ideas to the vast middle class majority enmeshed in the Indian cultural world? I'm not sure, but I don't really know how to begin. The problem is that Indian college students are so different from Western ones, that the whole nature of college life is different.

'Don't marry, Gail-*bai*,' says Tarabai; but in fact marriage is the destiny of all Indian women. This may seem to be true in the West also, but the difference is crucial. Western women can choose who to marry and they can also choose not to marry; they are 'free' in the same way that workers in a mature capitalist society can choose where to work and whether or not to work. In both cases there are real economic and social compulsions (the worker has to survive; unmarried women also find it difficult to cope economically on wage rates far lower than those of men; and an unmarried woman is considered to be an 'unfulfilled' person just as an unemployed male worker does not have the respect of being a 'productive' member of society). But the freedom is genuine. This is what does not exist in India. Though there are the exceptional women who break away, the normal situation is not only that a girl gets married, but that her husband is chosen for her and along with this every major decision of her life is made for her, not by her.

Along with marriage goes the dowry burden. Because the husband is expected to take care of the wife, because her own financial contribution is generally minimal (except among the rural poor and urban exceptions like the municipal workers) and with it her independence, the bride's family is expected to pay a sum of money, or its equivalent in goods, whose rate depends on the husband's education and career prospects. This ranges from 20,000 to 50,000 rupees for rich peasant and upper middle class families and much higher for the really rich. The dowry means that a girl becomes a financial burden on her parents by her very existence and this has its impact on her education. As a young student from a middle peasant family at another college has put it, 'Families don't want to educate girls because girls will go out of the family. And the more we are educated, the more our husband has to be educated and so the higher the dowry!'

Around marriage are also centred the whole paraphernalia of religious and cultural life — the particular forms of women's worship, the vows made to secure good husbands and not only in this life but for lives to come, the fasts undertaken usually once a week, and the continually told stories of the great mythological heroines like Sita and Savrita whose whole life is given meaning by their exemplary devotion to their husbands. With marriage a girl's ties to her mother's home are shattered so that her whole life henceforth will focus around her husband and his family, and all of traditional religious teaching seeks to condition her for this.

Finally, marriage defines what college is. This is not true in the West, where college is the period of searching and self-definition in a woman's life just as much as in a man's, a time when she is faced with the reality of choosing what she wants to do, what she wants to study, whom she wants to marry and when, even whether she wants to marry at all. She may be working and have a husband while carrying on her education. These are simple things; the point is they are not true in India. In India the college years are simply the period before a girl gets married, when she gets away from home for a few years, exposed to new people and new ideas but not set loose among them. The early upper caste social reformers who fought for women's education spent a great deal of time reassuring their contemporaries that education was not subversive, that an educated wife would be a real asset to the home, better able to serve her husband and teach her children. College life exists within the shadow of an expected marriage which is imposed from without.

I remember the prospective college students I have met in Pune, nine daughters of three rich landlord brothers, six planning to start college next year. Sheltered children of the rich, they are like caged birds, excited and fluttering, running around the house, eager to talk. They say they are bored because it is a holiday; school is the only chance they have to go out of the home and they look forward eagerly to college because living in a hostel will be the most free period of their lives. 'We would like to go out more,' one says, but our uncle won't even let us go to the cinema.' What about jobs after college? 'Oh yes, but it depends on whether our husbands will let us work.' They look over the city lights from their rooftop and sigh, 'We would like some independence . . . '

'Freedom' but not independence. College is the interregnum, the brief period of freedom from the control of the father before the new control of the as yet unmet and unchosen husband is asserted; college is *the time between* . . .

Nagpur is a relatively conservative city, and I look out at the girls of Bimzani in their bright nylon and synthetic saris, shiny black braids, glistening skin, and at their neatly dressed teachers, the women simply older, more settled editions of the students, those who have passed through their interregnum to a desirable (presumably) career and family life. And I wonder what to say. But I go ahead with what is to become my standard Women's Year talk. I say that 'the leaders of all countries' have admitted the exploitation of women and the necessity of doing something about it; I describe the varying forms of oppression in the US, including hard work for low pay, the unpaid 'second shift' in the home, cultural oppression which is different in the West (no joint family, no mother-in-law relationship, no dowry, free marriages) but still potent, still emphasizing that 'a woman's place is in the home', still leaving the women susceptible to rape and wife-beating. I talk of the sexual division of labour and argue in fact that women can do everything a man can do . . . And I stress, as we did at the beginning, that this is not a speech, that what I am most interested in is hearing their ideas, that we should have an open forum.

The teachers, not the students, initiate the discussion, as might be expected, and it is a free-ranging one with small speeches thrown in. The men are as vocal on the subject of women's oppression as the women; there are the usual assortment of liberal men who feel they know better than women exactly what is needed for their liberation as well as diehard, even reactionary, male chauvinists. The latter role in this case is filled by a rather aggressive and pompous man who, it turns out, is a teacher, returned from Germany, who seems to combine the most partonizing elements of both cultures and who repeatedly intervenes to ask the women exactly what it is they want. Topics range from why women work and their need for respect as workers to biological issues behind the sexual division of labour ('why is it the great chefs are men?' someone wants to know) but finally begin to centre around the issue of housework. 'Who is to do the work?' asks one man, implying that liberation would mean neglect of the home, that it is unthinkable that anyone besides the women can really take this responsibility. '*Both* should do it,' says a woman firmly. The German-returned teacher asks, 'What do women want? We have heard her idea of *American* liberation — what do *you* want?'

'We want one hundred per cent cooperation from our husbands. When the men come home tired we put a cup of tea before them — we want reciprocal cooperation.' The men argue that women really dominate the home and can get a cup of tea out of their husbands whenever they want; the women say that women are often afraid to make requests or to speak their minds.

The 'German' says again, 'Do they really know what they want, the womenfolk, I mean? If a husband gives her a cup of tea will that be sufficient to cool her anger? You want liberation, but from what?'

'Not *from*. We want liberation not "from" but at the root. No one says, "From what" are men independent? They just are independent at the beginning. That kind of independence is what we want. Men are never asked this question.' Another woman adds, 'Many times women can't express their feelings — and even if men listen they say it's just psychological.'

'There are twelve loudspeakers before you, just tell us.'

'We don't want loudspeakers, we just want understanding.'

'How can we understand if we can't listen,' says the 'German'. 'At least from so many women, at least one should tell exactly what she expects.

Mrs Vaidya, a young lecturer who helped to organize the meeting, makes a bold effort. She begins with biology and issues of human evolution that were discussed earlier. 'We don't mind biological differences, but they lead to a dependent status. The basic fact is that traditional *ideas* are hammered into our minds that it is due to biology that we are inferior.' A man tries to interrupt; she ignores him. 'From childhood on, there is the psychological impact of the idea that girls are inferior. Patriarchal social customs are the problem, but we don't hold with the reactionary idea of replacing these with matriarchal customs, we don't want just "women power".

'Child care is supposed to be a woman's responsibility but there should be equal participation. Women may earn, but in the family and society men are still respected more than women. Vows, *kum kum,* our gold wedding necklaces, being called *saubhagya,*' (the form of address for a married woman, meaning 'blessed') 'all these are only compensations to make a woman feel good. Indian women don't want freedom from men, they want to keep the family atmosphere but to share duties. Women don't have the right to decide about anything. Now people feel that when a girl gets married it is the end of her career, that marriage is the final goal. This should be changed.'

Then someone asks, 'Is there a discrimination between brother and sister in education?' and now the students become vocal:

'Yes, brothers get first preference in education. Girls should be allowed to go out, to see the world, to face the problems of life! We want equality!'

The 'German' says 'Yes, but what does equality mean?'

'Equality . . . ' says the student, a short, earnest looking girl, pausing to think, 'means, suppose we come home late. We are scolded. Why?'

A man says, 'This is parental care. They are worried about their daughters, about hoodlums . . . '

'Parents should not worry about their daughters! If boys can manage until twelve at night, we can manage. If hoodlums attack us, we will retaliate!'

Now the women, students and teachers alike, are in a combative mood, and when the discussion swings back to the issue of the sexual division of labour both express their scorn at the idea that men's and women's roles are really 'complementary'. This was a favourite notion of Gandhi and continues to be put forward by social traditionalists, but the Bimzani women are astute enough to note that it is like justifying the caste system by saying that different castes are really complementary. People used to say the caste system also was based on a 'division of labour', one student points out, 'But times have changed. The caste system must end. Male superiority must go.' Women's bondage to the home, the dowry are attacked. Someone says that in some societies husbands have to give 'dowry' and this also is rejected: 'Either way it's a marketplace.' And finally, at the end, when the 'German' says for the final time, 'Just tell me *concretely* what you want,' Mrs Vaidya replies:

'All right, if you want a *concrete* answer, I will give it. When we get up in the morning, we have to take care of the kitchen, make the tea, while our husbands sit reading the newspaper, even though we both go to work. Just once, for a change, we would like to be able to sit and read the newspaper while our husbands make the tea!'

And so the discussion ends. Bimzani is the first college discussion of my visit, but far from the last, and everywhere I find women and girls even in the so-called 'provincial' colleges and schools ready at least to discuss and assert new ideas. The difference in emphasis between the students and teachers is also striking. The final response of the teachers when asked about concrete issues centres around *tea,* that great essence of Indian sociability and, it is clear, a symbol also of the double work of woman, the countless seemingly trivial tasks that eat up her time. *Mul ani cul* ('child and hearth'), or 'a woman's place is in the kitchen'. In the traditional version the women sit with saris covering their heads, sometimes even their faces, hardly daring to appear before their husbands and other men, never going into the front rooms of the house. In the modern version women are simply too *busy* to fully participate in the man's world. 'Middle class women don't need liberation like we do because they can afford servants,' is another dictum of Tarabai's, but it is only partially true. Middle class women, especially employees like the Bimzani teachers, always can find maid service for washing dishes and clothes; they can get the help of relatives for child care much more easily than Western women; and they may have full time servants. Still, such maid service frequently only replaces the machinery available to Western women, and kitchen work remains time-consuming. 'Modern' men may be perfectly willing to include their wives and other women in their discussions just as Western men are, but invariably when guests come the women disappear into the kitchen to prepare the tea and edibles that go with it, and so find themselves on the periphery of the discussion.

The teachers, then, are concerned about lightening the burdens of work within a family and work situation more or less taken for granted, and to a large degree within the context of a woman's role that is taken for granted, though they may object to its more traditional features. The students are different. Many of them come from homes that have still hardly shaken the bonds of tradition, where even a woman's working is something revolutionary, but all are experiencing a bondage that the teachers have forgotten about, the bondage of not choosing for themselves. And so they talk of independence, the right to go out of the home, to assert their own strength against attackers, the right to choose. College may be simply a 'time between', but they are trying to make it into something more . . .

From Aurangabad, another Maharashtrian regional city, comes news of a new women's group formed by college students, the Mahila Samta Sainik Dal (League of Women Soldiers for Equality), which has published a manifesto (see Appendix 2 in this volume) which reads in part:

> It seems that men make all the decisions about how women should behave, how they should live, what fashions to follow and what to study . . . The idea of family purity is decided not on the basis of the purity of a special organ of men but only on the basis of the purity of a special organ of women and so she is confined to the home. The male caste has done a gross injustice to women by this mistrust. It is our firm opinion that men have kept women apart from freedom and apart from knowledge and have made them slaves only for sexual pleasure. Up to now we haven't even been given the right to choose our own life partners. Education is given up to marriage. Marriage is held up as our only aim. If love is expressed, bullets are shot as if we were animals . . .
>
> This hypocritical society has made us worship the men who have made us slaves. The strange system exists that the slaves themselves are given the job of protecting slavery. Because of this we have to fight against the thought of Manu which treats women and *shudras* as inferior, against the caste system which sticks the label of *karma* on everything, against god who puts women among the untouchables, and against the ideology of natural inequality . . .
>
> Those who rebel against slavery, the Dalits who aim for freedom, the Adivasis and the toilers are our brothers. We are battling for liberation along with men in the liberation war for human liberation called for by Dr Ambedkar. This is history. And so we wish every success to the workers in the American women's liberation movement, and to Angela Davis, and to the women's liberation army.

The members of the MSSD are students of Milind College, one of the best known Dalit colleges in the state, that is, a college particularly for the Untouchables aspiring to education and mobility and particularly identified with those who have converted to Buddhism under the leadership of Ambedkar. Their families are often as middle class as those of other college students, but their history of social struggles has given them a tradition of militancy; the conversion to Buddhism, which comes to them as a religion of humanism and atheism, has given them habits of questioning and secularism; and their low caste social background has often meant family customs of greater independence for women. The caste issue remains as burning even for the upwardly mobile as the race issue does in the US, and there has been a long tradition of untouchables identifying their problems with those of American Blacks — hence the reference to Angela Davis! Recently, militant young men of this group, students and city workers, formed an organization called the Dalit Panthers, with an ideology vaguely combining Marxism and cultural rebellion and with a focus on protecting Dalits from 'atrocities' — the violence exerted against rebellious low caste people by rural bosses, violence that often centres around such things as the rape and oppression of women. Feeling runs high on such issues, and there was one occasion at a mass meeting in Aurangabad when a young Dalit girl rose to hurl at the audience the bitter challenge, 'Now is the time for Dalit men to commit atrocities on caste Hindu women!' Hardly an expression of female solidarity — yet this girl was one of the founders of the MSSD!

Some months later, in May, I get a chance to meet the members of the MSSD during a visit to Aurangabad. About 15 girls and 20 young men, the latter including some college teachers, crowd into the front room of a small house. The girls are enthusiastic and militant as they talk with the same anger as appeared in the Manifesto about the confines of ideology, the atrocities committed against village women, the teasing of boys. They applaud the examples I mention of women ganging up to retaliate against men, the Chinese women's associations tackling wife-beaters, American women 'harassing' males on the streets. They react with enthusiasm to the mention of a new organization of Indian women, the POW (Progressive Organization of Women) of Hyderabad (whose manifesto appears in this volume in Appendix 1), which has conducted marches against the dowry and against male harassment of college students. But it becomes clear that the MSSD, perhaps the first militant women's organization initiated by college students in western India, is very much bound up with the girls' particular position as Dalits and Buddhists.

As is so often the case with middle class women and college students, our discussion of women's oppression comes to centre not so much around work issues as cultural issues. But for these young Dalit girls, with two generations of organized anti-caste militancy behind them, the issue of culture means religion. Hinduism is the cause of enslavement of women, they are firmly convinced; it is the essence of 'the ideology of natural in-equality'; all of the particular forms of binding woman to the home, con-sidering her inferior and impure, and taking her as an object of enjoyment derive from religion. 'Lord Buddha was the first to show the way to women.' I and Bhaskar Jadhav, the Dalit communist activist who has introduced me to the girls, argue that religion itself is of social origin, that ideologies of the subordination of women had their origin with the rise of class society, that concepts of the purity of blood and the consequent subordination of women to a family patriarch are connected with economic needs. Caste tension runs so high still that these girls would probably not listen to such ideas from Brahman men or women, but with Bhaskarrao as a Dalit and myself as a foreigner and outsider to their cultural conflicts the discussion becomes a lively one. But it remains unresolved.

The problem is that the girls are never left to debate alone. While the boys in the group with them are mostly silent, one of the male teachers, a

39

young lecturer in politics, intervenes consistently and aggressively. 'The basic problem is religion. First it is necessary to become a Buddhist – then we can begin to solve women's problems.' I say that I don't think the basic problem is religion, that in my discussions with Dalit agricultural labourer women (thinking of Kaminibai and others) they first talk of the rising prices, the lack of work, low pay, not enough to eat, the double burden of housework, before they get around to dealing with caste and religion. But this has no effect on him, and the argument about conversion continues to weave in and out of the discussion, with most of the girls supporting his point.

There is, it seems, a strong and very fierce trend among this section of Dalits to take a sort of 'Buddhism only' approach, to focus their anger against Hindu religion rather than on class issues and attempts to establish a wider unity, to argue that nothing can be done until all the low castes convert. In fact, the conversion to Buddhism has done so much for the self-respect of these groups that many are likely to yield to such arguments, which are carefully fostered in such colleges as Milind, and the dispute over 'Buddhism versus Marxism' (i.e. cultural issues first or economic issues first) has already begun to tear apart the Dalit Panthers. 'The Mahila Samta Sainik Dal is a Buddhist organization,' says the politics lecturer, and it does seem as if the girls have been encouraged and helped to establish it as a kind of women's auxiliary to the existing Buddhist/Dalit organizations which are mainly organizations of young men.

What does their organization plan to do, I ask. Here they falter a bit, for their Manifesto is new and as yet they have only vague ideas of action. Work among slum women, they say, as do almost all the militant social-minded college students – a kind of work that can be either reformist 'social work' or militant class organizing. 'First we will take a survey,' one girl says, 'to see what the problems are. Then we will have a programme.'

'The basic problem is religion' – at the end of the discussion, the lecturer and I have a final go at this issue. 'If you ask the women, they will say their problem is cultural,' he claims, and indeed the MSSD girls do say that, as college girls throughout the country tend to do.

But I refuse to accept this: 'I have asked women – women agricultural labourers.' And his final crushing response is, 'Oh, but you have to ask the *proper* people!'

It is clear that, for at least some educated Dalits, the toiling labourers of their own caste are not the 'proper' people. Further, the emphasis on 'culture' characteristic of the MSSD members is only a specific version of the tendency for all middle class women to focus on such issues. It seems that, though the MSSD girls are all Dalits, they belong mainly to the urban, middle class educated sections of their caste, and apart from a fierce and emotional response on the issue of atrocities, they, like other college girls, do not really have much identification with the daily traumas of survival that are the life of women labourers.

With the vagueness of programme, the lack of direction, the often contradictory influence of the men around them, the MSSD still has only a shadowy existence. Yet, as I am coming to realize, the issue of cultural enslavement that the educated continually point to is a real issue, and not simply a 'middle class' problem: the web of envelopment in family and tradition reaches to the depths of society. And the very existence of the MSSD, with its still-unfulfilled potential, is indicative of the restlessness and churning among the current generation of college students. New ideas and aspirations are in the air, and whether or not they get translated into action, the notorious 'indiscipline' of Indian college students, the frequent agitations which commentators and scholars try to attribute to manipulation by political parties or the problem of 'sexual frustration', is itself rather an indication that students are actively engaged in some kind of search, trying to make use of the relative 'freedom' of their 'time between' to look for real liberation.

Such a period of agitation has occurred in the past (when it was also lamented by social conservatives and political rulers). During the nationalist movement, Indian students were fired with social and political issues; they defied college authorities, joined the struggle, burned foreign cloth, donated their gold ornaments, left their education, went to jail, and became terrorists to shoot down British officials and risk hanging. They also defied their parents, ran away from home, and made love marriages. Today also, in a period of disillusionment with the results of independence and of rising poverty and mass turmoil, students are going into the streets, joining demonstrations, defying their parents, making love marriages, and leaving college to go to the villages to try to organize poor peasants in armed struggles against oppressive landlords. And in spite of their greater traditional bondage, and in defiance of this bondage, girls are as much a part of this process as the boys. It is clear that Sita and Savriti are not the final chapter in the Indian cultural tradition.

4. 'We never paid attention to women's problems as women'

Women and the Left

The Blood-coloured Red Flag

There is no grain in the sifter,
My child is starving in the house,
My husband's toiling in the woods,
My memories are of starvation —
      The red flag, the blood-coloured red flag.

My Raghu goes to school,
Without a shirt for his body.
He gets baked like a popcorn in the sun —
Giving a call comes the flag,
      the blood-coloured red flag!

The rich have all the power,
Their ways are alien to the rest of the world,
They grind up the poor to death.
The red flag will overthrow such power,
      the blood-coloured red flag.

Rise, woman, the dawn has come,
The cock has just crowed,
The sun with its pink rose also says
Take in your hand the red flag,
      the blood-coloured red flag.

The daughters of peasants have risen
They have gone to Bombay

And died toiling in the mills.
Until to survive they take in their hands
    the red flag, the blood-coloured red flag.

The rich and the government
Together have decided to beat up the poor,
So, peasant woman, take in your hand
    the red flag, the blood-coloured red flag.

Now we will no longer tolerate injustice!
Why should we be starving?
Why should we bear abuses?
The red flag teaches us to be the tigress,
    the blood-coloured red flag!

Whatever is left to us will also go,
So why do you worry now?
If you join hands in unity
The red flag will accompany you to battle,
    the blood-coloured red flag!

Throw away the false hopes in your mind,
Take the gun of unity in your hand,
Beat up the tyrannical rich!
Take in procession the red flag,
    the blood-coloured red flag.

by Amar Sheikh
Communist song of the 1950s

Leela Bhosle: If there is anyone who has helped me comprehend the inner life of many middle and working class women of India it is Leela, the big, broad, vigorous wife of A.D.Bhosle, the Lal Nishan Party's trade union leader in Pune and known affectionately as A.D. In my films of this period (for I spent a few months doing interviews and taking super-8 films of the municipal workers and some rural meetings) Leela can be seen, striding to a conference among a group of gaunt agricultural labourers, or sitting beside an old municipal worker, drawing her into discussion, commenting on the ways of women. None of the younger women, mostly students, who help me in my interviews or go to working women's meetings can communicate quite so well; none of the other middle class women activists can really share in quite the same way the culture and style of working class women or speak their dialect so effectively. Says Ajit, son of another LNP party leader (extensive family relationships among many of the top leaders give them an intimate familiarity with one another), 'Leela *mawshi* [Aunt Leela] is the one woman among us who chews betel nut and tobacco like the working women – and speaks their language too!' For me it is a vivid memory: Leela, pulling out her betel box and rubbing the tobacco and lime into the leaf as she sits chatting with Tarabai or Sitabai or other municipal workers; Leela intently reading a book on Vietnamese women or a new essay in Marxist theory as she silently chews; and Leela, teasing the younger women of her extended family about their orthodox habit of fasting on Thursday, slapping them on the back affectionately, 'You're a science student, that must be why you're not eating today! Why don't you pray to the gods too?' For, next to betel nut and tobacco, the other unique feature of Leela is her critical and sometimes humorous attitude to the traditional behaviour in which she is immersed.

Says her nephew, Madhav, 'Leela says *a-ho* to A.D., just like a "respectable" woman should – but she always makes it sound like *a-re*!' What he means is that Leela addresses her husband always in the respectful plural form (*a-ho* and its equivalents), but does it in such a tone of voice, with lifted eyebrows and occasional winks, and loudly indignant responses to his occasional indulgence in shouting, that their interaction always seems to me to be more modern, more affectionate than that of other families. What Leela does is to make the respectful sound, somehow, familiar.

Madhav's comment points to a major aspect of husband-wife relationships in India. Marathi, like other Indian languages, has both the singular (or 'familiar') and plural (or 'respectful') verb and adjective forms. Equals address each other in the plural form; close friends in the singular; social inferiors use the plural to social superiors and are spoken back to frequently in the singular – and husbands invariably use the singular form to their wives while wives, peasant or urban, working class or middle class, address their husbands in the plural. Wives are not supposed to refer to their husbands by name, except ritualistically in the 'name-taking' songs, and in general they simply use the polite form of impersonal address, *a-ho*, to get their husbands' attention. Only among the culturally radicalized sections of the younger generation will you nowadays find some young women addressing their husbands and other close male friends in the singular; the effect is shocking to an Indian ear.

Leela is of the older generation and at one with the overwhelming majority in her surface behaviour, but she is unique in her way of reflecting and commenting on this. Politically active since the age of 16, she knows and abides by the social rules but, unlike most, is intensely self-conscious of their implications. '*Bharatiya nari*, the "Indian woman",' she quotes mockingly, 'it sounds like a curse!' as she bustles about the kitchen preparing tea for various party leaders who are gathering in discussion. But she always makes the tea; she is not after all part of the Leading Committee. 'Make it yourself,' she will sometimes say to A.D. as he demands his afternoon cup, but in fact she always prepares it. 'I would like to wear slacks,' she sighs, holding up a pair of mine to her ample figure, 'but I'm too old. I'm stuck with saris.' And so she wears saris. And she is the one who emphasizes the linguistic rules: 'You *never* address your husband directly – just say, "he has come" or "he has gone" [where 'he' literally translated is the royal 'they'] or "that person over there".' And out of her years of experience and work beyond the confines of middle class life, she adds, 'It's not that way among the lowest classes, though. Among agricultural labourers both men and women may call each other "thou".'

In many ways Leela has become conscious of the political implications of social phenomena in a way that the men in her party are not. After all, she is the one who knows something of politics but continues to serve their tea and prepare their meals, providing the invisible but supporting domestic background for the serious political activity they carry on. Also, she is involved in the web of family relationships, acting as a kind of 'go-between' in marriage arrangements, entertaining and looking over prospective husbands for young girls of the extended family, disliking it, feeling the helplessness of the girls, but knowing there is no alternative. Leela herself has been and is in politics, originally in actual organizing among workers, for the last decades as a manager of the party press, working half time. But politics is not her only function; she is in the domestic world as well, and knows it, and at times feels trapped in it.

In fact, it was Leela who first drew my attention to the problems of women in left parties, to this one excruciatingly obvious example of the gap between egalitarian rhetoric and discriminatory practice. In 1971, sometime after I had spoken before the women agricultural labourers in Ahmednagar, after I had met many leaders from this localized but strongly based regional party, I had gotten into the habit of visiting the Bhosles' house. Not far away from the middle class flat I was sharing with another American student, their house was a centre for party meetings, and after they had finished their business I used to meet and discuss with them. Leela was of course there too, and we exchanged some words, but it was always difficult for me to know what to say, though I was conscious of the awkwardness of sitting down with men while a woman was fixing tea for us in the kitchen. From my point of view the main barrier was language, my stumbling Marathi and her faltering English. But from her perspective there was something more. One day she wrote me a note, lamenting that we hadn't been able to discuss much, and stressing that *'in spite of all the years of communist tradition women still sit in the back.'*

The truth is that in all the communist and socialist parties in India there are very few full-time women political activists. In Leela's party, the LNP, there are none among the older generation and only one young woman working in trade unions in Bombay. Yet there are very many politically conscious women, old and young, vigorous, energetic, capable, who have been involved in left movements for decades. Those Indian women who are in professional positions always seem extremely competent and self-confident, personally untroubled by any supposed 'role contradictions'; party women are much the same. Most women party members, however, are not in full-time 'politics' as such. They may be the wives or sisters of political activists; they may take part in occasional movements and mobilizations, they may be ready to talk

45

about politics, but for the most part they take care of the home and they work, as school teachers or as other professionals. Very often such women are and have been the main financial support of their 'political' husbands. In contrast, women full-time activists are rare, and there are a distressing number of men full-timers who seem to have traditional wives and home lives.

How did this all come about? Specifically, how did Leela, the wife of one party leader and sister of another, who entered politics herself at about the same time they did, come to be in such a secondary position? As we begin to talk more — and find that stumbling and faltering does not really prevent communication after all — we ask all these questions. Was there active discrimination against women? Here Leela and other members of the older generation of communist women are emphatic: there was not. Leela, in fact, stresses the emphasis on equality both in her parents' home and in early party life.

This home was a well-off household of a high court judge in the state of Kolhapur in the southern part of Maharashtra, one of literally hundreds of areas of India that used to still be officially under the rule of 'native princes' rather than being 'British territory'. Kolhapur itself was a fairly provincial small town, but in this period, in the late 1930s, its younger generation was swept with the fervour of Indian nationalism. And Kolhapur itself, though small-town, had unique features: it was ruled by a Maratha (the biggest non-Brahman caste), and Marathas and other low castes had gained positions in its administration in contrast to Brahman-dominated Pune and Bombay. More than this, it had been ruled by one of the most radically anti-caste Maharajahs in India, a man who had stressed education for all low castes, who promoted untouchables, who arranged inter-caste marriages for members of his own family. This social reformism, originally expressed in a bitter fight against 'Brahman nationalists', later merged into the nationalist stream to affect the atmosphere of Kohlapur and Leela's household:

'There was a lot of independence in my house for girls. I don't understand it, my mother being illiterate and ignorant, but her thought was never a barrier for us. Generally, in the atmosphere of a princely state, there were so many restrictions on girls — they couldn't speak with men, they couldn't go out of the home, they had to come back early in the day. Still, in our house there were no barriers. We had girlfriends as well as boyfriends, and since boys were politically more active than girls in the student movement, naturally boys used to come home. When I think about it now, I feel surprised that we had so much independence. That is, just as boys were given tea and so forth, so were we when we had boys and girls up to the room, and really, my entering into politics was out of this atmosphere. My father used to give educational help to poor students, untouchables and peasant boys. The arrangement was that such students would come for one or two days to eat with well-off sympathizers. My mother used to serve them, and she never discriminated in her behaviour between them and us. This was an education I got from my childhood.'

Perhaps what has to be stressed is that it was *unusual* for girls of a wealthy middle caste civil servant's family to have guests in their rooms, to have tea served to them, etc. In a way, the limits for women in the social reformism of Kolhapur were symbolized in the fact that the culturally radical Maharajah, who would at times force his own nobles to drink tea served by untouchables, still did not like his daughters to go out of his house freely 'like common peasant women', according to his biographer. In any case, Leela became a part of the spreading nationalist movement, and since her brother was one of the young communists who were core organizers of the students, she gravitated towards Marxism also. These Kolhapur Marxist youth remained separate from the official Communist Party for nationalist reasons (the CPI was collaborating with the British at that time — during the Second World War) and formed themselves instead into a separate group that was later to develop into the LNP. But the crucial point here is not the zigzags of this development but the fact that, from the beginning, both women and men were involved in it.

Of these ('there were about 100 boys and 20 girls') the most committed went to Pune to begin full-time political organizing among postal employees, railway workers, domestic servants and municipal workers; there was not much industry at the time. They lived then in a commune, and Leela and others insist that there was no discrimination.

'Three or four of us brothers and sisters were in politics from the days of the student movement. Then, for many reasons, only my brother and I stayed in, the rest got married . . . You could say I was free from all the problems of women from the beginning. My marriage was also with an activist from our party. And since both my father's and father-in-law's house were far away, I was free from household responsibilities. Even my son was taken care of by my mother-in-law after five months. When I was a full-timer my husband also did the cooking, washed clothes while I went out for meetings. So my husband also gave me freedom. However, when I began to work among women, we saw women only as workers, and did not pay attention to whatever problems they may have had as women.'

Those early days are recalled with nostalgia. Commune life, men and women of different castes together, domestic and political life shared by all, invigorating in spite of its rigours. 'Everyone did all the work,' each party leader would stress in talking about that period. 'Everyone shared . . . we couldn't afford servants . . . we men even washed the women's clothes.' This it seemed was of special importance, that men would wash women's clothes, even menstrual rags, showing that they could be as fervent as Gandhians in demonstrating equality and unconcern with pollution. To give the communist movement of the time its due (and this was true not simply of LNP, but in general) there seems to have been a kind of general moral fervour about women's equality in it. Opponents and traditionalists accused the communists of destroying the family; people talked about the defiance of convention; it was said that communist women would even smoke on stage during political rallies. They had indeed come a long way—but why not further? There *was* consciousness in the beginning about women's rights; the phrase — so much a part of left vocabulary — that 'women are doubly oppressed' was not mere rhetoric.

So what happened?

Was it marriage — which earlier had been the occasion for Leela's brothers and sisters to go out of the movement? Marriages, too, were in the context of the movement, of the mixed political-social life. They were mixed marriages, half 'love' (i.e. by choice), half arranged. But not arranged in the traditional way by parents, rather by party leaders as time went on and some kind of domestic stablization seemed required, as young women and men came to be attached to one another or to outsiders, in a period when not only were love affairs frowned upon but even the fact of unmarried girls going out alone was considered somewhat immoral. So marriages (including inter-caste marriages) were arranged, or chosen, with elements of romance, elements of pragmatic choice and simply the need for stable companionship, and occasionally even elements of compulsion when marriage or attraction to a non-party person was discouraged. Leela refuses to say what exactly was the case with her and A.D., but according to her nephew Madhav, 'she proposed to him one day, at a picnic, by a lake . . . '

What Leela herself says is only, 'Our marriage was not really proper, even though we're of the same caste. He is six months younger than I. The wife should not be elder to the husband!' And she goes on to talk about selling all their wedding gifts, including the gold *mangalsutra* necklace that is equivalent to a wedding ring, to raise money because the party itself was so poor. 'It wasn't until years later that I got a *mangalsutra*.'

If it wasn't marriage itself that altered the position of party women — for Leela had the privilege, unique to a more traditional society, of depositing her son with her mother-in-law while she continued work — then what was it? The clue perhaps is in her remark that 'we saw women only as workers and did not pay attention to whatever problems they may have had as women.' Somehow, among these early communists, the sense of moral fervour about personal life (equality in household tasks, treating women themselves as political equals just as they treated the low castes among them as equals) did not extend itself to their practical, political work where they functioned rigorously but narrowly on a simple class basis. Outside the sphere of production, the fact that there was caste discrimination, or that women were bound to household tasks, was in practice not treated as relevant to the task of revolutionary organizing. ('Well, we had to make a beginning, and we were so few activists,' they will say, when these issues are discussed; or, 'How can we organize the women when we've hardly begun to organize the men?') For women this was crucial: *workers* of course were overwhelmingly men, except for a few underprivileged sectors. (As a matter of fact, the inability to see 'social' issues as matters around which to organize politically also had a tremendous impact on the communists' relations with the Dalit movement, but this is another question.) And where there were women workers, party activists in practice had no programme for dealing with the fact that they rarely became union activists or leaders because of the heavy burden of housework.

And it was somehow more easy, more natural, for male activists to organize male workers, more difficult and more unnatural for female activists to keep going out. Gradually the natural processes began to establish themselves. Everyone should have equal rights, but there was somehow never an examination of the 'natural' bases of inequality, there was a theoretical blind spot, and the consciousness of women's rights remained at a mere 'moral' level because there was no analysis of the actual conditions for equality. The LNP group, also, was poor; it could not support everyone as full-time workers; some of its members had to take up employment. Somehow, very naturally, some of the men and *all* of the women in the group — particularly after people had married and begun to settle in family units, after finances became privatized along family lines and full-time political husbands found that they couldn't maintain full-time political wives — took up jobs. And once in employment, working a full day and enduring the long hours it often takes to get to work in India, coming home to take up housework and do some little political work, the women found it hard to have time to read, difficult to keep up with theory, and impossible to get real political training as activists. Becoming 'backward' in theory and political activity, then, they lost any claim to real participation in decision-making. And so it was that, out of the original group of enthusiastic Marxist-nationalist students, fervent about cultural and social reform as well as political and economic achievement, out of the original period of commune living and the sharing of domestic and public tasks, the 'natural' evolution took place, and husbands and brothers became well-known party leaders, while their equally intelligent and enthusiastic wives and sisters became working housewives. 'You can't blame the men,' the women say today; 'what else could they do?' What else indeed? It still remains a question whether the younger generation of activists can break this pattern of subordination of political women.

'We never paid attention to women's problems as women.' But, says Leela, 'during the famine days, when the women waged a struggle for equal wages and equal work, it began to come into our heads that women can give battle on women's problems and take part in a big way. After that I got some literature about Vietnamese women, then Chinese women, and about women battling in all areas. I was very impressed. The literature gave me confidence that we can do great work by going among women and taking up their problems as women, that we can link the fight for women's liberation with the general social struggle.'

A new wave of mass struggles, a new literature, new ideas, new images of women with guns. Vietnam, Mozambique, Guinea-Bissau, fighting imperialism and fighting social traditions, combating 'the colonialism of the Portuguese and the colonialism of men'. Women's liberation appearing as a new force at the heart of revolutionary upsurge. Are we really in a revolutionary new era?

From Hyderabad, in the state of Andhra Pradesh just south of

Maharashtra, come stories of a new women's organization that is both libera-tionist and left. POW, the Progressive Organization of Women, formed by women involved in a student movement that is itself rapidly becoming Marxist and revolutionary, marching against the dowry, attacking men who harass women students, organizing slum women and taking a new ideological step in making a link between 'scientific socialism' and the idea that women have special problems and must be organized specially as women. 'The majority of Indian women are slaves of slaves,' according to their draft manifesto. 'They are slaves to the men who themselves are slaves to this exploitative economic system. It is thus necessary that we women take a direct, leading role in organizing the masses of women in their struggles for a better life and a changed system.'

In the context of the Hyderabad area (known as Telengana, a name em-blazoned in Indian revolutionary tradition), it is more than just student rhetoric to talk of 'mass organizing' and 'revolution'. Over thirty years before, a whole wave of educated peasant and middle class youth rode the tide of radical nationalism into communism, just as Leela's group did. But in Hyderabad, which was ruled by a reactionary feudal king and not by the British or, like Kolhapur, by a reformist Maharajah, this took a different form. In the end, masses of peasants rose up in armed revolt against the feudal landlords of the area. 15,000 square miles and 3,000 villages in Telengana were enveloped in the communist uprising, ruled temporarily by peasant committees and defended by armed squads. And it took four years, 1948 to 1952, for the Indian army to finally crush them. Telegana retained its Marx-ist traditions, and years later, when a new tide of mass unrest began to gather after 1967, and a new call to armed revolt was given by what was known as the 'Naxalite' movement, it was natural for students in Hyderabad to sym-pathize and take up the call, some only in words but many also in action, going to villages to try to ignite the armed struggle, or going to slums to politicize and organize the people. Girls responded as well as boys, but the girls discovered they had to face different barriers to their participation from the boys — families who tried to hold them back, the weight of socially in-culcated femininity which made it difficult for them to have self-confidence, the complete lack of understanding of the men in the movement about all these problems. Like the women's liberation movement in the West, like the women's unions of Vietnam and Mozambique, the POW was born out of the special problems of women's involvement in a radical mass movement and in the context of a consciousness of those problems.

So the POW itself is something new, in its origin and its liberationist emphasis, and when word comes that a POW representative, Rukmini Menon, is visiting Pune, there is an eager response from a number of young left-oriented students. I am also invited to the meeting and go with just as much eagerness.

As I enter, a bit early, one of Pune's spacious upper middle class apart-ments I hear the soft singing of a Hindi film song. A typical scene . . . but this is a song from *Pyasa* ('Thirst'), a famous Hindi film of the late 1950s, a film in fact that, as one of my friends says, 'every generation of college students goes to see.' Like all Hindi films it seems terribly melodramatic to outsiders, a story of a poet crushed by corruption and commercialism, but its significance is in voicing the utter disillusionment of a whole generation. The massiveness of the Indian student rebellion has to be understood in the context of th hopes aroused by independence and then dashed by bitter reality, and films like *Pyasa* express this revolt in a romanticized and individualized form. And it is striking that the most famous song of disillusionment focuses on women, for it is a song about the prostitutes' quarters that the poet is wandering through:

> These lanes, these auction houses of loved ones,
> These caravans of people robbed of life,
> Where is he, where is he, the protector of God,
> Oh he who cares about India, where is he?
>   where is he?
>
> These alleys of watchmen, these ill-famed bazaars,
> These anonymous travellers, these clanging bells,
> These deals of fate, these blows against purity,
> Oh he who cares about India, where is he,
>   where is he?
>
> The ringing of ankle bells on empty carpets,
> The rumble of drums in defeated breaths,
> The rasping of coughs in bodiless rooms,
> Oh he who cares about India, where is he,
>   where is he?
>
> The saints have come here also, and the young
>   have come,
> Dumb sons, fathers and husbands have come here,
> She is a wife, she is a sister, she is a mother!
> Oh he who cares about India, where is he,
>   where is he?
>
> Please call the dwellers in this land,
> Show them these lanes, these paths, these temples,
> Bring the ones here who care about India,
> Oh he who cares about India, where is he,
>   where is he?

The singer is, of course, Rukmini. We exchange greetings, a few words, more people enter, young men as well as women, and Rukmini begins by telling us briefly about the student movement that formed the background for the POW. For, before they started organizing as women, all the girls were involved in fights against student fee increases, against rising prices, in mass agitations to protest the killing of a young student radical by college hoodlums, in the student movement's fervent turn to Marxism. And just as the MSSD has to be understood in the context of the Dalit movement, so this wave was the context for the POW.

'Why did we start a women's organization? When we went with boys to meetings — there were five or six of us to start with — other girls were afraid to go out. So we began to ask why. They were more interested in women's problems, they would come to a women's meeting. Aside from that, their level of consciousness is low, we have to admit that women are backward politically. And girls are afraid, if they are in a minority, to go out for a demonstration.'

'*Women are backward politically*': it is a different emphasis from what a Western feminist, 'radical' or 'socialist', would say. The POW women's ideological commitment to Marxism was never questioned, and their initial debate about 'whether we should stress women's liberation or social revolution' was quite naturally resolved in the direction of 'socialism'. But in those early days they were (like Leela) reading on women's movements and women's involvement in revolution; they were in contact with Western feminists and they were holding discussion forums. Out of this came something that really was new for the Indian left: not only a recognition of the 'double oppression' of women, but an effort to define it concretely and to grasp its cultural aspects, its specificity. 'Confined to the limits of the home,' states their Manifesto, 'the girl child receives pots, pans, dolls, mirrors etc as toys. She is taught to imitate her mother, to learn the art of housekeeping, and to prepare for marriage. She is taught that clinging tendencies, meekness, decorativeness, and a pathological fear of independence are feminine, and she is further degraded! Little wonder that women behave nearly always as they are expected to!'

Thus the girls identified themselves as 'socialist feminist', but like the early women's movement in the West they began to organize around cultural issues. Their first campaign was on a basic symbol of Indian women's oppression, the dowry. 'We created the organization in June with a meeting and a resolution, but not much was done for a while. The first agitation came in August, against the dowry. Ten students worked on this, going to different colleges, appealing to students and office workers.' Pamphlets were issued and September 13, 1974, was chosen as a protest day. 'Eight hundred turned up for the mass meeting, and it was really militant! Six hundred went with us on our march. A great victory!' And so this major focus of women's lack of independence in marriage turns out to be a spark.

'Then we had our organizational consolidation, a POW convention, the drafting of the Manifesto, an enrolment campaign. Now we have 500 members, mostly students.' The organizational structure of POW is elaborate, including seven basic committees for everything from seminars to cultural programmes to work in slums. The organizing spread from the big city of Hyderabad to the small town colleges in the rural areas of Telengana. 'The initial contact for going to the district colleges came from the girls themselves after they heard about our dowry campaign. In the districts the students are more of lower middle class and rural background, there is more oppression, and girls will put aside everything and work for this.' As in the case of Milind College and Bimzani College, it seems the 'provinces' are not so backward after all. Meetings of up to 8,000 and marches of 2 to 3,000 were held in these small district towns.

A month after the anti-dowry campaign came an anti-'Eve-teasing' march, 'Eve-teasing' being for some reason the term for general male harassment of girls. It was sparked off spontaneously when a gang of young landlords' sons mocked a POW activist, and the women decided to take this as a chance to attack both male chauvinism and their 'class enemies'. They marched down the college corridors, nearly *gheraoed* the vice-chancellor, and shouted, 'Down with roadside Romeos! Down with corridor Romeos! End police tyranny!'

And they began to organize women in the slums or *bustees*. Many of the young student radicals of this new generation have tended to devote themselves to experiments in slum work, rather than to the trade union organizing the traditional left parties have preferred, partly because they lack contact with organized workers whose party leaders (even when communists) are unwilling to let in competitors who disagree with them politically, but mainly because they are ideologically oriented to the most oppressed sections, the poor and landless in the rural areas, the unorganized, half-employed slum dwellers of the cities. The POW girls have been part of this, with attempts to establish a base through literacy campaigns, sewing classes, marches against high prices and for better water facilities. Here among the most desperately poor city dwellers, once their attention really turned to women's oppression, they made two discoveries: first, male support was necessary to begin work, to have some access to the women ('You can't organize women in *bustees* until the men are organized,' Rukmini tells us), but second, latent anti-male feeling runs high among the slum women ('Sometimes it seems they almost hate men; they like hearing about middle class women's agitation'). A new kind of contradiction was manifesting itself. In a situation where male domination is exercized in the extreme and direct forms of drunken wife-beating and total disregard of the woman's needs, in a situation where women are at best half-employed, working occasionally as casual labourers, making native cigarettes in the home, selling grass or a few vegetables in the market for a few pennies a day, they do not have the strength of even the well organized Pune municipal workers to stand up against the men. Behind this helplessness, the resentment of the women, though subdued, brews even more.

And as we discuss this in the bright, Pune middle class apartment, it turns out that the POW organizers have their own streak of real feminism. They too have found out that left male sympathizers don't really believe in separate women's organizations. Though Rukmini stresses the support the girls get from their 'comrades', she is equally ready to insist on the need for autonomous organization. 'Girls as individuals are not taken seriously, but when you're organized and have your section behind you, they take you seriously. So we educate girls first. Any oppressed section has to organize itself first.'

'Isn't there a problem of an anti-male danger?' asks a young man in the group. 'Will you merge later with a general organization?'

'No. Women's problems are special. We will work together but not merge. We will maintain separate organizations. There *is* a contradiction between men and women. *You have to accept that.* This division of labour that exists is unfair.'

And now other women in the group chime in to talk about the problems of a feudal culture which imposes on them the burdens of dowry and arranged marriages, which keeps women in the home; about the double burdens of housework; about the brainwashing of women to conform to stereotypes of frailty and femininity. The Pune women are tremendously impressed by the POW experience and self-assured insistence of Rukmini that women have to be and can be organized. As she talks, a sense of the dedication and energy of the organizers comes through, feverishly taking up one campaign after another with a feeling of working against time in the growing turmoil and polarization in India ('Really, we're so busy we hardly have time to eat, we drink endless cups of tea instead, then we fall sick —'). They are getting an undoubted response from the Telengana college students (POW's current campaign, against 'obscene' advertising and films making a commercial use of women's bodies, has been provoked by demands from new members: 'How can you claim to be a women's organization if you don't take this up?'). And adding to both tension and excitement is the very serious reality of participating in a left movement identified with 'Naxalite' communist rebels who are at that very moment involved in armed struggle in distant jungle areas, who have been confronting police shooting, jailing and torture. The POW women know very well they are being watched by police and see hope only in the possibility of building up enough mass support from students and slum dwellers to protect themselves for a time.

While it is true that many among the main group of POW organizers are in the process of identifying themselves as 'Naxalites', and with a specific Naxalite group at that, the 'Party' is not at this stage exercising any real guidance, and the impulse of their activity is coming from a different source. In fact, though the Naxalite movement itself involved women from the very beginning, the young revolutionary communists of the new era seem to have about the same attitude towards women as the first communists of Leela's generation and earlier had: a friendly welcome into activism, a blithe un-willingness to recognize the special problems of women, and perhaps a sub-conscious fear of having their own privileges challenged. In this sense, the POW with its insistence on organizing women around their own problems *is* new, a genuine, self-generated women's movement — and the 'Marxist-Leninist' links of some of its leaders (which all the Pune women and most people elsewhere know about but never discuss openly in politically mixed company) only lend it authenticity.

The POW leaders themselves are later to admit the flaws in their movement: too much identification in the minds of the public and the police with the Naxalite student left even though they were largely acting on their own; too much of a student orientation without any real mass base; too rapid expansion with just a few committed organizers. But it is undeniably the first real women's liberation organization in India. And Rukmini's visit and the accounts of the POW experience serve their purpose of sparking off the effort in Maharashtra. Two weeks later, an organizing group in Pune meets for the first time to start something similar. But there is one difference. In contrast to the POW, it includes not only the student radicals of the new generation but older women activists as well, not only those sympathetic to the Naxalite movement but also women of other left trends. In this meeting sit one socialist leader, women representing the two big parliamentary communist parties, independent leftist professionals, students, and finally, Leela and Tarabai. The Pune women's movement is about to begin.

5. 'Without the union we are scrap value'

Rural Women in Struggle

Throw Off the Burden of Debts

Chorus
Throw off the burden of debts,
The principles of capitalism.

Socialism they say they will bring,
With heaps of food their bellies swell!
Of the toilers' mountains of sorrow
Nothing will they see or tell.

For what, and for whom
They borrow money from abroad,
The profits are eaten by the capitalists
And inflation's our reward!

They give speeches against the great
And build up sugar cooperatives —
They hold the power and eat up the sugar
And *jaggery* tea to us they give.

In the mountains, on the river banks,
Tribal natives starving live.
What need do they have for
Palaces and luxury cars?

Goda, Pravara, Krishna, Koyna,
These are the treasures of white milky nectar,

The cream of the water, electricity's sparkle —
Who can get a share in this?

Battles have begun in the Congress Party,
The local boss grows fat in the middle,
Have you forgotten Maratha tradition,
These have become Black Englishmen!

In all directions I can see
The toilers' red flag flapping now —
To take the power in our hands
Now is the time to strike a blow!

by Bapurao Barde
Song of the agricultural
labourers' struggles
of the 1970s, from
Ahmednagar district

And so it begins. On March 8, 250 women march along the streets
of Pune to celebrate International Women's Day, red flags flying, municipal
workers striding along shouting slogans and college students joining in,
'Hail to the brave women of Vietnam and Mozambique!' 'Victory to
International Women's Day!' 'Victory to Toiling Women!' On
Leela's initiative a special issue of the Lal Nishan Party paper is brought out,
focusing on women's liberation and laying down the dictum that 'Without
social revolution there can be no women's liberation; without women's liberation social revolution is incomplete.' Because of this, consciousness begins to
grow among LNP activists that mobilizing women will release a new force,
and so I begin to get invitations from district level LNP organizers to visit
their area, to meet the women, to help stimulate interest. One such invitation
comes from Ahmednagar district where I had had that first early meeting wit
with women labourers in 1971, and so, out of a desire to once again come in
contact with the rural women who are at the base of the storm, who will be
the base for any real women's movement, I accept it.

Like the central India area where Bori Arab is located, Ahmednagar is an
overwhelmingly agricultural district, and has even more of a history of being
perennially famine-ridden. The same castes can be found as in Bori Arab —
peasant Marathas and Kunbis, the varied artisan castes, Dalit Mahars and
Matangs, an occasional group of tribal people. And the same toiling women
can be seen pulling up weeds, scraping fertilizer onto young plants, carrying
bundles of grass and fodder on their heads, nurturing the soil.

But the differences are crucial. Where Bori Arab and its neighbouring
villages seem quiet and relatively untouched by rural struggle, Ahmednagar
has been a centre of it, the 'red district' of Maharashtra state. From move-

ments of social and cultural revolt in which non-Brahman peasants fought Brahman moneylenders and priests, to anti-British underground activity led by socialists and young peasants, to Communist Party organizing in the 1950s and Lal Nishan organizing today, waves of struggle have crashed over the district, and women, the toiling women of the fields, have been a part of this storm. It was not accidental that I met my first group of women agricultural labourers in Ahmednagar, or that some of the most inspiring stories of women's militancy during the famine period have come from there. For while men and women poor peasants throughout the state went to work on government relief projects during those years and learned through bitter experience the necessity of struggle to get the projects in the first place and then to get their wages paid even after they had been working for weeks on these projects, it was in Ahmednagar district that the struggle reached its peak.

So, when I am invited once more as a guest of LNP organizers, I am ready. I meet Suresh Gawli, the young activist who told me the story of women tying the government official to a tree, and we start off from the dusty district town where the union centre is located, but not this time by bus, rather on a party provided motorcycle that is the fastest and most practical means of travel in the rural reas.

It is easy to see, as we ride along, what is different about Ahmednagar. Bori Arab and its surroundings show the scrawny trees, the fragmented fields, the barrenness of a 'backward' region, but Ahmednagar, at least northern Ahmednagar, is throbbing with progress. We pass rich green fields of waving sugar cane, travelling on roads busy not simply with bullock carts and buses and the occasional bicycle but also cars and trucks and the roaring motorcycles of the rich peasants, their white pyjama-pants flapping and white Gandhi caps set firmly on their heads. Here are the familiar mud and brick villages, but here also are smoking sugar factories surrounded by the huts of migrant workers, the imposing modernistic buildings of an agricultural university, an occasional gaudy rich farmer's house standing aloof in the middle of his fields. These are the signs of a transformed rural India, of India's 'Green Revolution' — the term for the government sponsored and Ford Foundation promoted programme of technological development that began in the mid-1960s with the aim of revolutionizing production through the use of irrigation, fertilizer and new varieties of seeds.

Truly speaking, Indian agriculture has not been revolutionized. By the 1970s food crop production is moving again towards stagnation relative to population growth, and sporadic famines spreading throughout the country reveal the fragile base and monsoon dependence of agriculture. Ahmednagar district itself, still plagued by famine, only half-developed, its southern counties still dry and backward, is witness to this. But there is no doubt that the northern area has been transformed. It is highly irrigated as a result of dam building projects, and this itself is part of its social explosiveness. When western Indian soils get irrigation, they blossom forth with cash crops and class conflict. As some peasants become rich and turn into capitalist farmers

riding high on green fields of sugar cane, the poor and landless become poorer
and turn into wage labourers on their farms. And so, the first wave of Communist organizing among Ahmednagar peasants in the 1950s was beaten back
as many newly rich peasant ex-Communists joined the Congress party, while
cooperative sugar factories, once organized with high hopes by social reformers and leftists, became bastions of the private power of village bosses. But a
second wave of struggle followed, and the poor peasants and agricultural
labourers mobilized mainly by LNP in the last few years seem to be fighting
with a new consciousness. Their very songs of struggle show it:

> They give speeches against the great
> And build up sugar cooperatives —
> They hold the power and eat up the sugar,
> And *jaggery* tea to us they give!

Songs like this, like 'Red Sun in the East' (which Bhimrao and I played in the
Bori Arab school), like 'Questions of a Woman Agricultural Labourer', come
from Ahmednagar. They describe the process by which one time 'peasant'
nationalists become capitalist exploiters and collaborators with imperialism
('Black Englishmen'), and ask new kinds of questions:

> Tall buildings rise before our eyes,
> The roads cannot contain their motorcycles and cars,
> On whose labour has all this development been built?

'Questions of a Woman Agricultural Labourer', while written by a man and
with no hint of the special oppression of women, still does illustrate the
extent to which political organizers were recognizing women's role in
struggles. And I remember its singer, the singer of so many of these songs,
Tanubai Barde, an agricultural labourer herself, the lead singer of a peasant
troupe, a woman of bold sweeping gestures and a proud stance, impulsively
grasping my hands after I speak of solidarity in a 1973 rally. Tanubai works
on a big capitalist farm in northern Ahmednagar, and I am eager to track her
down, anxious to find out what rural development and the waves of class
struggle have meant to women like her.

But first, riding north, we come to Rahuri and see on our left the tall
buildings of Mahatma Phule Agricultural University thrusting themselves
out of the fields. The Agricultural University pioneers and attempts to spread
modern techniques of agriculture, and trains as its students boys from rich
and middle peasant families of the area. But, working its fields, producing the
crops which are both experimental and highly profitable, are low caste farm
labourers, 1,100 women and 1,300 men. The difference is striking and visual.
In a Ford Foundation photo essay on India's 'Food Revolution', you can see
male agricultural experts, male rich peasants squatting to examine new crops,
and a whole cluster of young, suited male graduates walking forth into a new

world — but, working in the fields, bending, stooping, sifting grain, sorting ears of corn, are women labourers. Women, it is now universally admitted, were the original inventors of agriculture, but in the current era of technological advance they remain only manual labourers of the Green Revolution.

On the university farm, Suresh tells me, women earn 3.55 rupees a day and men earn 4.50, significantly higher than the villagers of Bori Arab but not much more than the rich peasants pay in surrounding villages. These are nowhere near the wages of any permanent government employee, and in fact, with a few exceptions, these farmworkers who have been working since the university was built are not 'permanent' and have no security of tenure, no leave, no paid holidays and no other benefits. And so in October 1974, under LNP leadership, they organized a union and went on strike over the main demands of status as permanent employees and application of the industrial relations laws to agriculture.

This seemingly simple demand met with ferocious resistance. There is a panicky nature about the Indian ruling classes in this period, confronted by rising demands everywhere and determined to hold the line at every point possible. A massive, nationwide railway strike in the middle of 1974 just before my arrival has been beaten down after 20 days of struggle and the arrest of 50,000 workers and union activists, and it is followed by a general renewed offensive by employers and the government. One part of this is the adamance of the management at Rahuri. In addition, the social ties between the university administration and the surrounding rich farmers, who have no desire to see any successful model of struggle that might inspire the labourers in their own fields, stiffened their resolve. And so the union leaders were warned by local police that, come what may, a 'policy level' decision had been made to break the strike.

One day, while workers picketed the farm, a group of students and professors ostentatiously walked into the field to work the land. The infuriated workers, led by the women, charged in — and the police, ready for exactly this response, retaliated with severe beatings and the first use of tear-gas the people of this area had experienced. The labourers, thinking at first they were being shot at, fled, and were chased by the rampaging police to their village homes, dragged out, beaten and arrested. The heart of the strike was broken, and though it continued for another week the labourers slowly drifted back to work and it had to be officially withdrawn.

Now, six months later, the consequences of the defeat are still visible. Suresh and other union activists are forbidden by court injunction from entering the university. When we stop on the roadside by the farm the labourers, on their way home, are at first fearful, reluctant to come to this equivalent of a 'gate meeting'. A university jeep filled with uniformed men drives conspicuously by and stops a hundred yards away. But finally the workers start together. They are more silent than usual, though, and the discussion focuses on the issue of women as Suresh explains my visit and gives what in fact is a militant feminist speech. By the end of it, in spite of the intimidation, nearly 150 workers have gathered and the meeting finishes with a song and some slogans of worker solidarity.

Later that night, as we visit two nearby villages, the people are more out-spoken. They talk of the speedup that has gone on since the breaking of the strike, the fact that if they are seen talking to a union organizer they will not be given work the following day, that if they resist at all or are the slightest bit late for work they will not be hired that day. 'Their whim is law,' they say of the university officials. 'They force us to work overtime. Before, we dictated terms and left at five, now they dictate to us and force us to do as they wish!'

Bhagubai, a woman strike leader who takes us to her house for tea, is depressed. Before the strike she had been one of about 100 workers on per-manent status; now she has lost this and with it most of her pay. 'Whoever goes out in front loses,' she says, echoing Kaminibai. But Bhagubai, out of her experience of struggle, adds, 'If everyone acts unitedly, we can win. Unity must endure!'

The problems of unity, though, are as glaringly obvious in Rahuri as in Bori Arab. There are caste differences among the farm labourers. About 40% are Dalits (mostly Mahar-Buddhists) while the rest are mainly Marathas, the large 'peasant' caste. Once repression came and the surrounding rich peasants and university administration resolved to break the strike, it was the Marathas who were the first to go back to work, while the Dalits stayed out until the end. Why? Perhaps because the Dalits were more proletarianized, with almost no land of their own and nothing to fall back on except the strength of num-bers and the militancy of desperation, while the Marathas, themselves poor but perhaps with a little land, were likely to have family or kin connections among the rich peasant landowners of their own caste and so were more wavering, more open to appeals to 'be reasonable'.

There is also the difference in women's position in the two castes. Among Dalits, where women have always worked in the fields and as labour-ers, they have more social independence and equality in decision-making, but among Marathas and other caste Hindus there is a greater tendency for the for the men to want to – and be able to – keep women in the home. Bhagubai, herself a Maratha, tells me that when the middle caste men decided to go back to work the women followed them: 'The men make the decisions'. Though women are more militant, 'if we start making speeches and take leadership, they say we are becoming "too wise".' Then how did Bhagubai herself become a leader? Because she is divorced and therefore free of the direct domination of a man. And it seems to be a pattern throughout rural India that wherever women emerge as active organizers they are women without husbands, widows or divorcees, or else the wives of party activists.

The next afternoon I am invited into the university grounds to hear the 'other side' in a meeting promoted by a local middle peasant who is trying to mediate what he sees as an 'inter-group' quarrel. The labour welfare officer of the university shows me around, claiming that the women workers in fact can finish up their work in half a day.

'Unions are all right,' he says, 'but not *goondaism*'. They cheat the workers of money, he claims; the local organizer gets 2,000 rupees a month. 'What do they need a union for anyway, when they have a labour welfare officer?'

He shows me a child care centre for the children of the labourers. But it is one of four on the entire farm, and only about 20 children are present, hardly enough, I feel, to meet the needs of 1,100 working women. He tells me that the workers get 5 kilos of grain free at every festival and a ration of milk every other day. 'Besides, they can keep goats and chickens.'

That night we talk to the labourers again. They are highly scornful of such claims of affluence and welfare programmes. 'That's because of our demonstrations,' the women claim. They have had marches and *gheraos* of all sorts prior to the strike, and the welfare programmes of the university were started after these. They say they have to pay for the festival grain and the milk — 'the money is cut from our wages after fifteen days.' They do indeed, or at least some do, have a few chickens or a goat, but it hardly seems fitting for a government to claim credit for 'allowing' its agricultural producers to afford some kind of milk and eggs. And as for the child care centre, there is no transportation: 'The kids have to walk both ways.' 'For one child they charge two rupees for two months.' So the women keep the children at home.

And women's fate of housework and less education seems always present. Why don't they try to educate their daughters? 'Boys study longer because boys should get jobs, good jobs. Girls have to do housework anyway, and young girls care for the babies in the home.' Added to the home burdens of the women is the long distance they have to walk to work, three to five miles for many of them, which means getting up even earlier in the morning. No wonder, then, that many of these women, when asked about demands for International Women's Year, say simply that 'Women should be happy, women should get some rest!'

But I press this point. 'Would you like to be like the rich peasant women, who don't work but have to stay inside their homes all day?' Not being able to leave 'the four walls' is one of the colloquial ways my friends use to illustrate women's oppression. The agricultural labourers shrug, they don't seem to have any aspirations or visions of such a life. 'This is our habit, our way of life.'

And what do they feel about the union? 'We are ready,' says one woman. 'We must have more pay, we must have permanent work, the union must remain. Without the union we are scrap value.'

From Rahuri we move on, after spending the night in the small house of Kale, the local organizer, to Mula Dam, the huge irrigation project of the area, source of the wellspring of life of these fields of waving sugar cane. Like many of the dams in India, in fact, its 'treasures of white milky nectar' are built on the sweat and blood, literally, of the poorest class of workers.

From colonial days to the present, 'development projects' have been a source of disease and death to those who have laboured on them. The projects, whether dams canals or roads, have been constructed primarily by migrants working under contractors, that is, by men and women drawn from far-away villages, from backward famine-ridden areas, and from the poorest most dependent sections of land-poor peasants in these areas. Contractors, going to such villages, would hire labourers by giving them advances, often negotiating with a landlord to whom the labourer was already in debt so that one kind of debt-bondage was simply substituted for another. The workers, hundreds of miles from their homes, often speaking a different language from nearby peasants, were helpless to demand higher wages and usually found that what wages they earned were going to pay off their debts. They lived in lean-tos or makeshift huts or even on the open ground under the shelter of trees, without adequate food or clothing, with barely one or two cooking utensils, afflicted by hunger, malaria and other epidemics that sprang up from the festering swamps often actually created as a result of the irrigation and road projects which destroyed the natural drainage systems of the area. Women were just as frequently found among such workers as men, for so low was the pay that without women's work as well no family could survive.

Such contracting systems still exist in the free society of post-war India. They mobilize labour for roads, dams, the massive work of gang-labour sugar cane harvesting, the mining of ore for huge modern steel plants, among other examples, and there is perhaps nothing more depressing than riding along a road, stopping to talk to such a group of migrant workers, hearing their litanies of despair, seeing their few possessions propped under trees, knowing that it is almost impossible for them to organize, feeling that it is unrealistic even to suggest that they struggle and fight because you yourself, and those with you, are in no position to help them organize. Government as well as private projects are contracted out, for, though the government lays down regulations and various benefits for its employees, it is quite ready to get its work done as cheaply as possible by using the service of contractors who can bid cheaply because of the low wages and non-existent benefits they give to workers. Such was the system when Mula Dam was begun, when nearly 2,500 workers from other Marathi-speaking districts and from south India were brought in after 1964 to take up the main work.

But 2,500 workers are enough to make a fight, and these too began to be affected by the waves of struggle that were starting to pound Ahmednagar and other districts of India. Kale, who began as a worker on the dam himself, tells me the story:

'In 1966 the project really picked up speed. At the start I was getting 2 rupees, after that, depending on the bosses' wish, it was raised to 2.25 or 2.50. Some of us got together and thought this was too low. The government supervisors were mostly Jan Sanghis, almost all Brahmans; they had the point of view of masters and servants, they thought they were the only ones who deserved a high standard of living, while the poor, the labourers, are from the lower class, uneducated, good only for manual work. That got us angry. We got together, went to Comrade Katre.' Katre was an LNP organizer, and from this point the unionizing started, with a march of nearly 1,500 workers in 1968 and the beginning of demands: for lunch hours, paid leave, pregnancy leave for women, an 8-hour day, cost-of-living allowances. 'Then in order to solve the problems of all those who work on dams we thought we should unite, so we sent our leaders all over Maharashtra and discussed with dam workers in at least six or seven different locations. Then in September 1969 the workers' union leaders held a conference.' What about women workers? 'At least 50-60% of all workers are women, and we took 60-70 men and 30-40 women workers with us to the conference.' Other conferences followed. As a result of the struggle and government legislation, the workers won part of their demands, about 25% of them becoming permanent with a pay of 75 rupees a month plus cost-of-living allowances. But the main crisis for the workers, the nearing completion of the dam and resulting unemployment, was approaching.

'Our demand was that simply because the dam is finished the workers can't stop living! The dam makes the land bear fruit, production will increase ten times, the surrounding district will benefit — and the workers who built the dam can't be let down! So we said. But it was no use. By 1970 we knew the layoff was coming. So we planned an indefinite strike. The supervisors brought in 500-700 police, and workers and police fought at the base of the dam. At 4.30 a.m. one morning 50 workers were arrested and put in a police van, but the workers came together and surrounded the van — and the women pushed the van backwards one-eighth of a mile. At that point the supervisors realized they had to retreat . . . '

But the workers did not win. Most were laid off, only about 70-80 remaining on a permanent basis. 'Four to five hundred people fought tooth and nail to the end, but others gradually went home, because of hunger and other problems.'

'Then what do you think is the use of all this union fighting?'

'Other unions were formed with this union's help, a settlement with the government covering all contract work was reached. On Mula Dam some workers got back pay owing, some lived well for a time.'

'And now?'

'Some of those who were laid off were hired at the Agricultural University. Now those who built the dam workers union have established the union at the university — they know the benefits they got from the fight. The university union was established because of the dam workers' union!'

So move the waves of struggle. But I wonder . . . how many of the thousands of workers got jobs, what of the now vanished workers from south India? And, halfway across the dam we stop once more, and Kale points below, and says, 'Nearly 100 workers drowned there in an accident.'

Small gains, costly struggle. But few signs of these epics of life and death remain. The dam itself stretches white and imposing under the morning sun with only a faint hum of machinery breaking the silence.

But there are still minor projects going on under the government employment scheme that has been started since the famine, and just down the road we meet the workers on one such project, 100 men and 200 women working on a canal. They are Marathi-speakers but still migrants, like the dam workers, living in lean-tos, searching for work constantly and finding it only for a few days or weeks at a time on projects like these, representatives of an increasing class of people in India's never ending *Grapes of Wrath* saga. In contrast to the labourers on the farm and to the women of Bori Arab who have settled homes, these are the real down-and-outs, the utterly destitute and desperate, and their despair shows itself immediately. But there is anger as well and the reflection of Ahmednagar's waves of struggle.

Thus, when I ask the women, they say that they rise at 5 a.m., an hour before the men, to do the work of cooking and then their paid labour, but when I talk about the universal nature of double work and the situation existing in rich countries like the US also, they react with, 'That may be true, but the people sitting here have only earth work! Women are uneducated. Without the earth we have no work. Those who have some education can get work elsewhere but this is our work!' Again one woman, this time old, wrinkled, ferocious, is emerging as a main speaker. I ask her, 'But when this work is over, what do you do?'

'If there is no other work, those who have land farm it, those like us who have no land have to die of hunger.' They are all landless.

What concretely do rising prices and the lack of work mean to them? 'Plenty of grain is grown in India. But we workers buy it at high prices. We have to eat one-half or one-fourth of a *bhakr* and when we remember the land we used to have we can't even digest that! We don't even have clothes for our body. As for food, if we get *jawar* we eat *jawar*, if we get *milo* we eat *milo*, if we get vegetables we eat them, if not, then chillies. We have to eat dry *bhakri*. There is no milk. Where would we get milk? We have to drink *jaggery* tea without milk. If grain is available we eat, if not we drink water and go to sleep.'

Why all this poverty? we ask. Why can't they get work when they are ready to do it? You have the labour power, the strength, you want work, the activists say. 'Yes, we are ready to work. But work is not available.'

Again Suresh launches into a speech on International Women's Year, the ability of women to do any kind of work that men can do, the right of women as well as men to have work. 'Women can work alongside men, they work on railroads, in factories, in many countries women fly airplanes and drive tractors, and if women are educated they can hold high official jobs. Then why don't girls get as much education as boys?'

But they are not inclined to be interested in high official jobs or education. 'The obstacles for us now are the lack of daily work and rising prices. How can we educate our children? If a single boy doesn't get education, then how can we talk of educating girls? There is no work, our stomachs are not full, so what is the sense of educating girls?'

From the perspective of these women, problems are reduced to bare survival. Casteism, they say (they are a mixed group, half Dalit, half caste Hindu), is no problem; remarraige of widows or divorcees is no problem. But the dowry custom seems to affect them still. 'If we can't make ends meet with 3 rupees then how can we give dowry? They want 1,000 rupees, a gold ring, a wristwatch, a feast, pots and pans, a necklace. How can we bring money for such things?' 'Do parents have to go in debt for these things?' 'If we don't have money or work at all, we can't get loans,' explains a man. Then what about the girls' marriages? They stay unmarried, people say, and all agree they don't like the dowry custom, that they are against giving or taking dowry for marriages.

They don't like dowry, they realize that girls get less education, they realize that women work more because of housework, but such issues have no salience for them at present. What stands out is hunger, and they are bitter about Indira Gandhi's slogan of *garibi hatao*, 'remove poverty'. 'Oh, where has poverty been removed? We have no food, no clothes, no home, we have to sleep on footpaths. What can we do? We have to fight!'

We talk about the struggles, the marches and *gheraos* of the famine period, the marches and *gheraoes* of the Women's Anti-Price Rise Committee in Bombay; stories of tribal women raiding merchants' houses to get food are told. They make their views clear: 'We are ready, but we need a leader.' The old woman says, 'With a leader like you by our side, then an old woman like me will come along to pull and drag a big sack of grain! I don't have a son or a husband. You people have to protect me. If we go to raid a big farmer's house and they arrest and beat me it's okay, but a leader like you should be there too!'

She continues with some excitement, 'Those who go out on marches, who act for the protection of their stomachs, they will survive. Those who have no hope, who give up and stay away, because they are afraid, they will not live!'

And so the tempo of the meeting rises, and it ends with plans to hold a march on demands for the houses that the government has promised to build for the homeless, with slogans and angry shouts that continue to echo behind us as we finally leave, by now under the hot sun of noonday.

'Where do we go now?' I ask Suresh.

'To Kathod Farm.'

'Isn't that where Tanubai works?'

'Yes.'

6. 'Once this land was ours'

Agricultural Labourers and Adivasis

Ballad of the Bhils

My first salute is to Mother India,
To the earth of India,
There is light all over the world
Each country has god's blessing.
My second salute is to the red flag —
Look, look at its glory.
The red flag reaches to the sky
And gives inspiration to our lives.
My third salute is to the heroes of revolution —
To Bhagat Singh
To Subash Babu
To Babu Genu.
For the country they lost their lives,
For the country they sacrificed themselves.
Their fame spread over the seven seas.
This land is the Adivasis',
It belongs to the Bhils, Kolis, Phasepardhis,
    Katkaris, Thakuris, Warlis, Gonds,
To these people.
In the dark forests on the banks of the Narbuda
Lived the Bhils,
And in the Satpudas lived the Bhils.
They were kings of the forest —
These landless people were once kings of the forest!
1857 became the time of rebellion,
The time of revolution.

The fire spread all over the country,
It spread in valleys and in mountains.
Adivasi heroes went to war
With bows and arrows in their hands,
This rebellion of bows and arrows
Made the white man helpless.
Gomaji in Pune,
Piraji Naik in Tarubag,
These made revolt, these made revolution.
The growing power of rebellion shook the
    Company Sarkar,
Then they became wise
And got hold of wealthy moneylenders —
They found a way out
To deal a blow to the poor.
The cunning white sahibs found a way out,
The cunning white sahibs used their head.
To some they gave a bribe,
To others they gave jobs,
And those who lost, lost because of their fate,
Don't even have shelter,
The hired thugs torment them.
How many of the Bhils, Kolis, Thakurs, Katkaris
Don't have a place to live today!
In the land that belonged to them
They can't protect themselves from the cold and wind.

by Bapurao Barde
Tribal ballad sung in
typical peasant style

So I am going to meet Tanubai, militant agricultural labourer, tribal (that is, a representative of one of the most oppressed sections of India's population), ballad singer of the movement, a woman who symbolizes much of my earliest encounters with the fighting rural women of India.

But it seems that there is a problem about Tanubai. And that is that apparently after 1971 she has dropped out of the movement.

When I ask about her in 1973 during a short visit and again in 1975, Lal Nishan leaders both in Bombay and Ahmednagar are reticent, even evasive. Her husband, they say, along with the leader of the singing troupe — also a relative and the writer of many of the songs, those militant red flag songs of revolution — has been wooed and won by India's ruling party, the Congress! He has gone over to the other side, and Tanubai has gone with him. Why? Well, these things happen. Even the most militant and purely proletarian can get corrupted. Little more is said and I am not willing to press the issue.

Instead Suresh and I talk about Kathod Farm. It is a notable feature of

northern Ahmednagar — a huge private farm owned by a textile magnate
in Bombay which at one time comprised 1,200 acres, organized on a factory-
like basis and growing the major cash crops of sugar cane and cotton. Of
these 1,200 acres, 400 were owned outright by the family and the rest leased
in from medium sized peasants of the surrounding villages, so that the
capitalists here were officially tenant farmers. There were several such farms
in Ahmednagar, and it was on these that the organizing of agricultural
labourers first took place, initially led by the CPI, then the Socialists, then
the Lal Nishan Party.

It is normal that such rural unionization would first occur on plantations
or on farms managed and run like factories. What is perhaps not so normal
is what has been happening recently. The big capitalist farms of Ahmednagar
are being broken up and sold off; the Bombay capitalists are withdrawing
their investments; the leased sections are being returned to their original
peasant owners. This has meant in many cases new pressure on the unions,
since the original peasant owners are not so ready to grow cash crops and
instead are reverting at least partially to food crops which employ far fewer
workers. In the case of Kathod there are only 400 acres left and 200 regularly
employed workers, though many others are hired on a contract basis. The
inability of the union to prevent such developments and save jobs has laid it
open to some demoralization, and in fact a rival union has been started by
one of its former activists who accuses the local leader, Bhauke, of being
dictatorial and discriminatory, and who is actively using caste divisions (he
is a Dalit) to build his own base.

In the case of Kathod Farm we could almost be entering a factory situation. Here are no 'semi-feudal' relations of dependence in which landlords
tyrannize over weak, fragmented labourers, but professional managers who
have grown accustomed like all Indian managers to dealing with strikes and
gheraos, to negotiating with unions, to manoeuvring and encouraging splits.
They are much more experienced than the managers of the Agricultural
University at this; they may even feel they have the situation under control.
At any rate they have to deal with the union leaders. And so we begin our
visit to Kathod Farm with a discussion with the managers. It takes place in a
long, low central building set under shade trees; even the buildings at Kathod
seem more seasoned than those of the Agricultural University.

I want to know about the issue of equal wages for women. On Kathod
Farm, of the 200 labourers most are Dalits and Christians, that is, converts
from Dalit castes, though tribal people and other castes are also there. Of
these, 85, all men, are on permanent status and earn 4½ to 6 rupees a day.
The others are employed on a daily basis: 47 are men earning 3 to 4 rupees
a day and 68 are women earning only 3 rupees a day. Besides these there are
the labourers hired on contract for the harvest and heavy work periods; their
women get 2 rupees a day.

Two things about these wages stand out. One is their relatively, even
abysmally, low nature, considering the long history of organization in the
area. For all the factory nature of the work and the unionization, these rates

69

are significantly below the wages of regularly employed and unionized urban workers. The other, of course, is the discrimination against women. Why?

It's customary, traditional, is the first response. One manager gives the main argument: 'Women don't give as much output.' Suresh points out that this is a meaningless argument since women do different kinds of work from men. The manager shifts ground: women's work is 'light work', work which can be done very comfortably. 'If men do the same work, they will do more of it.'

Then why was it, I ask, that during the famine period men and women were paid equally even though they did different types of work? This was a passing phenomenon, say the managers. 'The government was a little generous in giving equal pay,' says one, and they had to do this and to promise an equal minimum wage because 'otherwise the people will shout'.

This I feel is getting somewhere — then the main determinant of wages is political pressure and organization, I suggest. Perhaps the reason women have low wages to begin with is that they have not been organized in the past. Even the left parties neglected their cause up to the time of the famine period, and women have always been easier to exploit. (It is a discussion that is pointless to carry on with the managers, but it is an ongoing one. Elsewhere, a woman head of a middle peasant farm which hires labourers from time to time agrees with her nephew that men's work is 'superior' but adds, 'women also can do superior work, but they won't. They pass time . . . ' At half the wages, it is no wonder.)

Why has the farm been broken up, I ask. Because it's not profitable, say the managers. Land ceiling laws put too much pressure on them and make it impossible to maintain big holdings (though it should be noted that there are no ceilings on leases, and it was the leased, not owned, lands that were returned), while the high prices of fertilizers and other inputs versus the low prices of even the best crops make capitalist farming insufficiently profitable (this may well be true: it has been the central theme of all rich peasant agitations in India for some years).

After this we go out to a discussion with the workers, sitting in the shade of a large tree. There is a long debate on inter-union disputes, which I follow only partially, where Bhauke explains his position, the workers listen and give their responses. The workers, a group of about 100 people, are relatively outspoken. Tanubai is among them and taking part. Bhauke denies that he has been dictatorial or that he has financially benefited from his position. ('This must be true,' Tanubai intervenes, 'I've seen his home — he comes from a rich family.' What she means, somewhat paradoxically, is that because he comes from a relatively well-off peasant family and not a poor one he doesn't need to 'eat money' from the union; very often the poor trust each other's leadership the least.) Finally he says that he won't take an active role until he is sure that they want his leadership.

Then there is a brief exchange with Tanubai. We are reintroduced, and I ask what has happened to her in the meantime. 'Why didn't you go to Dahiwadi?' asks Suresh, referring to a recent state-wide conference of agricultural labourers and poor peasants organized by the LNP. Tanubai shrugs, complains that no one invited her, that they were not ready to pay her way, but says little more. We leave the subject.

What about this issue of women's work? Is it true that women's farm work is 'light work'? The women react with scorn and anger. 'What light work?' Their work — seeding, fertilizing, transplanting in rice areas — is stooping work, whereas men's work, though requiring periods of extreme physical exertion, has natural rest breaks. (And transplanting rice seedlings, the most typical women's work throughout Asia, is the primary example of this, requiring not only continuous stooping but also working throughout the day at least ankle deep in muddy water.) In fact the argument that men's work is paid better because it is 'heavier' or harder seems to me the most unjust of all, considering that there is no other area or country where 'hard' physical labour is paid more just because of that fact. In terms of the issues of productivity or skill, there is no evidence that women's work in the fields requires less skill or produces less output than the typical unskilled or semi-skilled labour of men, or that women cannot be trained for the more highly skilled jobs. Indeed, the last issue seems to be crucial. When it comes to a question of supervision or driving tractors, it is invariably men who are chosen and trained (and so all the 'permanent' workers at Kathod are men); or when dairy farms and sales cooperatives are set up, the women who traditionally have always milked cows and peddled the milk are relegated to a simple position of manual labour while the middle men and technical workers are all men. Modernization marginalizes women as the 'light' and better paid work of sales and supervision in the new institutions goes all to men. The women labourers, perhaps, know this instinctively, yet it seems they rarely make these points explicitly when the cliche that 'women's work is light work' gets repeated.

And what about housework? It is at this point that Suresh really works up a magnificent mood of challenge to tradition. 'Isn't it an injustice that women always have to do double work? This should be changed! Where is it written that only women can do housework? Men should help with this! If both women and men work in the fields, both should share the housework. Your husband has no right to go out drinking while you work!' And he concludes with, 'We are going to form a union of women, just like your union of agricultural labourers. And the demand we will make is that men should help with the housework!'

'That's one union we won't join, we will oppose it!' The reaction from the men is at least frank. A vigorous exchange follows. Suresh finally retreats with, 'Well, we won't make that demand right away. Later. But at the very least women should get equal pay for their work. Dowry should be abolished. Girls should have the same education as boys. Women should get jobs.' And all agree to this, though the women have not been very outspoken during the entire episode.

So the discussion closes and we leave the farm, but first the women show us to their homes, impressively clean, well polished mud-brick huts (to the extent that mud huts can be this), stocked with a number of cooking utensils, no luxuries, nothing close to urban middle class standards but clearly a long step above the utter destitution of the migrant workers and the uncertain hovering on the edge of hunger of the half-employed village poor like Kaminibai. This perhaps has been worth fighting for . . .

Whatever gains the workers have made on Kathod Farm, though, have to be seen in the context of their unionizing struggles and indeed far older traditions and memories. This becomes clear, in a way, during later meetings with Tanubai. For though I leave that first visit with a sense of mild frustration because we have had no real chance to talk, it seems that Tanubai is on her way back into the movement. She begins to turn up at various cultural programmes, held most often in nearby villages, or on short tours, and in one case – in Pune itself a year later – for the March 8 Women's Day programme when she is a great hit. My next encounter with her, though, is in a nearby village. A 'Toiling Women's Cultural Programme' has been organized. Tanubai has come; a newly formed local village troupe is there; and a group of young employees from Bombay who have worked up a repertoire of several new women's liberation songs have come. It is January; the city girls' voices are cracking with the cold, but Tanubai and the other village singers shrug it off. Something like a jam session begins in the afternoon, as she pulls out her well thumbed collection of songs (Tanubai is the only literate agricultural labourer I meet) and plays around with the harmonium, a kind of accordion without a keyboard that provides a background for singing. Her singing style itself, a vigorous, belting ballad style, is for me more reminiscent of the black musical tradition in the US than any other Indian music I have heard.

With 5,000 people gathering, the cultural programme itself is a roaring success, and there is something of an encore the next morning as special friends gather and again Tanubai sings. Once again we hear songs of the agricultural labourers and their revolution, devastating satires of rich peasants and the government (a new favourite seems to be 'The Minister Went Overseas' to live in ease and send back some imported rice and sorghum to the peasants starving at home). Then Tanubai sings her own special favourite, a song which centres on the story of the 1857 revolt against the British to weave together class and nationalist themes with the rebellion of the Bhils, a tribal group 'who were once kings of the forest' but are landless now:

> My first salute is to Mother India . . .
> My second salute is to the red flag . . .
> My third salute is to the heroes of revolution . . .

This 'Ballad of the Bhils' was written by the leader of Tanubai's former singing group, and it provides a major clue to her own personality and to many of the vital traditions of northern Maharashtra.

For Tanubai herself is a Bhil, that is, a member of one of the largest groups in India classified as 'tribal', who make up 7% officially of the population and together with Dalits constitute one of its most oppressed sections. There are points where the tribes are hard to distinguish from the lower Hindu castes, but by and large they are communities who up to the time of the British occupation remained outside the agrarian caste society of the plains, carrying on a hunting and gathering or slash-and-burn horticultural economy in the hills and jungles. Never fully conquered or absorbed, they sometimes paid tribute to Hindu rulers, sometimes engaged in raiding and plundering expeditions. Through a long historical process, the spread of Hindu culture and an agrarian economy transformed many such tribal groups into castes, but large numbers remained outside, preferring their own way of life, their own more egalitarian culture.

Then came the British conquest, and 'modernization' − the invasion of tribal lands by Hindu merchants who began to take control of the land in the process of grabbing the products of the forest, and by capitalists seeking to utilize the rich mineral wealth of the hills, and by bureaucrats wanting to ensure the sources of taxation and foreign exchange. The people of the tribes in most cases became transformed into debt-bonded serfs on the land they had once owned. Today, for the process has only intensified with independence, in almost all cases the original, relatively self-sufficient economy of the tribes has vanished. Their land has been taken over and transformed into farms or mines; they have been pushed out of many of their areas and can no longer support themselves in the old way on the shrinking territory left. In the process most of them have become share-cropping peasants, agricultural labourers, plantation workers on lands thousands of miles from their original homes, miners and a very few have become factory workers or educated middle class employees. But they have retained their unique cultural features, which include a lack of caste discrimination, a lack of social hierarchy, a great sense of romantic love and a strong element of song, dance and drinking in their festival life. And, the most important thing for the women's movement, much greater social equality for women. To find examples of women who have by custom held great social power, Indians do not have to look to the West; they can find it in the tribal communities of their own country.

The tribes have been more; they have been a centre of revolt − of uprisings against the Hindu moneylenders who oppressed them during colonial times, or uprisings against the British themselves, of communist-led class revolts more recently, and of movements for political independence. Tribes on India's northeast frontier, such as the Nagas or Mizos, have waged continuous armed struggle for national independence ever since the British were forced out in 1947. 'The question is not whether India should give us independence,' their leaders say fiercely. 'We are an independent country that has been invaded by India; India should get out.' The tribes in the interior part of the subcontinent have, by contrast, continued to think of themselves as Indians − Tanubai's 'Ballad of the Bhils' leaves no doubt of this − but many of them have been asking for a separate tribal state within India for at least as long as

73

the Nagas or Mizos, and behind this has lain an even longer, powerful movement of cultural revival and social independence. Around the 1930s began a
strong and conscious attempt to reject Hindu customs and the 'sanskritized'
ideas which were making inroads among them, and to revive their own
religion and social traditions. The tribal people began to call themselves
'adivasis' or 'original inhabitants', much as the North Americans now refer to
themselves as Native Americans, and to form their own autonomous political
parties. In the north-central region of Chota Nagpur and surrounding districts,
known by the *adivasis* as Jharkhand or 'the forest region', this political movement has been at its strongest.

Tanubai is a member of the Bhil tribe. With around three million people, it
is the third largest group of 'tribals' in the country. But unlike the people of
Jharkhand (the related Santal, Ho and Munda tribes), the Bhils are more
fragmented socially, with hardly a common language and no overall political
organization, spread out over far-flung districts of several states, and rarely
representing anything near a majority of the population. In most cases, as in
Ahmednagar district, they are only a small minority scattered among other
middle and low caste Hindus, speaking the general language (Marathi), working like the other rural poor as agricultural labourers, and with their cultural
distinctness muted. Tanubai's 'Ballad' shows this too, not only in its expres-
sions of solidarity with other Indians, but by the very fact that it is sung not
to any traditional Bhil tune but in the style of the customary ballad of the
Maratha peasant. Nevertheless Ahmednagar Bhils were also affected by the
cultural revolt, and in the early 1950s Tanubai became a member of a singing troupe that developed to spread among their people a pride in being
adivasis. And there is no doubt that this has become a fixed centre of
Tanubai's identity; as she tells us herself, '*Adivasi* means *mul rahivasi,* original
dwellers, the ones who were here first. Once this was all our land!' And
despite the landlessness, even despite the relatively complete proletarianization to be found in places like Kathod Farm, such a consciousness becomes
a powerful substratum of revolt.

Times change. The original cultural autonomy movement, and the political movement that went with it, could not do very much by itself. Its leaders
were mainly middle class and susceptible to electoralism and the appeals of
the more sophisticated ruling class of independent 'secular' India. The rape of
tribal culture and land went on, but the revolt faltered for a time. The
Jharkhand Party split, and most of its sections merged into Congress,
though a greater explosion began to form itself after 1967. As for the Bhils,
their initial cultural revolt seemed to have spent itself, and the leader of
Tanubai's singing troupe, the writer of the songs, began to waver and to
develop links with the Congress party also. The revival that began to occur
during the famine period — when I had my first encounter with Tanubai —
was of a different nature: class themes, exploitation as labourers were now
taking over. But the original leadership was not ready to stay with this new
form of the movement.

Why did Tanubai herself keep on? Possibly a variety of reasons — her own instinct for struggle, the songs she cannot give up, the fact that it was primarily her husband who decided to join the Congress party at the same time as he was taking a second wife. In fact, she says, her relations with her husband 'were fine' in spite of the new wife, but she was going back into the movement at a time when he was a strong supporter of the ruling party, and these political differences added to their mutual alienation.

Still Tanubai remains somewhat on the fringe of things. Her relations with Lal Nishan leaders are not the best, and the new singing group they form uses another lead singer. Why, I don't fully understand, not getting a chance to hear Tanubai's side of the story; they say she is 'too individualistic', that she has a kind of 'star complex'. The Pune women's group, on the other hand, might love to adopt her, but they remain for some time incapable of building an organization sufficently strong to keep some kind of contact with Kathod Farm, hundreds of miles away. And so Tanubai remains somewhat isolated . . .

Our last meeting, though, is at a women's study camp held at Kathod Farm itself, where forty women of varying ages and class backgrounds gather for discussion of basic theory and organization. Tanubai is present; though she never takes an active part in the discussions, her moment comes when one young enthusiastic factory worker of merchant caste background demonstrates a song that she and several others have written on the theme of women's liberation. Tanubai listens for a while, then decides to intervene. 'No, no it's too much like a Hindi film song.' It's too middle class, she means, 'too gushy' (she mimics the style which is one of delicately coy gestures). 'If you want to sing for *working* people, you have to be bold — like this,' demonstrating with sweeping gestures, 'as if you were swinging a scythe . . . ' The girls try to imitate her, and eventually five or six of them are practising proud stances, arms flung wide, sharp decisive movements. The whole thing reminds me of the Chinese revolutionary ballet I have seen on television, where there was a deliberate attempt to transform the delicate and fragile movements of the classical ballet into a militaristic and revolutionary form. Perhaps there is such a thing as proletarian art after all. And perhaps there is after all in India a rich and ancient cultural base for revolution, particularly among the low castes, Dalits, *adivasis* — and women.

7. 'Women have a tenacity to fight'

Urban Women and Rising Prices

Hey, Indira

Chorus
We have an invitation for you,
To see what will happen to us now,
Indira, the chaos of inflation lies
Before us now, before us now . . .

Wheat and carrots, rice and *jawar,* see the prices rising, hey,
Oil and lentils, cloth and sugar, vegetables are rising, hey!
When simple food cannot be found,
Daily life to dust is ground, Indira,
The chaos of inflation lies before us now.

When I heard you call 'Abolish poverty,' my heart was filled to
     bursting, hey,
Running I voted for your symbol, the cow and calf nursing, hey!
When will your promises be fulfilled?
When will happiness reach our homes, Indira?
The chaos of inflation lies before us now.

The rich are rolling on their sofas, luxuriously lounging, hey,
We are starving, half-exhausted, bitterness abounding, hey!
If you have any love, let it flow out,
Take a look and think about it, Indira,
The chaos of inflation lies before us now.

The landless now are organizing, building unity anew, hey,

If capitalism is not destroyed, we'll see that it's your funeral too,
   hey!
All now say, no more can we stand —
Then take revolution's flag in hand . . . Indira,
The chaos of inflation lies before us now.

by Dongre Javre
Song of the Shramik
Sanghatana in Dhule, 1974

The militancy of women workers like Tarabai, the aggressive and even vanguard participation of women like Bhagubai and Tanubai in rural class
struggles are not new things in the history of Indian popular movements. But
for the state of Maharashtra this emergence of fighting women reached a new
intensity in the famine period of 1970-73 and led directly to a new form of
the separate mobilization of women. This mobilization, the most massive yet
seen in India, has centred in the heart of Indian capitalism, the crowded textile mill and factory city of Bombay. Women storming into the streets;
women marching not in hundreds or thousands but in tens of thousands
beneath the crowded apartments and the endless tiny shops, beating their
steel or brass serving plates with heavy spoons to raise a thunderous din;
women barricading the cars of politicians and storming the offices of Bombay
merchant kings; women confronting the Minister of Food Supplies in his own
kitchen to find out if his family eats the ration food they have to eat; women
chasing after Indira Gandhi herself to call her to account for the unbearably
rising prices and food shortages that are driving their families into starvation.

This is the United Women's Anti-Price-Rise Committee. A militant mass
organization, it was formed as a coalition of various socialist and communist
parties at the end of 1972 in Bombay and has since spread all over India. For,
if women in the rural areas were proving their militancy from 1967 on by
coming out beside and sometimes ahead of their men against rich landowners
and the government, if men in the factories were staging rising waves of ever
more militant strikes, it is the women of the cities and towns, the housewives,
the managers of consumption who have been coming out in massive numbers
to protest the lack of the most minimal food and water, who have been
demanding price cuts and increased ration allotments, and showing that they
could be as fierce in the struggle as any men. According to government
statistics, 80% of all women are non-'worker' housewives (though many of
these work part-time at pitifully paid jobs) and it is these women, often considered the most 'backward' and tradition-bound, who have gone into the
streets in their tens of thousands, not on the issues of cultural oppression and
personal self-determination that affect many college students nor in efforts to
get wages or work, but on consumer issues. And in taking up these issues, the
Women's Anti-Price-Rise Committee has brought women into struggle on a
mightier scale than ever before.

The explosive bringing together of housewives against rising prices did not happen spontaneously, of course, but was deliberately organized by party leaders who had direct experience of the militancy of rural women in the famine period and who began to feel that such a force could be mobilized also in the cities. At the head of the Anti-Price-Rise Committee are the 'party women', that is, the leaders of such organizations as the Shramik Mahila Sabha, the Samajwadi Mahila Sabha, the National Federation of Indian Women (whose local branches are called the Shramik Mahila Sangh), which are in turn the 'mass fronts' of the left parties — respectively of the Communist Party of India (Marxist), the Socialist Party, and the Communist Party of India. The top women in these parties, who lead the women's fronts, are among the few women who have 'made it' politically, who for one reason or another have not fallen victim to the pressures of family and finance which have pushed other women party members into a secondary position. They have been through the struggles of the past, from the national movement to working class and countless social struggles; they have fought out ideological and political issues with each other as well as against the state; they are in their own way sophisticated and steeled women. Many have been to Europe or the Soviet Union or the US, and they think on a national scale.

The Anti-Price-Rise Committee is not really a 'women's liberation' group, and as an organization it is distrusted by many of my young radical friends who fear the domination of party politics in the organizations that have come together to form it, fear that women are being 'used' once again for other causes. But the Committee has succeeded in involving almost all urban classes from workers and slum dwellers to middle class employees, and in the process it has taken up most of the symbols of Indian women's traditional 'place' in the kitchen — but has transformed these into weapons. Thus the Committee began with a 'march of extinguished *culs*' (the traditional kind of stove used by women) in which nearly 1,000 women carried small stoves through pouring rain to symbolize the lack of food. It went on to hold a *thali*-beating march (the *thalis* are the traditional steel or brass plates) and it climaxed with the *latna* or Rolling Pin March of 20,000 women in the fall of 1973. And now the badge of the movement has become the rolling pin, brandished in a clenched fist as a weapon of revolt.

One of the party women leading the movement is Mrinal Gore, a vivacious Socialist leader in her middle forties. We sit in her home in the middle class Bombay suburb of Goregaon, one of those sections of Bombay that is hot and green, as if the jungle is relentlessly fighting the domination of the metropolis, where three- and four-storey apartment blocks and tree-shaded streets manage to dominate the countless small shops, workers' huts and crowded pathways that are here as everywhere in Bombay. Like everyone else, Mrinal is outspoken about the special militancy of women. 'We are organizing women to understand the problems behind price rise, so they can be prepared to agitate on a big scale to bring pressure on the government to change its policies — and if they won't change, we will change the government.'

'Do you think women can do this?'

'Oh yes, women can do this better than anyone! They are more firm once they decide. We experienced this when we went to Vartak, the Civil Supplies Minister. We organized uneducated ladies, those who were not active in any political party but were really agitated over the ration cut and the bad quality of rice supplied. When we went to Vartak we asked him, "What rice do you eat?" "The same as you," he told us. "No, I want to see," said one woman. Vartak tried to avoid this for an hour. Finally this woman got up, went into the kitchen, pulled out his rice and he had to admit that he was not eating ration rice but expensive free market *basmati* rice. "Why do you lie? Do you know what food we have to give our children?" She berated him continuously. He had called 500 police; there were only forty or so ladies, but we sat for five hours and finally he promised that the ration would be increased the next day.

'That firmness, that feeling from the heart of the way her children were suffering, made that woman speak!'

The organizing of the Committee is not simply a matter of spectacular mass marches, according to Mrinal. Part of the concept is to alternate the marches, which have up to 20 to 25,000 women, with smaller and more militant actions of thirty to forty women. These are mainly *gheraos,* a favourite technique of Indian workers in which they surround, or *gherao,* an employer or political leader, refuse to leave, refuse to let him move (sometimes denying him food or use of toilet facilities) until they are arrested or their demand is granted. Such *gheraos* can last up to twenty-four hours or more, and represent a kind of militancy that personally pinpoints an oppressor much more directly than the traditional strike or the 'sit-in' of the US civil rights and student movements.

'We had so many *gheraos,* and they tried so hard to evade us! We *gheraoed* sugar factory directors when they met in Bombay; we *gheraoed* the state Chief Minister even though he tried to hide — we got him after he came out of the meeting into his car. And we tried to *gherao* Indira Gandhi, but she managed to sneak out the back door.

'When Indira goes to Gujarat she wears a Gujarati sari and says, "I am a daughter-in-law of Gujarat," (because her husband was Gujarati, as you know), and when she goes to Bengal she wears a Bengali sari, and when she comes here she puts on a nine-yard sari; but she can't fool us, we know her.'

Part of the organizing technique in bringing women to demonstrations is to provide badges; the women then go in groups onto trains, brandishing the badges and demanding free passage for 'doing a public service' in fighting inflation. The militant railway employees, often on strike themselves and facing the same problems, are willing to oblige, and thousands of rupees in travel money are saved this way. And the badge itself, the rolling pin symbol, has become very popular. 'There is a great keenness in other states about the idea,' says Mrinal, who has toured Gujarat to organize marches there and has seen the rolling pin symbol taken up in demonstrations in the south as well. 'The movement is spreading to other states and it could become international.

Today price rise has become the major problem for each housewife from the poorer or middle classes — and we have certainly succeeded in involving the common housewife.'

Mrinal herself has a long history of activism with women. Since her student days she was in the national movement and its socialist-oriented volunteer corps, the Rashtra Seva Dal, which worked in the rural areas specially to involve peasants and sponsor some social programmes such as cheap and secular marriages. Then she joined the All-India Women's Conference (AIWC) and became the secretary for Bombay city. This was the original mass women's organization, but 'at that time they were mainly upper class women, carrying on their meetings in English. We fought for Hindi sessions . . . ' She and her friends also pushed such issues as family planning and, as early as 1952, moved a resolution at one conference to organize on the issue of rising prices. 'But no one then wanted to discuss it; they were not prepared to take up the real problems of women, only showy work.'

Still, in spite of the upper class orientation of the AIWC, it was a major national organization and included women of all political tendencies. And it did bring some agitation on women's questions. Members organized meetings to support the Hindu Code Bill, which sought to reform women's legal rights within the family; they tried to have study sessions on problems 'like the dowry and inter-caste marriage, and to urge women to give up old useless religious traditions — and so many of the same things we are discussing today! And women took part in a big way.' Later, when she left the AIWC and became involved in Socialist party politics, Mrinal maintained her work with women, helping to run women's organizations and promoting child care centres near her home in Goregaon. And during the Maharashtra famine, she was one of the party leaders who went out to the districts to see the misery and struggles of rural women and to become inspired to develop this militancy in Bombay.

But what does Mrinal Gore think about women's liberation? Is she questioning the basic position of women in the way that people like Leela, Tarabai, Rukmini, Kaminibai are ready to do? 'What do you think are the real problems of women?' I ask. She mentions price rise; changing diet habits ('women are losing the nutritious value of food in their cooking methods'), and removing superstitions about child care and family planning. I probe further. 'What about removing the burdens of child care and housework themselves from women? After all, this is a basic issue of women's liberation, as we say, in the West.'

'We are far away from that in India,' she responds. 'Child care is going to remain the responsibility of women and all that can be done is to lessen the burden. Society should take some responsibility, but ultimately child care will be the responsibility of women. You can't get away from that.' And she mentions the issue that is often put at the centre of a Marxist-feminist approach, the involvement of women in production: 'We have to find ways of supplementing the family income by part-time work for women. It will help the family and at the same time give the women confidence.'

This I find reformist, and muse about whether it is linked to an ultimately reformist approach of socialists in general (even though they may emphasize 'cultural' issues more than communists do), or if it has something to do with Mrinal's upper middle class background, the fact that she herself could afford to be a political full-timer in spite of marriage, unlike Leela and other lower middle or working class women. And I remember Tarabai's 'Middle class women don't need women's liberation like we do; they can have servants.'

But if Mrinal seems less than radical as a feminist, her own experience in efforts at providing part-time work for poor women is a fascinating one, and one that shows the essential honesty of her socialist convictions. The Goregaon women's group, it seems, had tried to get part-time work for women by a contracting arrangement with a local cardboard factory; the women would take materials from the factory, work in space provided by the organization, and make packages. 'But we found the result was that the owner fired many of his own workers because he could get the same work done by cheap part-time labour! So I closed down the project.

'Lots of women's organizations are doing this in Bombay. The factories give work on piece rates; you bring the material and the women do four to five hours of work and get a little money. They are satisfied and the factories get cheap labour. The fact is that the leaders of these women's organizations are connected with the general managers of the firms, and they will say that with their connections they can get work from the factory.'

Thus there are lots of what are, in effect, tiny 'factories' in India where women do part-time work at incredibly low pay under the name of 'co-operative projects' or 'women's organizations'. Their products, from woven handbags to electronic equipment, are often sold abroad or to big corporations. I think of the young girls putting together tiny electronic pieces for Philips in a similar socialist organization in Pune: from Mexico and Hong Kong to the 'women's clubs' of India, the 'runaway factory' has come a long way. Clearly, part-time work is not a simple issue.

Ahilya Rangnekar, the leading communist in the Anti-Price-Rise Committee, is, like Mrinal, from an upper middle class Bombay background. Like Mrinal, she came into the movement during her student days, when she was first part of the national struggle and then involved in the All-India Women's Conference, trying to raise issues affecting lower class and lower middle class women. Like Mrinal she is essentially a Bombay organizer, going in to the countryside mainly for visits on party tours and conferences.

But there are differences. Most important is the fact that for all the similarity in their backgrounds and experiences, Ahilya became a communist rather than a socialist, and from that point became involved much more intensely in organizing workers and working in Bombay slums, rather than among the lower middle classes. But the difference is striking also in terms of her approach to issues, which shows a harder, more class-oriented and analytical ideology, and perhaps at the same time a more radical approach to women.

She stresses, for example, the class focus of the Anti-Price-Rise Committee. 'Before that, there was tremendous feeling and militancy about rising prices, but the Shiv Sena and other right-wing forces were using it to attack small shopkeepers. They used to get a small crowd together and go and force the small merchants to sell at lower prices. We not only made it a women's organization, but we showed that the monopolies and government were the enemies, and we directed the fight against them, not the small merchants.'

She also talks about the new energy of the movement. 'The new forms of struggle appealed to me. Until now, the women's movement has been restricted to meetings, discussions, constructive work. Now there are marches, *gheraos,* women are unafraid to go anywhere, to enter any building or office for their demands. We could gain something concrete by fighting. In the cooking oil case we *gheraoed* monopolists and ministers. First, we *gheraoed* the president of the Oil Merchants Association, then the manager of Lever Brothers. The Tatas themselves, the biggest monopoly house in India, telephoned us to say that they had made a contribution and to plead for no *gherao.* The result was that 75,000 kilos of oil were given by the companies to the government.'

And she is as positive as Mrinal Gore about the militancy of women. 'You have to stress that where women take part in the movement its quality is different. Women are more militant, more lasting, women have a tenacity to fight. In one recent demonstration, the women were given one road for their part of the march, men were given seven, but the women's march was bigger.'

More than Mrinal, though, she analyzes the class base of the anti-price-rise movement. 'Twenty thousand women took part in the Rolling Pin March. They were lower middle class and working class women, and the working class were in the majority. They weren't factory workers themselves, but workers' wives. And in recent demonstrations we've also gone to Muslim sectors and to others not so far approached. There were 5,000 women in the demonstration against Indira Gandhi – that was a big step.'

'How do you reach the working class women?'

'First, we go to those women working in the factories, through gate meetings, but there is not much participation.' (In fact, it is clear that while the employed working class women may be more class conscious than the mere housewife, she has notably less, not to say no, time; thus women workers are very militant in strikes but rarely stay around for union meetings). 'The last time, middle class working women, such as teachers, doctors, bank clerks, insurance company employees, took part. These we can contact through unions. The majority of women are slum dwellers, and we can involve them through our work in the slums.' Ahilya, as a member of an established party, has one advantage over the younger groups like POW also trying to do slum work: she has been a member of parliament and the state legislature. 'I work in my constituency; and we have provided amenities for it, water and so forth. This gives an initial base for mobilization.'

Like many party women, Ahilya is privately critical of the lack of concern shown by the leadership and by other party mass organizations (such as unions) for the special problems of women. 'The unions are not taking up the question of equal wages for women. In the textile mills there is a contract system now; work is given out on a contract basis rather than done in the big factories themselves. Young, under-age girls are often employed. The Shramik Mahila Sabha has taken up this question and hopes to build up union support. We must have joint actions by trade unions and women's organizations. But there is very little on women in the general working class newspapers or the party papers. Maybe just a little . . . '

The Shramik Mahila Sabha ('Toiling Women's Organization') is the CPI (M)'s women's organization, but it is fairly recent. The fact is that, after communist women left the All-India Women's Conference, there was some talk about a women's organization, some brief attempts to hold conferences, but little was done for several years to really build a communist backed women's movement, and the women activists of the party were sent instead into general working class organizing. All sections of the now-split communist movement seemed to have shared the same approach, and women from all of them make similar complaints: 'We never paid attention to women's problems as women' (LNP); 'There was a lack of guidance from the party on how to unite class and women's issues, and those working in class organizations thought women workers' problems were only as workers' (CPI); 'Our main grievance is that the party has never taken an interest in organizing women on their own basis' (CPI (M)). Nevertheless, in recent years and as a result of the upsurge of women in general struggles, the party women's fronts have revived and grown, and the Shramik Mahila Sabha is one of these. But Ahilya feels it can do much more. 'Its main base is among working class women in Bombay. It has some rural base in Dhulia district, and a unit among the power-loom workers in Ichalkaranji; these are not exactly village women but small town women close to village life. And in Thana district among tribal women. I'm not satisfied with its development. My personal work is the main influence; there are not yet large sections of women taking part, and the trade unions are not taking an interest.'

In fact, it appears that Ahilya has something more of a 'liberationist' attitude than Mrinal, particularly when she describes some of her slum work. 'We are now propagating that women have a great part to play in changing society. We attack old beliefs and traditional religious ties. The child is a burden from birth in this society; we show that in a socialist society it is different. Women have a right to determine how many children they should have, and whether or not they should have children at all! We talk about this, especially the idea of the right to determine children, and the idea that the child is the society's responsibility, not just the mother's. We talk of socialist countries, especially China, and this appeals to people very much.' It seems that a concrete example, in another poor and developing country, is a crucial help for a belief in what is possible for women.

And when Ahilya speaks of women, much more than Mrinal or the socialists, she uses terms such as 'women's movement', and in comparing the nature of such movements and the position of women in other parts of India, she discusses cultural as well as economic issues, even though party work does not deal directly with cultural factors (the very name of its mass organization, 'Toiling Women's League', tends to show a belief that middle class or non-'toiling' women are not quite oppressed). 'There is much more progress here in Maharashtra regarding women's status than in other parts of India. In Bengal the feudal outlook is stronger, for instance on widow re-marriage. Formerly, women couldn't even go to restaurants, and they still find it difficult to move about in the streets in Calcutta. Here in Bombay we can go about at 1 or 2 a.m. Kerala is different again, due to its matriarchal traditions.' Kerala is a unique and beautiful small state in the south, famous for a large percentage of Christians, for a long-standing communist base (it was the first area in the world where communists were elected to power in its state government) and for the matrilineal – not quite matriarchal – customs of its major Hindu castes. 'But all the girls have to go out of the state; the poverty there is great, and they come to Bombay as nurses and such things. Among agricultural workers and tea plantation workers in Kerala, women play a great role; they organize and fight. In Calcutta [West Bengal] up to now, the women's movement has been limited to the middle class, and otherwise there is a total lack of women. In Kerala the most downtrodden women take part.'

Kerala and West Bengal are the CPI (M) strongholds in India, and it is clear that women's organizing there has grown up in close connection with the general movement and not so much out of a conscious party decision to build up a broader women's movement. But within this framework Ahilya is optimistic. 'Tremendous progress can be made. Two years ago in Tamilnadu state there was nothing, but recently as a result of the agricultural workers' movement 70,000 women attended the Democratic Women's Union rally in Thanjavur district.' Here she is referring to the December 1974 rally that mobilized masses of women out of the struggle of untouchable labourers who had experienced the brutality of landlords in the Kilvenmani incident. 'We have decided that we have to work in these classes, the working class and among agricultural working women.'

But who will lead this movement? Remembering Kaminibai and her request to provide leadership, remembering similar demands for direction from other illiterate rural and urban working class women, I ask, 'What about leadership? What about training women cadres from working class or slum backgrounds?' It seems they try to have some study circles for working women, but the level is very primitive. 'We need cadres, but the pace is slow, they are lacking. Middle class women should come forward; others don't even have primary education or literacy, it is very difficult for them. But young middle class girls are not coming forward these days.'

Seventy thousand women at a mass rally in an Indian small town; twenty thousand women marching through the streets of Bombay – this is mass mobilization of a type not often seen. The POW cannot match it; the Pune women can pull in only a few hundreds on their first 'women's day' programme. But is this really a 'women's movement'? If women involved in peasant struggles or unions or women in the electoral constituency of a leader who has gained them some government services are called out by their leaders to attend a 'women's meeting', are they really coming forth 'as women' to fight their oppression as women? Even though their unions or conferences may pass resolutions, what does this represent in the consciousness of the participants, who have usually not taken part in even the most elementary study circles and have no decision-making role in the process of passing resolutions? If the socialists and communists come together in an anti-price-rise movement, aren't they just 'using' women to strengthen the mass base of their parties and give a certain political weight to their claims? One day the communists may decide to pull 'their women' into such a united front, the next day they may decide to withdraw them because they have political disagreements with other members of the front. What then? In fact, this has happened in the anti-price-rise movement: while Ahilya's CPI (M) and Mrinal's Socialist Party have remained firm and militant organizers because of their continuing opposition to the Congress Party government, India's other Communist Party, the pro-Moscow CPI, has recently withdrawn from the front in order to support Indira Gandhi's government. Where in all this is the *self-activity* of women?

These are not just the questions of a Western feminist but are raised in India itself. They are raised by Marxist-oriented young women who would agree (as Rukmini and the POW agree) that the women's movement must be part of the general struggle of oppressed masses, but who feel that *women*'s issues, at a cultural level as well as at an economic level, must be taken up, and by an organization that is a special women's organization. They may wonder why socialists like Mrinal Gore simply assume that productive work is a 'part-time affair' for women and that 'children will always be women's responsibility'; and may wonder why communists like Ahilya Rangnekar, who can make more radical claims such as 'women have a right to determine whether or not to have children,' have never convinced their parties to take up women's issues like child care or even such basics as equal wages. Two women from such circles in Bombay have criticized the anti-price-rise movement for being a success not of rising sexual consciousness, but of the continuied deceptions perpetrated in both the economic and sexual spheres. The use of the demonstrations as a political weapon in the economic struggle focuses the attention and direction of the people towards economistic measures of price controls, etc . . . At the same time the participation of women is accepted and even encouraged because it is a logical extension of her role in the kitchen . . . The economic issues remain unresolved, essentially unchallenged, and the women's frustrations are channelled back into the same old patterns.'

These women radicals and their male friends profoundly distrust the parties, all of the established parliamentary parties. They say they are 'economistic', meaning not simply that they don't take up 'cultural' issues but also that they don't give a broader political consciousness to the women and men in their mass organizations, that they never go beyond the limits of parliamentary democracy, that they simply channel the masses they have organized into the direction of reforms. They say the parties themselves, even while claiming to be revolutionary, actually 'perpetrate deceptions', by increasing the hold of bourgeois ideology about 'women's place' or 'changing the government'. They say the parties are 'bureaucratic', meaning that they are controlled from the top down, that they don't develop or encourage real decision-making and leadership from below, and in particular that they are not serious about making an effort to educate urban workers or rural labourers so that men and women from these classes can really become dominant in the parties. Such young radicals are trying to work themselves — in slums, among peasants, among workers — and the women among them are meeting to discuss women's issues, to debate how to form organizations, how to build a mass base. But, whenever the question of participating in something like the Women's Anti-Price-Rise Committee comes up, they draw back: 'There is too much party power; how can we have any influence there?' And so the committee lacks the kind of dynamism that the young militants might provide, and correspondingly the party women, long-time leaders like Ahilya Rangnekar, feel a shortage of activists, an inability to build a permanent organization: 'There are not yet large sections of women taking part . . . Young middle class girls should come forward . . . '

8. 'The rain falls on everyone...'

Tribal Women Organise

Youth League Song

Chorus
You have to listen to the Youth League commands,
    brother, you have to listen!
Evils from the village we'll drive them away, brother,
    drive them away!

All these village leaders, who are they, tell?
Ah, my brother, I know them very well!
We have to break with their line, brother,
    break with their line —
Evils from the village we'll drive them away,
    brother, drive them away.

Throughout the county they gamble on numbers,
Filling the moneylender's gambling houses —
This filthy practice we must end, brother,
    we must end,
Evils from the village we'll drive them away,
    brother, drive them away.

Doling out law in every village square,
They wander holding liquor bottles there!
Youth League blows we'll deal them, brother,
    blows we will deal,
Evils from the village we'll drive them away,
    brother, drive them away.

For work worth five rupees you labour on their lands,
A rupee and a half you receive in your hands.
We'll have to win a raise in wages, brother,
    we will win it,
Evils from the village we'll drive them away,
    brother, drive them away.

Amassing private property they oppress us all,
Through it they suck and chew the workers all —
This private property we must end, brother,
    we must end,
Evils from the village we'll drive them away,
    brother, drive them away.

We'll have to build the Toilers' Union, brother,
    we will build it,
Evils from the village we'll drive them away,
    brother, drive them away!

by the Youth League of
Kharvad village of Dhule
district, 1973

In fact for about ten years now, radicalized youth, men and women alike, have not been coming forward to join the established communist parties like Lal Nishan or the CPI(M). The reason is not, as in the US or Britain, a general dearth of Marxist ideology or a suspicion about communism, and it is certainly not due to a swing to the right. Rather it is indicative of a split between the 'old' and 'new' left that in India has been different and more brutal than elsewhere. The significant event was not the party split in 1964 which divided the original Communist Party of India into the pro-Moscow, Congress-supporting CPI and the apparently 'centrist', slightly more pro-China and more militant CPI(M). Rather it was the Naxalbari revolt of 1967 which inaugurated an entirely new era in the Indian left. This revolt, occurring in a northeast section of West Bengal, the most militantly communist state of India, was an armed mass revolt (and, I was told long after, it was the poor peasant women who were actually the first to violently resist the police, something that was never commented on or analyzed in the literature which discussed the class structure of the Naxalbari only in terms of the traditional categories of 'rich', 'middle' and 'poor' peasants etc), and the revolt was led by cadres from the CPI(M), that is, Ahilya Rangnekar's party.

There had been armed peasant revolts in India in the past; what was new was that the Naxalbari leaders declared that they were not willing to compromise for partial economic gains, but rather that they were establishing 'red political power' in the region and that their goal was to smash the existing state. For its part, the CPI(M), whose party leadership was being defied, was leading a Left Front government in West Bengal state, and its leadership was faced with the decision whether to allow the police to be sent in to crush the movement its own cadres had started, or to support it. Supporting it, or allowing it to go on, would have meant being forced out of office and perhaps driven underground and into violent conflict with the central government. And so the police were sent in. As a result, there was tremendous disillusionment within the party ranks, who saw this as a final choice of electoralism over revolution. Between 15 and 30,000 members left or were expelled from the party. Many of these joined the newly formed, pro-China Communist Party of India (Marxist-Leninist), or CPI(ML), which was founded in 1969 with a call for armed struggle to smash the state, a struggle which was to begin with the 'annihilation of class enemies', a strategy of killing individual landlords and oppressors by small squads which it was thought would release the energy and enthusiasm of poor peasants and labourers and spark off mass uprisings. Other groups disagreed with this policy and considered it 'adventurist', but themselves also attempted to organize armed struggle in various forms. The Naxalite movement raised anew for the whole communist movement the issue of how to seize political power; it represented the most massive exodus of middle class youth to the villages in decades; and for a broader section of the Indian population, for millions of young educated youth and for many young workers and poor peasants as well, 'Naxalite' became a symbol of revolt, a call to arms.

But the movement could not achieve its goal of moving towards revolution through immediate armed struggle. The original struggles of 1967-70 were crushed by the ferocious repression of a frightened state: from the use of tear-gas and heavy beatings against peaceful strikers at Rahuri to the brutal slaughter of those who themselves took up weapons was not a long step. Tens of thousands of poor peasants and middle class youth landed in jail, to face the kind of tortures that had not previously been known in 'democratic' India, tortures that most people refused to believe existed even when they were documented by Amnesty International. Others were simply killed outright. The briefly established revolutionary peasant committees functioning in 'liberated areas' quickly succumbed to the army and police. The defeat inaugurated a new period of uncertainty for radicalized Indian youth. Most felt that the CPI (ML), whose organization was now in fractions, whose leaders were almost all murdered or in jail, had indeed been adventurist, had left its activists isolated out of unwillingness to really lead a mass movement. But the political atmosphere had irrevocably changed. It was impossible to see the old parties, even the most seemingly militant, as revolutionary, impossible to forget that the CPI(M) had 'betrayed' the movement. The old parties would not for a long time be able to recover their ability to attract young people.

Among the succeeding generation, there were many who, like the members of the Andhra POW and PDSU, were loyal to the 'Naxalite' movement and felt that somehow the party must be reorganized. Others wanted a new beginning totally; they felt that *all* existing parties, including the hastily organized CPI(ML) itself, suffered from dogmatism, petty bourgeois domina-

89

tion, and bureaucratic methods of work. New beginnings in theory had to be made ('there's never been a good analysis of Indian society since Rajni Palme Dutt'; 'there are not ten real Marxists in India' — meaning Marxist theorists — they used to say) and new experiments in organization had to begin ('the masses must be politically educated'). In Maharashtra this last tendency was strongest and radical youth began to gather around a new Marathi magazine, called *Magowa:* the Marathi word, difficult to translate, means something like 'search out, follow behind critically'. *Magowa* published poetry, stories, political analysis and theoretical articles; its core political group began to debate ideologies ranging from Maoism to Trotskyism and to involve themselves in organizing; and wider sections formed around it, 'Magowa Mandals', which sponsored forums, discussion groups and study camps in many small towns throughout the state.

Then in May 1971 came the Patilwadi Incident which, like the Kilvenmani slaughter in south India, highlighted the atrocities occurring against the rural poor. In Dhule district, tribal agricultural labourers — Bhils, like Tanubai — had gathered in the midst of the developing famine to ask for a share of the grain they had harvested, from the rich farmer in whose shed it was stored. The tribals, angry and starving, had brought their traditional weapons, sling-shots and bows. The landlords had guns. Two tribal labourers were killed in the clash, but when it was over no landlords were brought to court, rather some of the tribals themselves were jailed.

The affair touched the conscience of the liberal section of the Marathi-reading public, and a June conference called by a coalition of political parties (mainly Lal Nishan and the CPI(M), the only ones with some base in the district) plus local Gandhian workers and influential newspaper editors urged middle class youth to 'come forward' and take part in the struggles and sorrows of the poor. And many such youth did come. They came for a 'land liberation rally' (the *adivasis'* slogan was, 'the rain falls on everyone, the sun shines on everyone, and the land belongs to everyone') held in January 1972, and they stayed to work in the area. Some of these youth were from traditional communist families; others had come from a Gandhian experimental farm in the east where they had learned to work with their hands in the fields but were discontented with the lack of effort to organize the peasants; still others were from non-political or even right-wing backgrounds. But they came forward to work among the tribal labourers in Dhule in a way they would not have come to any established communist party; and they came forward vaguely influenced by the 'Naxalite' idea that the poorest, most oppressed sections in backward rural areas were the most revolutionary. They were also convinced that they should work with the parties but maintain a separate identity because these parties were hopelessly revisionist and bureaucratic. They were, in other words, a sort of Indian 'new left', and they became a crucial part of the wider *Magowa* group.

They were also, incidentally, all young men, because the movements of women were still so circumscribed that even the most socially conscious and militant young unmarried girls would not, like their brothers, dare to go alone to live and work in a remote village.

It was not accidental either that this new centre for a radical movement among the rural poor in Maharashtra was a tribal area. The *adivasis'* propensity for revolt was beginning to express itself again in these years, now under the most radical communist leadership. All the centres of the Naxalite movement up to 1970-71, for instance, were the jungly and mountainous homes of the tribals, including the most famous centres of Naxalbari itself and Srikakulam. In the case of Dhule, the *adivasis* were members of the Bhil tribe, like Tanubai; but unlike Tanubai's people, who were a minority in Ahmednagar district, in many parts of Dhule they constituted 40 to 50% of the population. Here they were genuinely on land 'that had once been ours', but land that was lost to rich peasants who had come down from the north a century before. Now these northerners or 'Gujars' were becoming rich capitalist farmers, growing cash crops, bringing in tractors, and employing the Bhils as wage labourers. Now about 60% of the Bhils had no claim to the land at all, not even as tenants or sharecroppers. No Naxalites had gone to work among the Bhils; nor had any established communist party built much of a base in this area; but followers of Gandhi had been long working there. Normally the Gandhians or Sarvodaya workers (the term means 'uplift of all') carry on only 'constructive work' such as education, anti-alcoholism and cleanliness campaigns, and eschew divisive 'struggle' as much as actual violence itself, but the turmoil of the period was beginning to affect Sarvodaya workers too. At least the Dhule organization was different. Its leader was a Bhil himself, Ambarsingh, and he was conscious enough of the needs of his people to accept an orientation to struggle and to welcome the young radicals who began to come to Dhule.

This, then, was the setting for what was to become the strongest rural mass organization in Maharashtra, the Shramik Sanghatana or 'Toilers' Union'. It was begun by the young radicals and Ambarsingh with the support of the Sarvodaya people — after an agreement that the Sanghatana would not be bound by Gandhian limitations to 'non-violence' and that decisions would be made only by the activists of the organization and not imposed from outside — and it increasingly incorporated young tribal leaders as well.

The Shramik Sanghatana began its movement with a campaign to win back land still officially owned by many Bhils but illegally occupied by Gujar landlords, the 'land liberation campaign'. After 4,000 acres were recovered, it began increasingly to take up wage issues, for the majority of the Bhils were wage labourers and as one activist pointed out, 'You can't have a *permanent* movement on such land issues, since those who get some land then tend to lose interest in the movement.' Strikes were organized in village after village. Police and landowner repression began to be felt, and while the Shramik Sanghatana often used such Gandhian methods as *satyagraha* and going to jail, they also occasionally met violence with violence and there were a number of notable clashes in which the *adivasis'* skill with the slingshots and stone throwing made itself felt. Through the *Magowa* group a good deal of outside publicity and financial support was organized to maintain the movement, and this wider support proved helpful on occasions such as the time activists discovered plans by landlords to organize a massive private army known as the 'Crop Protection Society'.

The unique feature of the Shramik Sanghatana was not simply this mass mobilization, but its effort to form stable village-level organizations of the tribal workers themselves. Agricultural labourer committees were formed in each village of struggle to negotiate as a democratic representative of the people, and youth leagues were formed as nuclei of the most politically conscious young men. Marxist study circles were carried on with the idea of developing leadership from among these most oppressed sections of labourers themselves, in an attempt to go beyond the bureaucratism and middle class domination that existed in the established parties.

In focusing on building up permanent organizations of agricultural labourers and creating leadership at the village level, the Shramik Sanghatana was attempting something relatively new. Up to now the communist parties have agreed that the rural poor (agricultural labourers and poor peasants) represent the most revolutionary rural sections and *must* be organized, but few stable organizations have in fact been built. There have been sporadic mobilizations on a single issue basis, such as the famine period fight for work projects or 'landgrab' campaigns at a state or national level; there have been periodic conferences and 'marches on parliament'; and there have been agricultural labourer unions formed on large public and private capitalist farms employing hundreds of labourers like those I saw in Ahmednagar district. But the countless millions working as wage labourers on the innumerable farms of middle and rich peasants and capitalist landlords in the far-flung villages of India have hardly been touched. Why is this? The agricultural labourers who make up nearly 40% of the rural work force are *not* in the same position as urban workers: even if they are permanent workers, they are scattered in tiny groups ranging from two to twenty on countless farms, and if they are not, they may simply go from farm to farm as temporary gang workers. These are usually hired only by the day, and not every day, and can be easily replaced by others of the half-starved semi-employed; with many still owning a bit of land they are not fully proletarianized in the Marxist sense; and they are sometimes even linked by kinship and caste to the farmowners themselves, as well as being nearly always divided internally by caste differences. By and large the communist movement has not been able to find enough activists ready to go into enough of the countless villages to organize, and has not been able to build up activists or leaders from among th poor and landless themselves. (Most of the established parties' village leaders are rich peasants and thus reluctant to really organize the rural poor.) And the movement has not found a way to really overcome caste divisions, and divisions between the totally landless and those with some land.

In trying to overcome these difficulties, the Shramik Sanghatana had the advantage of working in an area where a single and very militant community, the Bhils, made up the majority of wage labourers. But the problems of organizing toilers scattered on many farms, of facing not simply one or a few big non-cultivating landlords but a larger section of rich peasants and capitalist farmers who thought of themselves as the 'peasants' who had built up the land (a common situation in areas of capitalist farming), of overcoming caste feeling between the Bhils and other smaller groups of labourers and poor peasants – these obstacles remained. But whatever the case, youthful energy and innovation in methods of work were producing something new, and by my first visit in 1973 the Dhule example had itself become a famous movement in the state.

What I found interesting in all of this was the way women were involved. When I made my first visit to the area in 1973, their participation was already evident. Visits to Shramik Sanghatana villages at that time by outside 'guests' were something like a triumphal tour. While landowners sat grimly under the banyan trees in the village squares and stared at us, while their wives peered surreptitiously from the back doors of their huge stone houses in amazement at tribal women sitting on cots in a position of equality beside guests, we marched from one tribal hamlet to another to sit at each, discuss, take interviews of women or young men eager to tell of their struggles. And always we were served the inevitable tea – for even if they have nothing else, even if they have no milk to put in the tea, the poor of India still serve it to guests; it cannot be refused, and so I drank endless cups of heavy and usually milky tea, able to cut down only by pouring half of it into a saucer and handing it to someone else.

If the collective spirit of the people was impressive, it was the women and young girls who seemed to embody it the most, as they sang sitting in huts or marching through the village. They were more free and spirited, more collective in their singing, than other village women I had met, and this reflected the somewhat greater customary freedom for women among the Bhils. But it also reflected Shramik Sanghatana organizing. Here were young girls, thirteen or fourteen years old, singing as I and my friends used to sing in Girl Scout camps – but these were not love songs or religious ballads but political songs, songs of struggle. They sang about their confrontations with the landlords and about going to jail, about how they were no longer afraid of the police, and had succeeded in getting prices lowered by the local merchants. And they sang of the 'new wave' that had come to the villages with the Shramik Sanghatana: how, because of organizing, drunkenness had diminished, husbands were not beating wives so much, and it began to appear that although 'war is unhealthy for children and other growing things', class struggle on the contrary is healthy!

Behind this activity of the women, an interesting process was going on. The activists from the beginning had worked to build up local leadership, to give some kind of political education; defeating the landlords meant also changing the social and political consciousness of the people and replacing a traditionalist, accommodating leadership of tribal elders by militants from among the youth. But the organizers were all males; they found it easiest to mix socially, joke and communicate with the young *adivasi* boys as they sat around smoking *bidis* and discussing late into the night; they didn't quite

93

know how to handle the tribal women, who were unlike any city girls they had known. And perhaps subconsciously they expected the new leadership to come only from among the young men. As a result, though women were included from the beginning on the labourer committees (the organs of democratic representation), the youth leagues (the political nuclei) were entirely men, and the orientation was male. 'You'll have to listen to the Youth League commands, brother, you'll have to listen − !' Yet while this was happening, at the same time adult women as well as the young men were merging as a new political force in opposition to the collaborationist leadership of male tribal leaders.

But let Ashok, one of the organizers, tell the story as he told it to me in August 1973:

'The women were really militant, especially during the famine period. They were the ones who would be the first to stage a *gherao,* and when the men were ready to accept a promise and leave, it would be the women who insisted on having it in writing. They wouldn't give up! So we decided we should have some concentration on women, and to hold a special study camp for them.'

That was April 1973. 'We expected 25 women − 125 showed up. None of us really knew how to handle it; all the organizers, including Ambarsingh, were men. So we simply let the women take over. One by one, they stood up and told their problems. At the end one woman gave a summary. She said: 'The problem is, we need unity, we need organization. But the men won't organize themselves! Why? The answer is − *daru*! Alcohol. They drink too much. They become incapable of doing anything. *Daru* is preventing them from acting and we must smash it!'

Daru is the traditional 'country liquor' of the area. Once it had been a simple part of tribal culture and ceremonial life. Now it was spreading as a social evil, infecting them as it infected all the poor and working class sections. All moralism aside, I was beginning to understand as I talked to tribal women, to women factory workers, to slum women, how the prohibition movement in the West at one time really was a 'woman's movement'. The fact was that among the poor, faced with unemployment and misery, it was primarily the men who could escape into drink: women, always more mindful of domestic responsibilities, did so much more rarely. And when people are at the economic margin, the men literally drink up the food money, and then come home to beat their wives. And so an anti-alcohol campaign was almost always popular with women. But in Dhule something more was going on: the campaign to protect the family and fight a social evil was being linked up with the theme of class struggle, and the women were the first to show that *daru* must be fought in order to help build the organization!

'Then another woman stood up and said that her village was only a few miles away, that she knew all the liquor shops, and that the headman was taking bribes to let it all go on. Let's go there and break up the shops, she said. And all the women were ready!

'We organizers opposed it. We said, it's 10 p.m., how can you start something now? But the women wouldn't be stopped. They walked to that village, found the liquor shop, pulled out all the jugs and smashed them and let the liquor run into the village mud. Then they *gheraoed* the headman and forced him to apologize, one by one, to every woman. Only then would they return.'

The immediate lesson for the organizers was a demonstration of the militancy and special fervour of women, their orientation to immediate practical action. As with many sections of the left at that time, the Shramik Sanghatana activists were realizing that women could be a major force, that they had to be somehow more involved in decision-making and brought into leadership. More women's study camps would follow, with special efforts being made to invite women activists from outside Dhule. Even more important — and reflecting the group's theoretical openness — it is perhaps not accidental that the first Indian Marxist magazine to have a 'women's liberation special issue' was *Magowa,* which devoted its September 1973 issue to the problems and struggles of women in India and abroad. Rather uncertainly, the left movement in India was beginning to take up problems — caste, the special oppression of women — which all sections of it from the CPI to the Naxalites, had neglected in the past.

Two years later, 1975, it is International Women's Year and events are moving at a rapid pace. Throughout India people are stirring, and a disjointed left — from new groups like *Magowa* to the fragmented Naxalites and the loyal activists of traditional left parties — is attempting to cope with surging popular turmoil and police repression. And women, with the famine period struggles and peasant organizing behind them, with the massive anti-price-rise movement still reverberating, with the new ideas of equal rights coming not only from the West but also from newly liberated countries where Vietnamese and African women are rising up with guns in their hand, women are also part of the ferment.

January and February: months of discussion, ideas brewing. Discussions with Kaminibai, the Pune municipal workers, Bimzani college students, meetings with factory women and life insurance company employees, interviews with Ahilya Rangnekar and Mrinal Gore. Discussions also with women in Lal Nishan and the Magowa Mandals — for while women have not yet gone to work among the *adivasis* in Dhule, there are still many associated with the *Magowa* group in Bombay and Pune and elsewhere, and some of them really do not feel that *Magowa* or the Shramik Sanghatana have done all they could to face the problems of women's special oppression. 'They want to emphasize class as the main contradiction, and they ignore everything else,' says Chhaya Datar, a young upper middle class writer, a Bombay sophisticate but one beginning to come into the movement with a good deal of bubbling energy, raising funds, organizing forums, meeting political leaders when a crisis comes up in Dhule, writing articles. 'I'm not even part of the core group, I'm on the periphery, and all they have me doing is running around collecting funds. Support work . . . ' It is, for me, reminiscent of the early experience of US women in the civil rights movement, assigned to do the 'shit work', the secretarial tasks of organizing. I mention this to Chhaya. In the meantime, there is Rukmini's visit followed by a new wave of enthusiasm and the formation of a Pune version of the POW, which aims at being more working class oriented and broader in political scope.

March 8, Women's Day: the first-ever 'International Women's Day' march, organized in Pune by the new Progressive Women's Organization which by now has emerged as a kind of coalition of local Lal Nishan women, some *Magowa* people, the Naxalite-oriented college students, and independents, and by the CPI. One day later, the 'Women's Special Issue' of the LNP party paper is published, another mark of the new consciousness beginning to filter through to cadres in the country districts. Most of the articles are written by men. 'You shouldn't have an issue like this until women can write it,' a German friend argues with Leela. 'We're not ready yet, I'm not ready, but I will write,' she says. 'Meantime, we need this.'

April: a month of gathering storm. The momentum that started with popular upsurges in the northern states of Bihar and Gujarat in 1973 and with the massive railway strike in 1974 is not halted. Strikes and agricultural revolts continue. On April 3, 30,000 poor peasants, agricultural labourers and city workers gather for a giant march in Bombay which has been organized by five left parties. Its special demand is the removal of police camps from the tribal areas of Dhule and Thana districts and so it is known as the *Adivasi* March, but the general popular demands for work, higher wages and more food rations serve to unify all sections of toilers behind it. The turnout is impressive. From nearby Thana come thousands of Warli tribals organized by the CPI(M), with bright red scarves around their necks and flowers in the hair of the women. From faraway Dhule the Shramik Sanghathana, a poorer, younger organization, cannot afford the transportation for so many, but about a hundred Bhil labourers walk on foot for nearly a hundred miles and take the train the rest of the way. No women are among them; the organizers still have doubts about their capacity. Endless rolling waves of people and red banners above them, a demonstration to mighty Bombay, India's capitalist centre, of the rural presence . . . And meanwhile, the rural women labourers at Rahuri farm and on the Mula Canal began to turn again to their struggle.

And discussions go on among the Pune women: how to proceed, whether to do slum work, take up the question of dowry as the focus for a campaign, try to organize around the issue of employment for women, do working class surveys, or what? What section of women should be organized first, who will be the most militant, who will be readiest to respond, where can the most solid base be built? Chhaya and I are invited to the small town of Barsi by a socialist organizer for a special International Women's Year programme; she gives a lecture and we meet local working class and agricultural labourer women. I go to other small towns; colleges and schools are vociferously demanding lectures for 'Women's Year'.

April 17: Indochina Victory Day is proclaimed by a student group as the triumph of the Vietnamese seems assured, and they bring together a coalition of all union and party leaders, including the Dalit Panthers, for a march and a rally. Tarabai and I leave in the middle of the rally to go to a small town in a nearby district for a 'Baglan County Women's Rally'. The rally's guiding hand is that of an LNP local organizer, but its official sponsors are 20 local *mahila mandals* or women's clubs. This is Tarabai's first trip outside of Pune as an organizer, and she is entrhalled with the discussions and meetings though not yet ready to do much speaking herself. It is my first experience of a major women's rally in a rural area. A small march winds through the streets of the town to come to a hall filled with people, all women, ('men to the outside, men to the outside, let the women sit first,' yell the organizers), students, workers, peasants, tribal women, all classes, a demonstration of the possibility of mobilization, of the potential massiveness of women's unity. On our return we stop in Aurangabad to meet the Mahila Samta Sainik Dal and then to meet some working class women who are organizing a march to demand water facilities.

May 1: *May Day,* celebrated always in India as it never is in the US, its original 'home', is more turbulent than ever this year. Thousands march in Dhule; in Bombay the factionalized left parties hold three separate marches. The Pune march is more united, and striking state government employees join it, middle class clerical workers for the most part, who are taking a big organizational step and uniting with blue collar workers with new shouts, 'We are all one! *hum sub ek hai!*' As always, the Pune women street sweepers form a special and large contingent, surging together, the more flamboyant among them dancing as some of the men dance, dancing along the march route to the beating of drums and the rhythm of shouted slogans . . .

In the midst of marches, rallies, meetings, discussions, strikes and *gheraos* comes the news that in Dhule the Shramik Sanghatana is planning its third 'women's study camp'. 'This time,' says Chhaya, 'we are going to discuss the oppression of women as well as general Marxist theory.' It is unclear if she or the Dhule activists are planning this, but outside women are invited, including many who are not part of the Magowa group. So, Chhaya and a few others from Bombay will be joined by socialist women from Barsi, by Leela and Tarabai and other Lal Nishan women from Pune and elsewhere. Distant Dhule district, nearly in the hill country along the border of Maharashtra state, is about to become a focal point for a different and newly developing movement.

9. 'Listen to the toilers' call'

Women Call for a Conference

Come, You Poor, Come

Chorus
Come, you poor, come,
Take the flag in hand,
Listen to the toilers' call —
Moneylender's rule, capitalist rule,
Now we must smash them all!

Inside the purple cars see the painted dolls,
Comfortably they go on the road —
Thorns in the jungle, bare feet are mangled,
The poor walk with their load.

Storey upon storey, decorations gaudy,
Their houses are blinding our eyes —
Huts made of mud, darkness inside,
Heavy the poor men's fate lies.

Plates made of silver, designs surrounding,
Sweets to eat their fill —
Pots made of clay, the food is decayed,
The poor have no holiday meal.

Now comes the summer, curtains are scented
To keep the hot breeze at bay —
For the poor only a tree's umbrella
And a dog for company today.

The hookah needs lighting? a servant is waiting,
There is wood for the winter around –
The poor have hardly a rag for their body
And sleep on the stony ground.

The flag of revolution, the call to insurrection,
Listen to the toilers' cry!
For ending injustice, destroying oppression,
The moment of truth is nigh!

> *Nationalist song from*
> *the 1940s, adapted by*
> *the Shramik*
> *Sanghatana*

It is night when Leela, Tarabai, Suman and I – the 'Pune delegation' – arrive
in the village of Nandurkheda on the banks of the Tapti river in Dhule district.
Milling throngs of women and girls can be seen in the large, thatched-roof
open-walled site of the camp; kerosene lamps cast flickering waves of light
and shadow on the faces of the girls rising in ordered streams to eat; surges of
choral singing in the tribal dialect erupt from one group or another.
'Zindabad, Zindabad', the tribal women greet us with clenched fists.
Zindabad, meaning 'long live', is really a short form of the familiar *inquilab
zindabad,* 'long live the revolution', and has been taught to the women as a
greeting in order to replace the more traditional custom of touching a visitor's
(or superior's) feet. We can see glimpses of other outside visitors, Bombay
women, Barsi women, Chhaya looking tense because she is in the middle of a
debate with the local activists over how to organize the meeting, how much
time to give to 'women's subjects'. But beyond a few songs, there is little
desire to argue out issues that night. Everyone is too exhausted from journeys
of ten to twenty hours on jolting buses, and we fall asleep outside the hall to
the accompaniment of the fierce wild wind that howls through the night and
is to continue whistling and blowing dust over everything during the following
days . . .

Morning comes. We rise with the dawn, go to the river to bathe, sort into
groups for an exercise session and begin to feel a kind of emptiness in the
stomach that is the signal that really tea time has come – for even if break-
fast does not always come in the early Indian mornings, tea inevitably is
served. Leela, with her usual good-natured lack of inhibition, complains: are
the conference organizers expecting people to do without tea? 'Are we
supposed to be self-sacrificing? Sacrifice is a Gandhian notion, not a communist one. These youngsters' (meaning the activists and *Magowa* people
generally) 'are so enthusiastic they won't even take care of themselves. Look
at them, they'll all end up sick. Not me.'

Tea seems to symbolize a good deal in India. I remember Chhaya once
arguing with an agricultural labourer activist in Barsi that she should *not*

serve tea to us as 'honoured guests', that tea is a middle class and not a working class custom. This was naturally ignored. I remember another enthusiastic new activist, Gita, inviting a group of housewives for a discussion on women's liberation, determined not to serve the usual tea for the same reason. This also was a total failure; the women simply sat around and sat around until tea was brought, for tea is not only an expression of hospitality but also functions in such cases as a kind of social signal: the meeting is over and now you can go home. Middle class, even imperialist in origin tea may be (its first spread in India was the result of a British advertising campaign), but it has become so universal that, apart from a very few who have given it up on principle, no Indian woman who had it in her power to make tea (or in the south, coffee) would leave it aside.

Leela complains, but it is Tarabai, the Pune worker, who moves into action. She disappears and after a short while reappears and says to us, 'Come on' — and we go next door into the hut of a neighbouring Bhil family to have our morning tea. Tarabai, it turns out, has gone out, bought tea, sugar and milk, and made their acquaintance for 'stove' service. And so for the next three days we enjoy both special morning tea and discussions with the family. But other *Magowa* women, the Bombay people, give us rather curious glances as if we were making something special of ourselves. I can imagine their thoughts, 'middle class communists' . . . and tea has become the first, if minor, source of tension in the study camp.

Then, after the camp-provided tea (the Shramik Sanghatana is not really going to do without it), the morning session begins, under a brightly decorated canvas roof featuring posters of women in other countries, including two of Vietnam, a large map and a peasant woman shown sitting guarding her baby with a gun. A brief argument, however, precedes it. A familiar argument, which re-enacts all the old themes of the left-feminist debate now reincarnated among the young left organizers of oppressed tribal people in India. It seems the activists have already set the themes of the camp — Class, Exploitation, Organization and Revolution — and 'women's liberation' doesn't quite fit in. The other topics are of *urgent* importance to build up consciousness; as for Dhule, they have won near equality in wage rates for men and women; women are included as representatives on every agricultural labourer committee; *daru* has become a special focus for organizing women. Even food for the study camp is being cooked by men. Why is there a need for anything more? Why discuss 'women's oppression' as a special topic when there is so little time? Why try to do too much? First have the revolution, then after . . .

Chhaya argues that this is a liquidationist tendency, that it represents mechanical Marxism — 'Even if women's oppression is secondary, that doesn't mean you can ignore the secondary contradictions!' She is carrying on most of the debate; Leela is involved with other matters outside, studiously ignoring the whole thing more or less on the belief that every woman has to fight out the issue in 'her own' group. But Chhaya is not immediately successful; the Shramik Sanghatana activists seem to feel that she is giving a 'petty bourgeois' line.

In fact, though the activists have created a militant class organization rooted in the villages and have succeeded in building up a degree of political
consciousness, they are still having problems with 'secondary contradictions'.
Are the Bhils agricultural labourers first, or *adivasis* first? Although the
Shramik Sanghatana defines its membership as agricultural labourers and poor
peasants of any caste, and works hard to include non-Bhil labourers, it is still
a largely Bhil organization, and slogans like 'victory to Ambarsingh Maharaj'
(after the dead Bhil leader) are central to it. Also, are the Bhil women agricultural labourers first, or women first? In fact, the women do get lower
wages and less work than the men; a 1973 survey has shown that they got
1½ to 2 rupees a day while the men got 2 to 2½, and 80% of the women but
only 37% of the men had work for less than four months of the year. Shramik
Sanghatana organizing has brought these wages up, but the differentials
remain. However, in the face of the difficulties of relating class identity,
tribal identity, and sex identity, the first response of the Shramik Sanghatana
seems to me little different from the classic Indian communist response: to
hammer home the concept of 'class'.

This is clear in the first session. After a discussion of the Vietnamese
revolution and a valiant attempt to give a sense of world geography, an
initial, simple but effective lecture on 'class' is given. Then the eighty or ninety
women present are broken up into small discussion groups, each led by a local
or visiting activist. The discussion groups themselves are a relatively new
thing, an effort to get around the 'top down' type of political education that
seems universal in Indian study groups. But there is a tendency to turn these
into a rote drill:

'Landless agricultural labourer: whoever has no land of his or her own and
has to work on land of others is a landless agricultural labourer. Say it — ' and
the women are made to repeat this three or four times. 'Number one class:
landless agricultural labourer.' Then a 'poor peasant' is defined, and each
woman and girl is tackled separately: 'What is *your* class?' And at this point
the tribal women — who are voluble and vigorous in informal discussion, who
are able to memorize a whole Marathi song after one hearing, even though it
is not their mother tongue — fall bashful and silent, forgetful or un-
comprehending, hiding their faces or muttering the answer. 'Say it louder . . .'

Some of the 'rote' character may come out of the inexperience of outside
visitors in the face of the genuine difficulties of teaching women who have
almost never been outside their home village. Local activists are more free
and easy in their groups. But this is how the discussion is directed, and there
seems to me to be something elitist about educated middle class youth asking
tribal women to analyze their class positions without discussing their own
petty bourgeois, urban (and upper caste) background. I begin to have my
doubts about the innovative character of the Shramik Sanghatana. Beneath
the activists' tendency to think of 'women's issues' as 'distracting' from the
'basic' concept of class identity, isn't there a demeaning view of the tribal
women as being somehow childishly unable to handle more than one idea at
a time? Is the theoretical openness of the group only limited to their Bombay

comrades, or to an orientation to new Marxist philosophers? Doesn't maybe the revolutionary fervour about giving political education only hide a slight brahmanical tendency to turn every village into a classroom?

Chhaya meanwhile is ignoring instructions. After half an hour her group diverges into a lively discussion of women's work, wages, past struggles, harassment by husbands. One woman reveals that she had to 'run away' from her social responsibilities in a wedding ceremony in order to attend the study camp. This woman, Bhuribai, is in the process of becoming a local leader and this has been possible, she tells us, because she has no heavy family responsibilities — she has no children herself and does not live in a joint family — and because her husband, loyal to the Sanghatana, is willing to have her away from home for periods of organizing even at the occasional expense of her work on the few acres of land they own. But to leave a close relative's wedding seemed to everyone too much, and Bhuribai shows us the deep scratches on her arm made by bangles breaking as she tore herself away. Clearly, political participation in itself requires a defiance of social convention, and this leads to a fairly in-depth discussion. But then a male activist comes by to check up: 'You have two acres? Then you are a poor peasant. Say it, poor peasant . . .'

Tarabai's group also diverges from the prescribed pattern. After the morning session of drill and a similar beginning in the afternoon, she is asked to say something — and Tarabai moves in an easy flow and semi-random fashion from tales of union organizing to the need for women's liberation, and her group settles into a discussion of the significance of the fact that most Bhils still pay a bride-price rather than having a dowry given by the girl's family. Until, once more, the inevitable male organizer appears to have a local boy repeat the afternoon lesson ('Organization') in the Bhilori dialect.

At this point, women's liberation and class education have clearly been put into a kind of confrontation. Chhaya again argues with the local activists and this time they surrender. Whether it is because they are genuinely non-dogmatic enough to agree to an experiment, or because they are convinced by Chhaya's somewhat overwhelming persistence, or simply because in the face of so many reluctant women they again feel, as in the first women's study camp, that they 'really don't know how to handle' the situation, they give in. The next morning is to be devoted entirely to women's issues and the women activists as a group can organize it.

And so, rising again before the sun, bathing in the brown waters of the Tapti, taking our special tea with Tarabai and our Shramik Sanghatana tea with the group, we begin. Now it is a different kind of meeting — no long lecture or rote drill or random group discussion, but rather a kind of combination of rally and encounter group.

All of the outside women — four from Pune, two from the socialist group in Barsi, two from Bombay, one the wife of a union leader in a nearby town — and as many of the Bhil women who want to, speak. Few are experienced speakers; most simply recount their experiences of struggle and of their particular form of women's oppression to the group, and in so doing take inspiration from the group. It becomes clear why the 'outsiders' are brought to Dhule — not simply to help in the process of educating the tribal women, but to be inspired and educated themselves.

In a way this process goes beyond the original vision of the organizers, for the 'outsiders' emphasize not only how impressed they are with the collective militancy of the tribal women and the need for a broader united struggle, but also, with simple eloquence, the relative freedom of tribal customs in contrast to the semi-slavery of women in traditional Hindu families. This is a new theme — and a contrast to the usual middle class, rather puritanical and moralizing Hindu attitude that tribal customs are barbaric and inferior, that the villages are culturally backward in comparison to the cities and so forth. (It should not be surprising after all if women should have a different attitude in these matters; there is a well-known anecdote about Irawati Karve, the famous Indian anthropologist, who was asked by the government for her help in erasing the 'deplorable' custom of polyandry — multiple husbands — found in some tribes. 'Why should I?' she reportedly said, 'I think it's a fine idea!') And so the two Barsi women begin. Hirabai talks about struggles, anti-price-rise movements, attending rallies in Bombay and about the oppression of women, and her friend Suman fills in a personal and eloquent account of this with the story of her husband who has taken a second wife but refuses to let her, the first wife, have any freedom. Suman Gokhale of Pune also talks about the anti-price-rise movement and going to jail; for her it is the story of a woman fighting the fear of public action instilled from childhood in a severely repressed brahmanical upbringing.

There are songs — some by the tribal women, some by us 'outsiders' — and Tarabai rises for her first public speech. Rather excited, she forgets to say anything at all about 'women's liberation' (though it has by now become a favourite theme of hers), forgets even her usual argument that because of their ability to do double work 'women are stronger than men', but instead taks about the militant union struggles of the Pune workers and ends with a call for unity. 'We treat others as sisters. We, the city municipal workers, the sweepers and other workers, support the struggle of peasants and labourers. And among those we give the most support to agricultural workers! Whenever we hear about an agricultural workers' struggle, we take the red flag and go and do whatever we can ... Coming to a session like this, we take you as our sisters, and you should also take us as sisters, and we should build up an organization together!'

There follows a speech by a Bombay *Magowa* woman, who tries to tell, in oversimplified terms and without mentioning the petty bourgeoisie, about 'class' in the big city. It is too didactic; it brings the rally/encounter group back to the classroom and the audience becomes restless, women start to rise and go out for the toilet, and order finally has to be restored with a song. But then it is Leela's turn — Leela, who is capable at her best of really gauging the mood and orientation of a crowd and taking up people's sorrows and struggles in their own language to give them an exciting transformation. She begins with Vietnam 'where the toilers' state has been established' (the 'toilers' state' is the way the revolutionary left describes the goal of peoples' struggles, and it has a strong appeal for those already disillusioned with 'parliamentary socialism'), and she moves on to the history of women's struggles in India, particularly the fights of the women textile workers of Bombay. Then she takes up the theme of the militancy and social independence of these Bhil women:

'I want to say one thing: I've been watching you and deliberately have asked questions of every woman, and discovered that many here are un-married girls. I was surprised. Because in the villages I've been to, twelve-and thirteen-year old girls are either married or kept in the home. And their parents feel that they are a stone weighing on their head. Why? Is it the father's fault? Not at all. Because a daughter means dowry! Behind every girl lurks 200 to 1,000 rupees debt' (a low figure but she is gauging her audience). 'He has to bear the expenses and so the father and mother will think, what is she born for? who knows, it might have been better if she died, truly! If a boy is born, hooray, happiness, give a party, hand out sweets, ice-cream, presents! But not for a girl. Because things get more difficult day by day . . .

'But among you, I have seen that if a daughter is born people are happy! I asked, don't you feel worried? They said, why should we? Because you don't give dowry. The situation here is that a boy gives money for a wife — so what reason do you have to feel bad about a daughter? Truly, the burden on the mind is so much less here. You have girls fifteen and sixteen years old who are unmarried and they go about freely. Aren't you worried? No — because you have many kinds of independence, freedom of behaviour between boys and girls. Earlier I was hearing about your traditional custom of boys and girls running away together. They could just go away, and if the girl wanted to get married after that she would, and if she didn't she wouldn't! You have many kinds of independence, and that is a very good thing, in my opinion!'

A very good thing . . . For a Hindu woman to praise the traditional sexual freedom of *adivasis* is something new, after decades of being exposed to, if not bombarded by, the moralizing educational practices of Christian mission-aries or Hindu reformers who bring with them, openly enshrined, the nuclear family and, more subtly hidden, even more feudal values. The tribal women listen attentively, and Leela goes on to the theme of women's oppression, the theme of struggle:

'Today women are coming to the fore. Why? Because of today's condi-tions. Women have to care for the household. Who does the cooking? Women. Who cares for the children? Women. Since you are *adivasis,* you have more independence, you can behave freely with men. Among us that is not possible even in the villages. If the husband comes, the women still cover their faces. Why? Because women from generation to generation are slaves! Why? We also work, we also earn, but still as women our inferior status has not ended.

'But today the situation is such that we have to care for the homes and feed our children, but there is nothing to fill our stomachs with, nothing to eat. Suppose tomorrow someone says, "Mother, give me something!" What can we give? Where is the money? On 3 rupees a day how can we live? What shall we feed our husbands or children? And there is a remarkable thing among women: first we feed our husbands, then our children, and who eats last? We do. This has existed from the beginning. But today's conditions are such that we are starting to think. After generations and generations, how much longer can we endure? And you will find everywhere agricultural women coming forward. Especially in the villages the movement is strong. As women we are beginning to feel solidarity. What problems, what sorrows . . . !

'And here, the remarkable thing is that you listen the whole day, in the evening you sing, really your enthusiasm is tremendous, and it is worth seeing that women can toil the whole day and still their minds are filled with enthusiasm, they don't get weary. If the women's movement becomes strong tomorrow, the toiling women will rise up. We have heard the examples of Vietnamese women, Russian women going to battle. It may be difficult to tell what will happen in our country, but truly after seeing your organization, your unity, I am certain that you will also, and women in other areas will also, definitely come into the vanguard!'

And she finishes by taking up Tarabai's theme of unity and worker aid to struggles, turning it into a call for a new and wider organizational beginning: 'Truly, the municipal workers of Pune have donated *lakhs* of rupees for the struggles of the rural poor' (this is true) 'and they have decided to sponsor a conference' (in fact they haven't, but such petty details can be worked out later; Leela is seizing the moment) 'for toiling women – you all come!' And so it is in this way, though it has been floating around before this, that the idea of an all-Maharashtra women's conference, designed to spark off and organize a new women's movement, gets its first public airing in this distant tribal corner of the state among the militant women and girls of the Shramik Sanghatana.

But the meeting is hardly over. Now it is the turn of the tribal women to speak; they are if anything less fearful of public speaking than many of the visitors from outside and sometimes grab the microphone as if it were a weapon – but for most also the experience is new, they are only beginning to come into a self-conscious leading role in the struggle. An exception is Bhuribai, who has been active since the first women's camp; she speaks passionately in the local dialect of the movement and its problems, of the need for organization and the special contribution that women can make. There are more songs, and finally Chhaya as the leading *'Magowa* feminist' takes the opportunity to have the last word.

It is, like Leela's, a long speech, though tending to be middle class in vocabulary and didactic in approach. But at the end, dealing finally with the issue of class and sex, she makes her direct reply to the male organizers who have been implying that focusing on women's oppression is somehow a distraction from class organizing: 'There are many contradictions besides class contradictions: contradictions between castes, between Gujar and Bhil, between Brahmans and untouchables. And there is the contradiction between men and women. All these can become obstacles to the building up of class unity. And those who put obstacles before the full participation of women, those who try to keep them in the home, bound to housework, those who do not encourage them to come forward as leaders — *they* are the ones who are breaking the unity of the class!'

Back in Pune, after a final session of lessons on 'Exploitation' and 'Revolution' and after a series of *'Zindabad! zindabad!* come again!' farewells, the question of organizing a women's conference is taken up seriously. The problem is to put some organizational force behind it. The students in the Pune Progressive Women's Group, who by and large lack rural contacts, are not particularly enthusiastic about a mass conference. Chhaya on the other hand is, and the help of Shramik Sanghatana and *Magowa* people elsewhere seems assured. Potential contacts with a wide variety of independent, leftist and some Dalit women leaders throughout the state have also been built up. But it is LNP, with its widespread union base among rural and urban workers, that can form the backbone for mobilizing working class and agricultural labourer women for such a conference. Their leaders have sensed the potential in women's militancy; they are at this period a growing organization — though still like other 'old' CPs, lacking the ability to inspire the new generation of youth — and anxious to build on the new wave. Leela and other women close to the party have been doing their part in pushing the issue. So the men of the 'Leading Committee' spend time listening to my various tapes of women's meetings; the whole 4½-hour tape of the Nandurkheda study camp discussions and speeches is played for them. And in one of their meetings they make a decision to 'support' such a conference. But they have their own suggestions: don't work through the Pune Progressive Women's Group because it has already become too narrow and has not yet established its name, rather begin with an *ad hoc* organizing committee including women of every left group, from the Socialists and CPI to the Naxalite-minded students and vaguely Marxist professors. And make the conference one oriented to mass mobilizing, 'a platform for spreading our ideas, for giving a push to the new movement'.

Symbolically, the forthcoming 'Women's Liberation Struggle Conference' has been born out of a call given by the working class, given at a session and under the inspiration of that special group of women, the militant and organized tribal agricultural labourers of Dhule. The reality of course is more complex. Funds will be forthcoming from the Pune minicipal workers' union because their LNP leadership has decided it is worth doing; rural women labourers will be able to come to the conference because LNP and other groups organizing among them have made such decisions. And the leadership of such groups is still largely male — not to mention petty bourgeois in class origin, a fact still true of every single left organization in India.

Dependence on men, in other words, is integral to the very process of organizing women. But behind this process still is the force of women which has in the last decade and especially in the last few years impressed itself upon the party leaders in various ways, which has at local levels and in hesitating forms produced its own initiative. So, with all its ambiguity, the first meeting of the 'organizing committee' for the conference is held on June 1; once again women from the whole spectrum of political groups are there, and a new thrust begins. October 18-19 is decided on as the date for the conference, and preparations begin immediately.

10. 'Go to the women'

Organising Begins

Go to the Women

Chorus
To the women of this country, mothers and sisters,
We must go, and say,
Unite together, take up the battle,
We will smash this prison!

This prison —
This prison in whose walls daughters and daughters-in-law
    are buried alive
In a web of slavery woven with the webs of cruel laws,
We will no longer die trapped in this prison!

This prison —
This prison on whose stones the songs of religion
    are written
Dividing one from another, sowing destruction,
    reaping the fruits of our labour
We must grab them by the throat, throw them on their faces,
Take back what we have lost!

This prison —
This prison whose every brick is made of mud
    taken from our land.
By bringing liquor to the villages, peddling pot and pipes,
They have sapped the strength of our men!
We must surge ahead, banish liquor and together

demand back our land!

This prison —
This prison in whose defence sit the priests,
    the *mullahs* and *pujaris,*
And with keys in their hands and sticks on their shoulders
    the money men and sugar kings.
Come *adivasi,* come Devadasi, Buddhists and Dalits
    to the forefront —
To the women of this country, mothers and sisters
We must go and say,
Unite together, take up the battle, and we will smash this prison!

by Madhav Chavan,
for the Women's Liberation
Struggle Conference, 1975

And so the campaign begins. Now I become part of an organization. No
longer am I simply interviewing women, or taking information-gathering tours
with enthusiastic young union activists interested in providing new stimulation for their membership, or merely observing the complex process of a
developing Indian women's movement. I am part of it. Go out to meet
women in the fields and factories, throw out the message of 'women's liberation' and the new realization of oppression, bring women to the conference,
let a process of mass struggle begin . . . This is the mood that begins to catch
people up in those days.

I go to Bombay, where Chhaya and Sharda, a young LNP full-time worker,
have got together a group of young women, friends and relatives of LNP and
Magowa members, most of them employed in banks and offices in the city.
Sharda, a small, sharp-faced woman, a quiet and regular worker, has in her
own way been a feminist for a long time: she has kept her own name after
marriage and refused to wear the *mangalsutra,* the gold necklace that is the
Indian equivalent of a wedding ring. But until recently she has seemed un-
interested in women's liberation as a cause. Then in April, during a discussion
with a group of hospital workers — low-caste women who work in the kitchens, clean the floors and are generally, like Spanish-speaking and Black
women in North American hospitals, on the bottom rung of the hospital
hierarchy — Sharda bursts into a long speech about Vietnam and the US and
the proven ability of women in that war to do anything, literally anything.
'She's become a raving feminist,' comments one LNP leader with a rueful
grin on hearing the tape of the meeting. Sharda says that she would like to
have more time for organizing working women as union members as well as
in a women's movement. But she is a legal worker for the party, caught up
in the endless round of workers' court disputes that are such a time-
consuming part of established trade unionism. 'It's the housework of the
movement,' she says, but she can't seem to get out of it.

But she does have time to help Chhaya organize for the conference and
hold one or two meetings a week and now, as I walk into the building that is
both the LNP office centre and home for several of its leaders and full-time
workers, the women are spread over the floor of one room, clipping pictures
and pasting them together to make posters that will eventually become a
picture exhibition of women around the world. And as I come in, so does
Madhav, Leela's nephew, with sheets of paper in his hand. 'How does this
sound?' he asks, and begins to sing —

> To the women of this country, mothers and
>   sisters,
> We must go and say,
> Unite together, take up the battle, and we
>   will smash this prison!
> This prison . . .

'Let's hear the whole thing,' says one of the women, and they join in — the
song in its process of composition is clearly familiar to them — now transformed into a singing group. Madhav in fact has been writing women's
liberation songs ('unfortunately women as yet aren't used to writing songs,
but someone has to, so why shouldn't I?') and the songs, picture exhibition,
a skit and films are all being planned for the cultural part of the conference.

Chhaya in the meantime is bustling about from poster to poster. 'Come
on, Gail, hello, did you just come? Do you want to go down to the fort area
with me this afternoon and meet some people?' And after a bath and some
food we take off, walking to catch the local train as Chhaya talks of organizing in Bombay. 'We'll have at least some textile workers coming, and we'll
go to some of the factories next week. You know we were invited to go out
and meet the salt pan workers — the women who work gathering salt, they've
been unionizing and have a lot to say. I was never able to go, so Sulabha went
finally — her first public speech and it seems she did quite well! But she
doesn't get to the study group regularly. We've already met some of the LIC
employees [LIC is the Life Insurance Corporation] , probably the same ones
you talked to in January, through Dev and Bhat. We want to meet the bank
employees also but the CPI people, the ones who control the union, won't
cooperate. CPI(M) won't really cooperate either, Gail, you know how the
parties are. But I've been to see Prabha Sawant and she likes the idea of a
picture exhibition. Ahilya and Mrinal are both out of town, but you said
Leela was going to meet Ahilya in Pune? But you know, they're really reluctant to give any kind of access to trade union members, they want to hang on
to their unions about everything. LNP I guess is the same, but they're co-
operating a lot now. You have to meet women workers through their unions
if you want to get them at the workplace, otherwise they just scatter when
the day is over. We must build a base in the working class, don't you think?'

Build a base in the organized working class — for this, some cooperation
from the unions is necessary. And this means cooperation from the party

leaderships which control the unions! And of course, 'Party politics' has already affected the Conference Organizing Committee. The aim is unexceptionable: to build a broad-based, working class-oriented mass organization of women with the united participation of the left. But the left, as usual and as everywhere, won't unite. Why? First of all, there is mutual suspicion, that one party or another is going to capture this new thing that is being created, is going to be able to use the coalition to increase its own hold. Already the conference is being identified as a Lal Nishan affair, though all recognize that other individuals and groups are participating. Then there is the political question. However much it is said that 'we will unite on *women's* issues and put political disagreements aside', everyone knows that the conference will have some kind of political thrust. And the parties at this time differ so tremendously in their politics. Already the CPI is withdrawing because they think the conference is too 'oppositional' to the government which they support, though this decision must be disappointing to the Pune activist who was so enthusiastic at the first meeting. And the Socialists are staying out for the opposite reason: they have been throwing all their energies into uniting with right-wing parties in the new anti-government movement for 'total revolution' led by Jayaprakash Narayan (J.P.), a movement that is attempting to pose a real bourgeois alternative to Indira Gandhi's increasingly discredited regime. Then there is the CPI(M), the party in whom the young revolutionaries and the 'new' left put the most hope as being a bit less of a sell-out, a bit more militant than most, the party that if it wanted could give the women's movement a truly India-wide thrust. (LNP is stronger than the CPI(M) in Maharashtra, but it is limited to this state.) But the CPI(M) is also aloof, looking things over, it seems, and inclining towards an alliance with the Socialist and the J.P. movement. And in the meantime, Chhaya, who wants to go and meet the women members of CPI(M)-led unions, is frustrated. 'Really, they talk about a broad movement but they would rather build up their own women's fronts, and they don't even really put much energy into that . . . '

With the big parties not yet drawn in, the conference has thus come to centre around more or less the same groups that formed the Pune Progressive Women's Group: the LNP, *Magowa,* and the Naxalite-oriented students and Marxist independents. This core group shares certain common ideas. Women are specially oppressed and, therefore, there is a need for a special mass organization of women. Such an organization should be broad, i.e. not tightly bound to any one party, not an arm of a party in the way that the trade unions and party women's fronts have become. Instead it should have 'democratic functioning': people of varying (left) political views should be able to work within it and decisions should be made democratically and not imposed by party leaders. It should be an organization uniting women of different classes (at least up to petty bourgeois or middle class women) but with an emphasis on women of the most exploited working classes and rural poor. It should take up cultural as well as economic issues. And it should be an organization which can build up a powerful mass women's movement that can be an integral part of the Indian revolutionary process.

Such at least is the common vision of almost all the participants along with their shared horror at the truly miserable conditions of the masses of Indian women. In spite of this, there are an amazing number of remaining disagreements and tensions. Some of these are petty and personal; some are political, centring around whether to focus on economic or cultural issues, and whether to build up a core group or to emphasize mass organizing. There is a kind of class suspicion between Leela and the students and professors: Leela, for her part, expresses an insecurity about being uneducated and thus less 'competent', feels the students are aloof and don't know how to mix with the masses and don't really want to. The students see Leela as part of an older generation of politicians, bureaucratic and manoeuvring, anxious to maintain control of, for example, the Pune municipal workers' union. Leela stresses the building of a mass movement; the students feel that what is really meant is a process of continually 'giving leadership' to a listening crowd of people who are there to be mobilized. The students themselves say they want to develop leadership and train activists from among the masses, even if they don't know exactly how to go about it. So they argue for a conference that will be small, involve a good deal of political education of 'delegates', of 'activists' who can then form a core organizing group. Leela in contrast feels that this is exclusivist and a result of the students' inability to mix with the masses, and she pushes for a conference that will be wide open, that will involve as many people as possible even at minimal levels of political development, that will inspire the masses of women already involved in struggle. The students in turn feel that this will be just a useless one-shot affair if there are no trained activists to maintain the momentum of the movement, or that in the end the LNP workers here and there will provide that core and thus 'control' whatever comes out of the conference. And so it goes, with the *Magowa* women like Chhaya and others often coming in the middle, seeming to be a buffer and intermediary in an ongoing often acrimonious debate.

Yet amazingly little of this is really argued out explicitly. Instead, people discuss among themselves and not collectively, and there is grumbling and complaints ('they always remain aloof'; 'the old communists just want to build up their own leadership') and ongoing speculation about political affiliations ('is *Magowa* really splitting?' 'which Naxalite group do you think they really belong to?'). But in spite of the simmering tensions, it is not worse and somewhat better than the US and many other places; after all, some rather diverse people with very widespread contacts and union work are continuing to work together.

These disputes, running through my mind as Chhaya chatters on and we move onto the train platform, are interrupted by the sight of a local train coming out from the fort or downtown area. Though it is barely 3.45 p.m., it is already filled with men and women literally bursting through the doors of the carriages at this stop which is a major transit point. Masses of people hurl themselves onto the platform and flow on up the stairs, and the plat-

112

form and flow on up the stairs, and the platform crowd in turn, which up to this point has been a diverse, relaxed, newspaper-reading and chatting collection of people, is suddenly transformed into a clawing mob of all-against-all, pressing to somehow edge through the door, to get a seat if possible and, if not, a place to stand and a strap to hang onto. Once inside, tired shoulders sag and everyone relaxes, no hard feelings for the few moments of brutal competition. These are the local trains of Bombay; every morning the flood pours into the city from the outer neighbourhoods, the suburbs and beyond, carrying men and women packed in until they can hardly breathe, lucky even to find standing space, many dangling by a hand and foot from open doors, trains packed for four or five solid hours – packed, and yet somehow, miraculously, the hawkers whose own desperate existence depends on a few sales manage to keep moving through the pack, stepping over people or ducking under arms, selling fruit, pens, sunglasses, toys, gadgets or simply singing religious songs and begging. Then in the evening the reverse torrent, office and factory workers going home, tired and hot but still packed in, sometimes holding a strap or sitting on the edge of a seat, sometimes held up only by the mass of bodies around them swaying to the rhythm of the train. Chhaya and I, fortunate ones who do not have to work, find Bombay tremendously convenient for travel, for there are trains and buses nearly every fifteen minutes going almost everywhere and quite comfortable as long as you are going in the opposite direction from the commuter flood. But for those in the flood, it is a daily routine of exhaustion.

And, as we step into the now very spacious interior of a 'ladies' compartment' (there are still special compartments for women and though the fight in them is almost as vicious as in the general compartments they are a trifle less packed and nobody grudges the favour) leaving a now quiet platform behind us, I realize that here in the trains can be seen nearly all the panorama of Bombay working women. Not the non-working slum women, who cannot afford even this much travel, whose huts in endless rows in the slum colonies can be seen from the carriage doors and windows. But nearly all the rest are here, including the fisherwomen, Kolis in bright saris and heavy silver or metal bangles, going into the fort area to sell their fish, and other vendors of fruit and foodstuffs; factory workers; textile mill workers; and the endless throngs of office workers, middle class employees and students.

For Bombay, the capitalist hub of India, is also a city of working women. Unemployment and misery as everywhere stalk the streets. The majority of women still live homebound, traditional lives. And yet, the presence of women moving out of their homes, reaching for some kind of independence, seems visible here as nowhere else. In Bombay, 8.7% of the working population are women, a figure that seems abysmally low and lower than in the rural areas; yet it is higher than any other major city in India and by universal testimony Bombay has less male chauvinism than Delhi, more indepent and bold women than Calcutta.

The incidence of working women varies. There are the women of the textile mills, the oldest industry in India and one where women had a place

113

from the very beginning. And they fought from the very beginning; you can read the stories of their struggle in old communist newspapers or hear the accounts of those who worked among them. Such women, along with the wives of workers, still come onto the streets during strikes in the face of tear-gas and police baton-charges, and yet they are losing out to the impact of 'modernization'. Male workers are getting the new jobs created by auto-mation, and with maternity benefits and other laws employers no longer find it so profitable to exploit women. The number of working women has shrunk, activists tell me, from something like 40,000 in the early years to under 5,000 among perhaps 200,000 textile workers. And though every left union and every strike makes 'fighting retrenchment of women' one of its demands, nothing happens to change this — just as nothing happens to change the continuing discrimination against Dalit workers in the textile mills. But women, unlike the Dalits, are not yet organized and conscious enough to be even very cynical about this.

At the other extreme, among the new, modern, high technology and highly organized 'engineering' factories, women are also an insignificant minority outside the clerical staff. These desirable factory jobs are also a a male preserve. In a company like Kamanis, which makes metal tubes and employs some 4,500 workers, there are only 40 non-clerical women, limited to one department. These earn almost as well as the men, some 600 rupees or so a month, fantastic by the standards of their slum dweller sisters, but the money is often eaten away in supporting relatives and the drinking habits of men, and like the others they seem to remain caught in the bonds of tradition and male domination. I remember one meeting at Kamanis, in which the problem of 'native' Marathi-speakers versus south Indian 'outsiders' is a topic of fierce controversy, as are union-busting efforts by a Marathi chauvinist organization. The women listen throughout the meeting as the left-wing leaders patiently try to beat back the tide. Afterwards, when I ask one woman to explain, she comes to the essence of the politics of the thing: 'Really they're out to break the union.' She tries to explain linguistic differences: 'There are Marathi people, Malayali people, Bhaiyyas and others — these are all different "castes", that's the problem.' And then adds, 'But really there are only two castes, men and women.' Such women are usually loyal union members and militant during strikes; but their role is marginal to the process of organizing the workers.

Where are most of the women factory workers, then? In a few industries like pharmaceuticals, in numerous tiny food processing plants like the ones that freeze and package frogs legs caught by shivering tribal people at night in the hills near Bombay and then ship them off to the luxury restaurants of the US, and above all in the small factories, factories which cluster together in government provided industrial estates and manufacture components for the big companies or gadgets for sale in the streets. Such a process of 'putting out' a part of the manufacturing process is deliberately done as a means of getting cheap parts, manufactured by cheap labour, labour in which there is a high percentage of women and low caste workers and which is cheap because it is unorganized and because factories are deliberately kept small to evade the factory regulation acts. One man may own five or ten such factories (or a single big corporation may make use of hundreds of them), but they all employ under fifteen workers, and one can see girls and young women bent over minute assembling processes, seated on floors in tiny crowded rooms.

But more visible than the classical Indian working women I have come to expect from sights in towns and villages are throngs of seeming middle class women and girls. Somehow it is the office workers, bank employees, clerical staff of the big companies, teachers, nurses and the multitude of other middle class employees who seem to set the tone in Bombay. Girls and women in flowing, bright coloured synthetic saris, bangles, a bit of make-up, keeping in touch with 'fashion', somehow incredibly managing to keep themselves undishevelled and smart after coming through the inferno of the trains, these are the most numerous working women of Bombay. The young workers of the small factories, themselves often from low caste and working class backgrounds but literate and often matriculates, discard the nine-yard single-coloured saris of their mothers for the gaudy new nylons and synthetics and aim at the 'middle class' standard. This, for the working woman, is 'city culture'.

The middle class employees, women moving out of their homes and into a more independent, if brutal, world, are often the object of male wisecracks in the same way that Western women are: 'they're only trying to earn pin money'; 'they only spend it on clothes and lipstick'; and 'there should be only one job per family — why should men be deprived of work when there is a shortage of jobs?' Partly women do work to get a little more, to move a bit closer to a higher standard of living — where that means something like having a pressure cooker, being able to send the kids to college, etc. Some have husbands who are earning well, but others barely manage to struggle along by themselves as the main support of a family. All would say they like the independence of working and prefer it, but only if there could be more help with child care, a job closer to home. For it is not an easy life, being part of the commuter flood. Waking at 6 or earlier in the morning to feed the baby and children and prepare the day's meal, hurriedly straightening the house, then dashing off at 8.45 to catch the bus to make the 9.35 fast train, lucky to find a seat on the train, elbowing through the mob to make the transfer at Dadar, out at VT to walk ten minutes to the office. Then in the evening off at 5 p.m. to begin the reverse flow, two trains and one bus, now no chance at all to find a seat in the madness, home exhausted by 7 p.m. or later. Even with lax working hour discipline, even with easily available maid service, it is a gruelling routine that leaves me wrung out the one time I go in with a friend. Is this why so many of my Bombay friends seem to have miscarriages, I wonder.

There are other hazards on the trains — the purse snatchers, the men who grab the gold wedding necklaces from a woman's neck or, more brutally, tear gold earrings from their ears. And occasionally, late at night, the danger of rape, for though Bombay is considerably safer than any American city and though men are less obnoxious to the now familiar working women than in north India, still cases continue to occur. For most middle class working women, though, it is the sheer exhaustion of work and travel which makes life difficult.

Such women, like the factory workers, have been involved in unionizing efforts. The bank employees' and life insurance employees' unions are communist led, and the latter is renowned for its militancy. Women are part of these struggles, though their daily schedule makes it difficult for them to get to meetings. Women, mainly in the clerical staff, were also part of the big 1974 railway strike, while their slum dwelling working class sisters, the wives of the workers, suffered the brutality of police raids that tore apart the workers' homes, fighting back fiercely. But most recently it has been the state government employees, a vast category ranging from clerks to teachers to nurses and low-level janitors, who have been organizing; a memorable event in Bombay was a huge demonstration of striking employees in April when nearly 100,000 women and men, from middle class staff to low caste peons and sweepers, marched through the streets with their slogan, 'We are all one!'

It is this vast panorama of women that Chhaya and the Bombay group have been trying to meet and now, as the train, bright coloured in the muggy afternoon, rumbles through one stop after another, she talks about their experiences. And we spill out into VT, Victoria Terminus, Bombay's vast oriental-gothic railway station, pushing through the streaming mob. ' . . . concentrate on working class women to build their leadership,' says Chhaya. 'Gail, you are saying that rural women are the base, but don't you think that it's a mechanistic way of looking at things, just because that's where the greatest numbers of working women are? Rural women may be a force, but how do we create a leadership section? Rural women simply don't have the consciousness, the experience, it's too big a jump for them, they have to do everything at once. Here in Bombay, look around you – ' There are vendors of every kind, the barefoot pedlars of a poor country; there are modern animated product displays of giant Indian and multinational corporations; there are the book and magazine racks, Gandhi literature displays next to sex and film magazines; ads for Hindi films, blaring music. ' – And they are exposed to all the stimulation, ideas, contradictions of modern life, forms of collective work and factory production juxtaposed to the traditional atmosphere of the home. They can see the products of Western countries and the films and products of the factories, the fifteen-storey apartments next to their slums, they experience at the same time exploitation in the factories and the homes, they are in touch with it all in spite of themselves. The rural woman may be a fighting woman, really fighting to rise up from her oppression, having to deal with sexual exploitation at the same time as she is fighting class oppression, and so she is a force. She gains feminist consciousness and class consciousness together. But the urban working woman already has class consciousness, she takes part in collective struggles but can't become a leader because of her home oppression. But if you add feminist consciousness, she will begin to play a leading role everywhere. We need to create a broad vanguard of activists, leaders, and if we can reach working women on a massive scale, women who are already involved in struggle, we can find and build this vanguard, a large core group, ready to give leadership at all levels, in the factories, in the neighbourhoods, the homes . . . '

She pauses for a moment — Chhaya hardly ever stops — and I realize that this too is part of the great debate. Rural women or urban? Core group of activists or mass movement? Where to begin? It is in confrontation with the concrete, living problems of exactly what to do next with the organization that the ideological wrangling turns into serious debate about how to go about it . . .

Leela, for instance, thinks in terms of building a base among rural women who are beginning to fight for wages and the very ability to survive and who find that in this fight itself they have to confront and partly overcome sexual discrimination. Make the women's movement an indissoluble part of the great process of organizing the unorganized rural and urban poor — especially the agricultural labourers — and build consciousness of cultural and political issues around the economic struggle for daily existence. Go out to the masses, build the mass movement, and your core group of activists will develop not so much out of the masses themselves but by learning from the masses and taking part in the movement. The problem with this is that it does not really deal with the issue of developing activists and leadership from below, of how to spread political consciousness, and so this approach is in danger of perpetuating a situation where that consciousness and leadership simply come from above.

Chhaya wants to build a base in the industrial working class, to raise the consciousness of those already working and involved in union struggle and so develop on a wide scale a whole section, a vanguard, of militant women who will be ready to take leadership. The problems with this are the difficulties of access to the party controlled unions and the pure lack of time for working women to have any social and political activities. It is not by accident that it was mainly working class and middle class housewives, not working women, who were the basis of the huge anti-price-rise demonstrations.

Others among the young revolutionaries want to get around this by working in a single area — a slum neighbourhood — with an intensive programme to involve both working women and wives of workers, those bound to the home and those who go out; with the idea of developing both middle class students and educated outsiders as activists through their experience with the slum women while at the same time training leaders from among the slum women themselves; with the hope of creating a solid base. The trouble with this is that the city is a jungle, not a prairie; light a spark (i.e. build a base) and it does not explode to engulf surrounding areas but is rather smothered in the pure massiveness and impenetrability of the jungle. Your base may even become famous among the conscious radical circles, visitors may go there, students may work there, you may hold demonstrations and organize meetings — but it requires conscious attention, long-term work that is often more than impatient students and middle class leftists can manage; withdraw your activists and it all seems to collapse. ('Every radical group has gone to work in Matunga labour camp – and not one has left a mark.') Maybe this is too harsh, the remnants are there, Bombay does after all have some very politically conscious slums, but they never remain politically conscious in quite the way the groups working there want.

One of the student leaders wants to solve the problem of developing a core of activists by building a movement among students themselves. Throw energy into a concentrated state-wide campaign against the dowry and, like the explosive growth of the POW in Andhra, students can be aroused throughout the state and from the most active and conscious of these you can develop a core of educated activists, conscious of Marxism and of feminism, who can then go to work among the toiling masses. The problem with this is that it not only postpones the question of exactly how to work among the masses, but also that radical students sometimes are enthusiasts of the moment and wither away, or rather, drop out and get married, in the absence of real living contact with a mass movement.

And so the debate comes full circle. It is a dilemma of Bombay itself, of all India at the time. Everywhere women as well as men are on the move, reaching out of their traditional bondages, going into the streets to march against the government, *gherao* officials or fight the police, attacking their oppressors physically – whether managers of companies, liquor sellers, merchants or supervisors of government relief projects – and everywhere the left is fragmented and in a dilemma about what to do. Young radicals are throwing themselves enthusiastically into the movement, engrossed and rapturous about the militancy and readiness of the workers, the tribal agricultural labourers, the women, the Dalits, to fight and even die, feeling the throbbing heat of the movement and its need for direction but themselves not knowing what direction to take. From the slums and working class tenements of Bombay and from the very depths of the most backward, hierarchy-bound villages, there is a developing, spiralling process, women no longer mute, untouchables no longer passively accepting degradation, agricultural labourers fighting for wages, young working girls in small factories going on strike even though they have a family of five depending on their meagre wages, students rejecting arranged marriages, and all of this basically leaderless or led by factionalized left groups at odds with each other. The villages of India seem endless and baking in silence under the sun; Bombay seems massive, incomprehensible, mile after mile of three- and four-storey apartments or endless stretches of miserable slum colonies, and yet all of this is stirring, the upper classes in both the cities and the villages are in a state of nervous tension that even the most elite visitors from the West can sense as the Mukherjees did in their 'days and nights in Calcutta' and Bombay.

And those who aspire to be the leaders of revolution don't really know what to do. Everything, by the middle of 1975, seems to be hanging in the air, a huge question mark, Indira Gandhi defied and almost disgraced among the masses, a right-wing oppositional movement shouting about 'total revolu-

tion' but itself falling into division and stagnation, the parliamentary communists divided about whether to ally with Indira or the opposition, the
Naxalites and the new left plunging into the cauldron but with a consciousness of impending doom, a feeling that something stupendous is about to
happen but with everything beyond their control . . .

The crisis has to be resolved, the spiral has to have a climax, if only temporarily, and sure enough this comes, but not when I am in Bombay, rather some
10 days later when I am in a village to the south, near the city of Kolhapur.
Banage is the last village in a short three-village organizing tour, for Leela,
Tarabai and I have become a kind of team, usually with the addition of another worker or student from Pune, going out to nearby villages and small
towns to rally women to the movement and the conference.

Such meetings have by now fallen into a pattern. Women are gathered. If
it is a small town these are mainly union members of whatever small factories
or government employment exists along with just about everyone the local
organizer is in contact with, from schoolgirls and school teachers to wives
and friends of activists to agricultural labourers from the surrounding
villages. If it is a village, the representation of poor peasants and agricultural
labourers is much greater, but in all cases women from almost every class
and section come, a panorama of Indian women from the rugged, often
ragged, poor peasant and labourer women to the students with their shiny
black braids to the local nurses and teachers to the conservatively dressed
upper peasant or merchant housewives, half the women holding sucking or
squalling or sleeping infants and with half-grown children raising a ruckus
on the outskirts. The local organizer begins with an introduction, then I
come on with my 'interview' technique in which scholarly information
gathering has been transformed into a method of organizing:

'How many hours a day do you work?' And the women, nearly always
interpreting 'work' in the usual, male chauvinist, productive labour sense, say
'eight'. 'Oh, really, well, what time do you get up in the morning?' And so
we go through the day, just as I have done with Kaminibai and the municipal
workers and the women agricultural labourers and the canal workers of
Ahmednagar, and by the time we get to coming home from work, doing the
housework and cooking, taking care of the children and all, the women
nearly always, like Kaminibai and all the others, catch on. 'Work' now takes
on a new meaning as they begin to count the hours of their day and murmurs
and even grins break out. I go on to a rap about 'double work' and the double
shift of women, cultural oppression, rape, always careful to take my
examples from the US (I am still a foreigner and not supposed to 'interfere'
in Indian 'politics'), and ask them about the concrete conditions of their
life: how much they are paid, what do they eat, how they can manage
to survive in these days of rising prices and stagnant wages . . .

Then it is Tarabai's turn, and talking rapidly, sometimes randomly but
always in the vigorous, colourful, low caste dialect of the working women,

119

she flays into the wickedness of merchants, capitalists and men, the bitter work of women, especially that of the municipal sweepers, the necessity for solidarity in struggle, the problems of alcoholism, the fact that women are after all stronger than men because they bear all this. Local women activists follow, perhaps the wife of the local union or peasant leader, herself often a school teacher or government employee; other school teachers or middle class sympathizers speak; a particularly bold student gives an impassioned call for freedom. And finally, Leela comes to the front to pull the threads together in a talk on the oppression of Indian women, the social roots of that oppression, and the need for organization. 'Why do we hand out sweets for the birth of a son but keep quiet when a daughter is born? Why are women considered inferior? This is not a natural thing . . . '

The listening women are then asked to speak, and some do, illiterate poor peasant women or agricultural labourers, talking briefly because it is their first time for a public speech, but inspired to tell of their needs. And then, with a concluding speech by the local organizer, the meeting finishes with resounding slogans and admonitions to carry on with local organizing and to come to the women's conference.

Such village tours often bring us into contact with the most poignant and pathetic examples of social oppression. There is the small town of Sangamner and its nearby villages where we visit *bidi* factories where Maratha and Muslim women toil throughout the day rolling tobacco into leaves to make the cheap native cigarettes or *bidis*. It is a kind of work still not open to untouchables whose handling of the cigarettes is considered polluting, but there is no lightening of the oppression because of this. 'In such 'factories', two- to three-storey buildings, a hundred women or more sit packed into a room, their small children beside them, half sleeping, half whining, sometimes a baby on their laps, the air dark and musty, the fumes of tobacco rising.as they endlessly roll the leaves. 'There is an 80% tuberculosis rate here,' says a local unionist, and the women, who work twelve hours a day and more, desperately trying to roll 1,000 *bidis* to get the now legal minimum wage rate of five rupees (which they rarely really get due to systematic 'rejections') complain of alcoholism and wife-beating, but give us their attention only briefly: the work must go on.

And there is the small town of Bhor where, after an enthusiastic meeting of women mainly from small peasant families in the town hall, we go outside the city to meet women migrant workers on a dam project, and it is the Mula Canal story all over again. Migrants from perennially famine-ridden districts who live in makeshift tents in a nearby field and walk up and down the steep incline of the dam site all day with loads of soil on their heads, dump them, come back for more, an endless procession of despair, the women complaining that they have no food at all, that they have to live on roots. What does *women*'s oppression mean? Very little — at the moment they only want more to eat, and here there seems to be little hope in their anger.

But the major impression that comes to me from the meetings is not one

of despondent suffering, but rather one of stirring militancy and a respon-
siveness even, or especially, from the seemingly poorest, the agricultural
labourers. Thin as they often are, saris torn and ragged, children looking like
thin dusty bones with bellies, tiny babies clinging to hips, these women have
somehow managed to grow up rugged and vigorous, and from all appearances
the talk of women's suppressed position in society really hits home. Perhaps
because it is my first experience of mass meetings, riding on the wave of a
popular massive indignation, learning how it feels to stir and lift it up; but I
find the expression on the rural women's faces as they listen to our speeches
and their eagerness tremendously inspiring.

Banage, where some five to six hundred women have gathered, has been
one such visit, and afterwards I am in a mood of tired elation as we walk
down the dirty road, filled with huge muddy ruts, through the glistening
fields — rains are intermittent now and the countryside is gleaming green,
lush and fertile in this area — past bullock carts and an occasional tractor,
to the house of a local sympathizer who is providing dinner for the organizing team. Here we sit, drink tea and wait, and Santaram Patil, the local LNP
leader, talks of the famine organizing days, a period when there was a tremendous wave, even flood of popular indignation, mobilization and struggle
which has now, at least in these areas, subsided. 'The problem was that we
could not build up an enduring organization. That was where we failed.' It
is as if people rise up, respond to a mobilizing call, then when the crisis
vanishes, sink back again into their traditional subservience . . . I don't stop
to worry if this will happen with the women's conference, we are all too
enthusiastic at the time about the potentiality of women. But the problem is
there.

Banage, 26 June 1975. As in Bombay, questions hang in the air. How to
really develop a mass movement, how to unite and build up a core of leaders,
how to root a stable and widespread organization among the very poorest
and most militant of the toiling masses, how to unite the caste- and class-
divided and disparate sections of the exploited people . . . the same debates
that the women are having over mobilizing are, after all, only part of the
general problem of the left in India. As we muse, we are called for dinner.
Cotton mats are spread beside the walls of the room, we sit down with legs
crossed, gleaming stainless steel plates with small dishes and water jugs are
placed in front of us, women and boys of the household walk by putting
down heaps of rice, chapattis, ladlefuls of hot spicy mutton and the raw
onion and yoghurt salad which goes with it on our plates — the spicy special
dish of Maharashtrain peasants. As we eat, the evening news comes on, in
Marathi. I only half pay attention to it, until I notice everyone else suddenly
looking up, faces fixed on the radio speaker as if they could discern more
meaning that way, and then I too try to piece out the phrases . . .

' . . . *a state of internal emergency declared* . . . among those arrested Shri
Jayaprakash Narayan, Shri Morarji Desai . . . conspiracy to destabilize the
government . . . reactionary and fascist forces . . . the press to submit to
government censorship . . . no public meetings without police permission . . .

Mrs Gandhi to announce a new programme of action . . . '

What does it all mean? I am aware that the Constitution gives the President (now a tool of the Prime Minister) the power to declare a 'state of emergency' against internal or external subversion, that India in fact has been under 'external' emergency for many years as a result of the wars against Pakistan and China, giving the government rights of arrest and censorship over people and actions considered traitorous . . . but 'internal emergency'? No, surely not. 'Indirabai has taken control,' says someone with a raw laugh. I think of the radical intellectuals who have been talking for some years now about the onslaught of fascism, the journalists who have been writing about the erosion of democracy. 'It's the death of democracy,' I say. And no one seems to dispute this.

Riding back in the car to Kolhapur city, there is subdued but tense discussion about what the new Emergency actually means, to what extent democratic rights have vanished, whether this is temporary or permanent, and what the left — by and large unaccustomed to anything really resembling a police state — will do now. What do 'democratic' rights mean in a situation where millions daily go to sleep half-fed? This question, so long a rhetorical one for radicals, suddenly takes on concrete meaning. Santaram, who like other LNP people is inclined to dismiss the issue of 'bourgeois' democratic rights as being irrelevant to the organization of a revolutionary mass movement, says, 'You want to fight for democratic rights? Bring 20,000 women into the streets to demand their democratic rights! That will be a fight!' But this too is left hanging in the air because, in the new conditions, no one knows quite how to bring 20,000 women into the streets. Almost as if all the problems of Indian women have been reduced to the one woman who is at the top . . .

Map of India: Places Mentioned in the Text

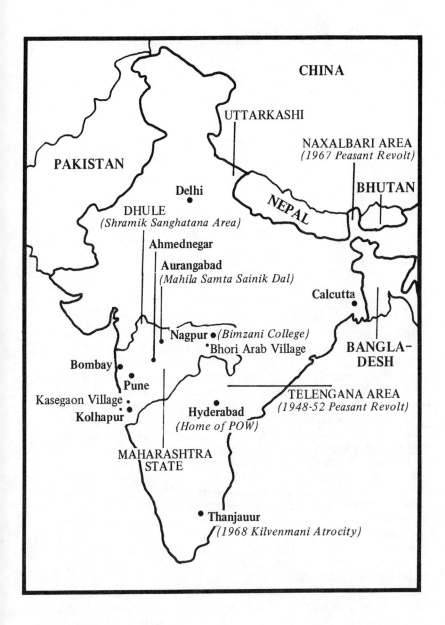

CHINA

UTTARKASHI

NAXALBARI AREA
(1967 Peasant Revolt)

PAKISTAN

BHUTAN

Delhi

DHULE
(Shramik Sanghatana Area)

NEPAL

Ahmednegar

Aurangabad
(Mahila Samta Sainik Dal)

Calcutta

Nagpur ●*(Bimzani College)*
●*Bhori Arab Village*

BANGLA-
DESH

Bombay

Pune

TELENGANA AREA
(1948-52 Peasant Revolt)

Kasegaon Village

Kolhapur

Hyderabad
(Home of POW)

MAHARASHTRA
STATE

● Thanjauur
(1968 Kilvenmani Atrocity)

11. The Empress of India
A Political Interlude

Indira Gandhi, a woman, now unquestionably at the top. But how did a woman get to be prime minister of this male dominated society in the first place?

Part of the answer is easy. She inherited it. Indira, only child of a wealthy and aristocratic Brahman family whose ancestors eight generations earlier had come down from the valley of Kashmir to become high-level administrators first for the Muslim and then for the British rulers of India, was born into power and affluence. Like many of the educated elite, her grandfather Motilal Nehru became an early nationalist, and his son Jawaharlal Nehru was the most famous leader, next to Mahatma Gandhi, of the Indian independence movement. Unlike Gandhi, Nehru was resolutely secular, a Cambridge-educated sophisticate, an inveterate intellectual, vaguely socialist, attracted by the Russian Revolution and drawn into the newly organizing peasant leagues and trade union movement of the 1920s to experience what he himself described as a 'discovery of India'. But Nehru was never so socialist as to be unacceptable to the most far-sighted Indian capitalist, never so rationalist as to be outside the spell and thus control of the more socially conservative Gandhi. He became the first prime minister of India after independence, and led the country not to socialism but to the building up of heavy industry and a 'public sector' along with a 'non-aligned' foreign policy, all programmes which angered the West though they were in the interest of and even demanded by Indian capitalists. At the same time he oversaw a growing police and military force that was used for such matters as crushing the communist rebellion in Telengana.

Politics was embedded in the family tradition. Had Nehru had a son he undoubtedly would have trained him first, but as it was he had only a daughter. Indira was also brought up to a political life – Nehru's memoirs recount such events as sitting in court during trials with his four-year-old daughter – but even though women do inherit in the aristocracy (remember Queen Elizabeth) they still inherit differently from men. It seems that the businessmen, civil servants and political leaders of Nehru's generation – men like J.R.D. Tata, the big Indian capitalist, and Morarji Desai, the Janata party leader – never really took her seriously. Rammanohar Lohia, the Socialist leader, called her a 'dumb doll' which was repeated by socialists time and again; Morarji Desai kept referring to her as a 'mere chit of a girl', and the Hindu anti-feminism which lay hidden in all of this added fuel to later political feuds.

Indira, in other words, never fitted into the *social* world of the political leaders as a man might have; she was torn by the ambivalences of a woman and the emotional strains represented by her long-suffering mother and a marriage that never fully worked out; she experienced the real chauvinism of the sophisticated modern upper classes. Consequently, she never became a comfortable Cambridge intellectual or a secular idealist like her father. And this is the second part of the answer to the question of how a woman attained the position she did: she had to fight her way up through a morass of contemptuous, too familiar elites and in so doing developed a contempt, maybe almost a hatred, for the class of politicians and bureaucrats who considered themselves, more than her, the true heirs of power. She found she had political skills, the kind of stamina that could take the gruelling electoral campaigns of twenty or more rallies a day even when she was past sixty, a talent for manoeuvring, and above all the ability to enthral and arouse the masses and to find the kind of simple slogans that really spoke to people. Just as Mahatma Gandhi (her namesake, not a relative) could take an extraordinarily common demand, such as the right to make salt without paying taxes to foreign rulers, and turn it into a major nationalist campaign, so Indira found that something as simple as providing free glass bangles to peasant women who had broken theirs while lifting rocks on famine relief projects could win her a place in their hearts. In this political world of the masses, being a woman helped her even though she may have suffered from it in terms of acceptance by the established elites. She could identify as a member of an oppressed section, and at the same time she could appeal to the deep emotional responses of a mother-figure and the vast and ambivalent Hindu tradition of the mother-goddess who is both the benevolent Durga and the ferocious destroyer Kali. 'Generally the concept of energy and power is female in our mythology, and this is why this is accepted, you see,' she said to a reporter for the American fashion magazine *Vogue* in an interview on the Emergency; 'this is the world of *shakti*.' And weaving this all together, she was able to develop a powerful personal style that included a traditional and modest dress in the regional style of whatever area she was campaigning in and a careful elegance that could equally impress *Vogue*: 'Tired or not, she looked fresh. Her white and ochre-printed cotton sari falling in unrumpled folds. The skin of her arms and neck prettily white and smooth, her handsome face composed, the blazon of white in her hair more dramatic than her photographs suggest. More an accomplished hostess she seemed, than a school mistress . . . ' Which in its own way was as adulatory as anything her personal sycophants produced.

But her appeal, her 'identification with the masses', was backed by no real ideology, according to the universal testimony of almost all who knew her, but only a ruthless pragmatism. 'We spoke of Socialism because that was what went down with the masses,' she told Indian journalist Kuldip Nayar. 'Sometimes I feel that even our parliamentary system is moribund,' she said to writer Ved Mehta. 'The inertia of our civil service is incredible . . . Sometimes I wish we had had a real revolution, like France or Russia.' And Italian journalist, Oriana Fallaci, remembers how, upon seeing a beggar, Indira remarked, 'What can I do? I'm surrounded by a bunch of idiots. And democracy . . . '

Does all this explain why Indira Gandhi declared a state of Emergency, arrested her upper class political opponents, rode roughshod over the niceties of bureaucratic regulations, imposed censorship on the press and headed a government in which the torture of young revolutionaries became a new feature of Indian democracy?

Many people seemed to think so. So much of Indian politics, for so many years, seemed to centre around the figure of Indira Gandhi that many thought she was personally responsible for all that happened. To many she did in fact seem to be Durga and Kali. This applied not only to illiterate poor peasants and workers who were encouraged to rely on 'leaders' but also to many of her educated and even Marxist political opponents. In particular the socialists, such as Mrinal Gore and her fiery trade union colleague George Fernandes, tended to personalize politics and blame everything on her personal dictatorship. More strangely, this applied also to Ahilya Rangnekar's party, the CPI(M), which had conceived an almost vituperative hatred for her as a result of having borne, along with the Naxalites, the brunt of vicious state repression in West Bengal in the years after 1970. Ahilya herself could be heard making speeches which were colourful attacks on Indira but which were oddly un-Marxist because they implied that things would be basically different if only certain people (like Indira Gandhi) or a certain party (the Congress) were replaced by another set of people or another party of the same sort without any more fundamental changes in the system they were running.

Indira Gandhi, of course, did not determine events. It was the relentless unfolding crisis of the Indian social and economic order which produced its political convulsions; it was the relentless pressure of mass turmoil in strikes, peasant uprisings, even middle class employees coming out into the streets to agitate for their demands which made certain measures necessary if the Indian state was to maintain any sort of stability. It was millions of men and women like Kaminibai, Tarabai, Tanubai, Leela, Rukmini, Mrinal and Ahilya themselves, who were in their own fashion – from the most obscure to the most well known – as much the makers of history as Indira Gandhi. 'He who rides a tiger cannot easily get off' is a famous Indian saying; and if Indian society was a plunging ferocious tiger in these decades, Indira's talent was to ride it, not to drive it.

The story really begins in 1966-67. In 1966 Indira was chosen as Prime Minister by a set of party bosses, each of whom had a base among the rural landlords and rich farmers who dominated the politics of the various states, who considered her the least unacceptable person and one they could control. 1966 was also a year of major famine in north India, a year in which the economy began to take a downturn that would last for at least ten years, and the year in which workers began increasingly to apply such techniques as the *gherao* and to go on ever longer strikes in ever greater numbers. In the following year, 1967, the Naxalbari Revolt occurred, and the Congress party suffered a humiliating electoral defeat, losing control of many state governments to a varied collection of right- and left-wing oppositional parties.

'I want to take the wind out of the sails of the Communists and I can do that only by moving left of centre,' Indira told Kuldip Nayar. Her inclination, in fact, was to respond boldly to the crisis, to search for something to capture the imagination of the frustrated millions, and she aired the possibility of a few apparently radical steps, things like bank nationalization, taking away the financial privileges of India's ex-Maharajahs, firmer limits on the amount of land one family could own. But this put her in conflict with many of the party bosses. The steps were not new; many had been in some form part of the government's strategy for years. They were also far from being *really* revolutionary; they modified but did not actually threaten the power structure. But they upset many of the party bosses, especially those who had their social base among the most conservative of the rural elite. Indira was itching for a fight anyway; drawing ideological lines was in part a means to form a party and governmental machinery under her control by bringing in new men (and women) often from low caste and minority backgrounds and, partly because of this, without a real power base of their own and thus more dependent on her.

The result was a battle royal that resulted in the first real split in the Congress party since independence, taking place over the issue of Indira's unwillingness to accept party 'discipline' in choosing a new President. (That is, she successfully pushed her own candidate over the choice of the party bosses.) Though sections had left the party before, this was the first time in which the major part of its organizational structure appeared to range themselves against the top leader. But Indira did not mind; she was aiming at a wider audience, the masses of Indian people. She characterized her opponents as 'rightist, reactionary and retrograde' (by 1978 this was to become even more specifically 'casteists, communalists and capitalists', but this showed the developing political consciousness of the people as much as anything) and claimed they were the major force blocking her progressive policies. She took up the slogan of *'garibi hatao'*, 'remove poverty'. It was an impressive success; in the end it was the 'mere slip of a girl' who proved to have the formula for political success in India. For, what the hungry masses demanded was at least the appearance of a solution; what the entrenched power structure could not stand was its reality. The formula promised to satisfy the expressed (that is limited) demands of the masses without a real revolution. But it was more than just political rhetoric; it also embodied real economic needs of the elite.

Indira did not invent the formula. Her father Nehru had been applying it in his own way for years, and in fact every enduring non-communist Third World leader has used it in varying fashions. A stress on the public sector not because it is 'socialist' but because native capitalists are too weak to build up the needed industrial infrastructure on their own. Foreign policies of 'non-alignment' not because revolution really appealed to them but because the Soviet Union represented an important bargaining counter to play against the US-dominated Western capitalist world. Carefully orchestrated land reforms not to give power to the poor in the rural areas but to check the power of the most backward feudal classes of landlords who were unwilling to take enough of an entrepreneurial interest in their land to become capitalist farmers, and to strengthen a much broader though just as exploitative section of rich peasants. Militant, socialist rhetoric to convince the poor in cities and villages that all of the above was being done directly to help them. And the fostering of an ever stronger police and military to handle those who did not believe the rhetoric, who could not believe it because it went counter to their everyday experience, who rebelled against the poverty and misery that continued to engulf those at the bottom levels of society.

The secret of the formula was that it linked real, even radical changes in creaking, ages-old social structures, often further warped by colonialism, with an unwillingness to allow even a minimal challenge from the bottom to the new classes of businessmen and political entrepreneurs who were the real inheritors of power. It was applied by Nehru; and also by Nasser when he nationalized all the main industries and threw the communists of Egypt into jail; even, in a more extreme form, by the Shah of Iran when he wiped out the power of feudal landlords (turning them into capitalist shareholders in the process) and came forth as the 'modernizer' of his country while developing SAVAK to spy out and torture the rebels against his rule. And, of course, it was applied after 1969 by Indira when she promised to 'remove poverty' and appeared to be leaning toward the Soviet Union while at the same time trying to ensure the complete crushing of the Naxalite rebellion.

'Radical' changes in the position of women were quite naturally part of the formula. In fact they seemed an ideal, progressive, 'anti-feudal' measure so long as no one took them to 'extremes'. So it was that women were often granted more equality in rhetoric and in law, with more legal benefits (child care facilities, maternity benefits) than in some industrially advanced Western societies — and a small upper class stratum of women like Indira Gandhi were able to realize some of these formal gains. The fact that these benefits did not did not reach the vast majority of unemployed or underpaid women toiling in the fields, on road projects and in homes and factories except as promises or the equivalent of a few glass bangles made little difference, because the opponents of the formula offered even less to women. A parallel case, of course, was that of Dalits, who were given an Untouchability Offences Act that was almost never enforced and a percentage of reserved seats in colleges, government services and legislative bodies that gave real if ambiguous benefits. An illustration of their reality was the position of Jagjivan Ram, an Untouchable politician with real political power; an illustration of the ambiguity was that he had gained it by acting all his life at the behest of Gandhi and other caste Hindu leaders of the Congress party and serving as a protege of the Birla capitalist family.

The formula had two effects (beside antagonizing the leaders of the West for over a decade until they were forced to live with it and figure out that it was better than any possible alternative and not harmful to their interest). One was that sections of the privileged classes who could not understand its necessity or tolerate its sometimes 'disciplining' attacks on their power often went into political opposition, thereby increasing the threat of political chaos in the country and constituting further pressure towards the dictatorship which was often the only way the formula could be applied successfully. In India, for example, with the exception of the Hinduist Jan Sangh party and the Communists and Dalit or tribal-based parties, *every* political party after independence was formed from discontented members of the Congress party which had been India's 'broad national front' leading the independence struggle against the British. These — discontented landlords, merchants, rich peasants, businessmen — left the Congress at varying times, calling themselves things like the 'Kerala Congress', 'Bangla Congress', 'Socialist Congress', 'Congress for Democracy' or 'The Indian Revolutionary League', the 'United Revolutionary Front' and so forth, but their main purpose was to oppose one or more aspects of the formula. The socialists, who were the first to split off in the 1950s, by and large opposed its repressive aspects, later groups more often its 'radical' measures, but they all came out of the Congress. Perhaps that was why it was quite natural for them to come together in opposition in spite of their seemingly disparate policies and social origins. Third World countries like India never developed genuine 'two party' systems; at the level of ruling class politics there was really only Congress and Anti-Congress — and the latter became, after 1969, Anti-Indira.

A second result of the formula was that it helped to split up popular movements, particularly because the left, including the communists, failed to understand it. The communists saw what they thought were 'progressive' policies (building up a public sector, programmes of equality for women and the low castes, land reforms) on the one hand, but on the other they experienced police attacks, jailing and repression, and worsening poverty. They failed to see the link between these. Instead, they thought that the progressive policies and repressive measures came from different classes or different sections of classes, and tried to figure out a way to ally with the 'progressive' ones to defeat the 'reactionary' ones. (The Naxalites, born in a total fight against the state, were a partial exception; they saw nothing progressive in a 'public' sector or in a foreign policy favourable to the Soviet Union, and their first chairman, Charu Mazumdar, was the first Indian communist to formulate a united front policy that excluded the bourgeoisie.) Only they differed in their view as to whether progressiveness or repressiveness was the main aspect of the Congress party. The CPI thought that the Congress, and especially Indira, represented mainly a 'national bourgeoisie' with whom alliances could be formed, and defined the Opposition as representing mainly reactionary merchants and landlords. So they allied with Indira. The CPI(M), in contrast, either ignored the progressive policies (but agreed in seeing them as progressive), perhaps assuming they came from somewhere else besides the groups in power, or else characterized them as simply rhetoric, and thought that the growing dictatorial tendencies represented the main aspect of Congress and so allied itself with the Opposition against Congress. Thus the Indian communists divided themselves even further, and managed to tail not one but two essentially bourgeois forces.

1969, then, was the year that the Congress party split into Indira and anti-Indira factions (though after Indira's success it was her section that kept the name 'Congress') and also the year that some of the Naxalites formed their party, the CPI(ML). The latter, however, could not find a way to spark off a real mass revolt, and it was Indira who managed to take the centre of the stage. And hold it. The Opposition made its first major attempt to come together in something called the 'Grand Alliance' that included the Jan Sangh, the socialists and all the various rural landlord/rich peasant based parties. It took up the slogan 'remove Indira' as a cute answer to 'remove poverty'. This proved to be a huge strategic mistake. At a time when the progressive aspects of the formula were being stressed and the masses still looked hopefully to Indira, it was an act of political stupidity to further focus their attention on her. Indira rode to victory on a wave of popular support in central and state elections in 1971 and 1972, with a significant number of votes coming from the minorities, Dalits, women and the rural poor. It was about this time that the jouranlistic world, significantly ahead of the academic world which was still caught in the fantasies of 'faction-ridden' India the 'soft state', began to moot the possibility of India taking the same kind of road to dictatorship that other countries had, and one of the journals, *The Far Eastern Economic Review*, began to run features with such titles as 'Empress of India'.

So the formula resulted in Indira standing at the centre of Indian politics. But, as a prescription for capitalist development and political stability in the face of economic crisis, it could not really prevent that crisis. This deepened. Prices, unemployment, famine, inequality, the cost of dowry demanded by parents — everything seemed to be rising. Disillusionment increased and this too now centred on Indira. Kaminibai's plaint ('she's doing politics . . . and it's not for us . . . whatever the state does it does for them, it does nothing for the poor') echoed everywhere, and as an indication of the level of consciousness of the most unorganized sections of low caste rural women, it was an illustration of the existing revolutionary potential. If Indira Gandhi had a massive victory in 1972, by the very next year she was losing it, and strikes, peasant revolts and agitations were breaking out everywhere. The revolutionary non-parliamentary left was again surging up among youth, often in new forms – a Naxalite revival here, the Dalit Panther movement there, the *Magowa* group on one side complaining about the lack of theoretical development in the Indian communist movement, a 'Phule-Ambedkar-Marx' organization on another charging the movement with being Brahman-dominated and neglecting the problem of caste. The middle class as a whole was becoming as restless as workers and peasants. A revolt occurred in the state of Gujarat, unique because it was the home and stronghold of Mahatma Gandhi, highly conservative in politics and without a significant left. Yet here, in the heartland of Indian non-violence, youth were storming into the streets, facing tear-gas and police firing, hurling stones and breaking into buildings, vaguely defining their enemies as corruption, rising prices and the wickedness of the government, and forming what they called *nav nirman* ('new life') societies.

It was at the end of 1972 that the Women's Anti-Price-Rise Committee was formed. It was, in a way, a signal. In response to rising popular unrest, the left parties were uniting. A 'Trade Union Joint Action Committee' followed, then a 'Struggle Committee' of the left political parties themselves. By 1974 all of India seemed ablaze, and the railway strike of that year was a climax. All the left parties were in it, from secret organizations of the Naxalites to the Socialists, CPI and CPI(M), all charging one another with crimes ranging from sell-out to recklessness, but uneasily working together. Indira responded with appeals to unorganized workers on the one hand – with the familiar theme that the organized industrial workers were 'privileged', a labour aristocracy – and with brutal suppression on the other. 50,000 workers and leaders were arrested, police stormed into their housing settlements, beat up and molested their wives, burned and scattered their possessions. It was a demonstration to Indian capitalists that her heart was in the right place.

The railway strike was a climax, but it was also an end. The various communists could unite in a particular struggle, but they were incapable of giving an overall political direction to the movement. Both big Communist Parties believed essentially in a version of the 'national democratic' revolution in which the first step would be to complete anti-imperialist and anti-feudal tasks in alliance with the 'democratic' section of the bourgeoisie. But they couldn't agree on what was the 'democratic' bourgeoisie, or how really to present this as an alternative to what Indira was doing – for Indira was successfully projecting an image of carrying through land reform, self-reliant development and all such good anti-imperialist and anti-feudal things. The CPI and CPI(M) could not give an alternative revolutionary vision and remained stuck in parliamentary politics; dissident parties like LNP were floundering; the Naxalites were ideologically confused and organizationally fragmented; and new left groups like *Magowa*, which were groping towards something different, were small and still immature. A political vacuum was forming.

Into this vacuum came Jayaprakash Narayan, an old Gandhian socialist, but more Gandhian than socialist by then, with a reputation as a man of morality and a long history of anti-communism. J.P. had been a one-time exponent of armed struggle in the nationalist movement of the 1940s, but afterwards had left politics altogether to find 'peaceful' means of solving India's problems, joining the *bhoodan* movement which consisted of urging landlords voluntarily to give up their land to the poor. In a negative way, the *bhoodan* movement was communist inspired: it came as a response to the communist revolt in Telegana and only gained any support in areas where there was a communist threat and landlords felt, as a result, that they had to do something. J.P.'s political participation had the same sophisticated anti-communist character to it when, in his last major act, he came out of the 'constructive work' of *bhoodan* to organize a political movement in his home state of Bihar. In the simmering cauldron of India, his role was to unite the Opposition and turn it into a movement – but not of course the potential, working class-based left movement which the communists could have built, rather a movement based on the traditional anti-Congress opposition which brought together right-wing and often reactionary parties with a section of the left.

If a storm was roaring over India, Bihar, a huge state of nearly 60 million people in north India, was at its centre. Here the most feudal land relations could be found – landlords with no notion that an age of democracy had arrived, thousands of acres held by religious monasteries with peasants in a state of serfdom, low castes held in bondage, with their women subjugated to every sort of oppression from male beatings to the seemingly unquestioned right of upper caste landlords to their bodies, middle caste peasants on the rise and fighting against the 'advanced' high caste landowners but ready to adopt the same methods of feudal terror against the landless. In the most backward and jungly tribal areas, massive iron and steel plants were built to take advantage of the state's abundant natural resources, and consequently militant unions and *adivasi* demands for a separate tribal state and relief from Hindu moneylenders (the Jharkhand Movement) sparked each other off. Bihar was one of the few parts of India where guns, often homemade, were common, were carried by landlords and their thugs openly on buses and by agricultural labourers and left activists at night as they took revenge for oppression or sought to protect themselves. A dozen contending student groups existed, the working class was on strike as everywhere, in the tribal areas militant unions were beginning to unite with militant *adivasis*, and the centuries-oppressed Dalit agricultural labourers were beginning to stir in a massive if disorganized revolt.

Into this cauldron moved J.P. with a message of 'total revolution'. Learn from Gandhi, Marx and Mao; take the best of all. Students, youth, go to the villages and organize the people. Let parties and parliaments die away, build a new politics of 'partyless democracy' based on the village. Throw out politicians, suspend the state machinery that was responsible for so much anti-people repression, stop corruption, dissolve the Bihar legislative assembly. This was the call to build a movement – what the left could not form out of the wave of massive popular indignation and the violent scattered elements of India's contradiction-embroiled social system, J.P. was trying to do: build a political alternative.

What was wrong with all of this? From the point of view of the communists, of course, much. A class basis was missing. The working class was said to be incompetent and privileged, youth were urged to be the vanguard. Youth were told to go to the villages, but how would villages embroiled in internal class and caste conflict be organized? How could students as such lead a movement for the poor and downtrodden when they were so often from the rich and high caste families of the villages? In fact, the movement deliberately ignored the working class in the cities and, when it reached the villages, it most often coalesced with landlord interests. But, while all communists more or less agreed about its class base, that it was at best petty bourgeois, they disagreed about how to assess this. The CPI decided that, since this new movement was against an essentially progressive government and since it included right-wing pro-American parties, it was reactionary and even 'fascist'. The CPI(M) vacillated but basically began to ally with it as a democratic petty-bourgeois movement. The Naxalites also vacillated – in fact one of the issues in the 1971 split in their central committee was over whether or not to ally with J.P. Left unity broke down once again and the J.P. movement took the centre of the stage. By the end of 1974 it was no longer the working masses who were confronting the state, it was J.P. confronting Indira in a gigantic, personalized political drama.

'Queen of Delhi, vacate the throne!' thundered the Opposition in a massive rally in Delhi in 1975. Indira began to be hounded by the dogs of dissent, attacked in Nagpur, hunted by women in Bombay, greeted with black flag demonstrations everywhere and with sandals thrown at her head, the ultimate in Hindu insults. A lawsuit was brought against her for personal political corruption, essentially marshalling government resources to fight an election campaign in her own district. In June 1975 the Allahabad High Court made the dramatic decision that she was guilty. Conviction meant that she was ineligible for her poliitcal post. The Opposition demanded that she step down. Indira refused; the case was on appeal to the Supreme Court. The Opposition threatened a nationwide civil disobedience campaign, and now the CPI(M) as well was throwing its forces into the battle to stage a half-million strong rally for J.P. in Calcutta.

But it was not enough. The Opposition had united but the movement was floundering. If, from the point of view of the communists, J.P. was building up a petty bourgeois based movement that was providing support to merchants and landlords, from the point of view of the capitalists he was not building it well enough. The movement had not gathered nationwide support.

J.P.'s tours of the south aroused little interest; his visit to Pune (in the west) drew a huge crowd of 40,000 but most of them middle class and upper caste – and even there women workers whom the socialists had brought to the rally staged an unconscious 'walkout' at 6 p.m. because they had to go home and cook supper and they could see no point in staying at the rally. There was no nation-wide party machinery or band of activists with a mass base to provide a force capable of governing the country. The slogans of the movement themselves were personalistic and vague, implying only that the people in power had to be replaced by other people – but there were no others who really looked different. There was talk of corruption but not of what economic programme would follow. 'Queen of Delhi, vacate the throne!' was incapable of rallying enough people and it gave absolutely no clue as to what would come next.

Vacant thrones are not good for business. J.P. had the support of some sections of India's industrialists, including major newspaper owners – but the group was clearly worried, and their fear showed itself in a dramatically sinking stock market rate. After the Allahabad High Court decision against Indira, it virtually plunged.

It was at this time that the women of Pune were beginning to come together, that the Dhule tribal women were gathering in their study camp, that an initial decision was made to organize a Maharashtra-wide women's conference. The Allahabad High Court decision was on June 12 and it was a little over two weeks later, on June 25, 1975, that Indira Gandhi seized the initiative, declared a State of Emergency, arrested J.P. and the major Opposition leaders, arrested as well some of the people in her own Congress party who were his secret supporters, threw in an assortment of smugglers and black marketeers, imposed restrictions on public meetings, gatherings and strikes, and clamped down on all major sources of instability. The next day, after assuring businessmen that there would be no immediate further nationalizations, she declared that the Emergency was not simply directed against opponents conspiring to overthrow the government but that it had a *purpose*, to get the country moving and to help the poor. There would be a '20-Point Programme' including minimum wages for agricultural labourers, debt relief and tightened land ceilings, free books for students, houses for the homeless, liberalization of import licences for business, a whole combination of goodies thrown out to every section of the population and designed also to creak some life into India's gasping economy. With the repression went 'action' – this was the nature of the formula, and with the Emergency the formula reached a still higher point.

J.R.D. Tata, India's wealthiest businessman, sipping tea from a silver cup, told a reporter for the *New York Times Magazine,* 'Things had gone too far. You can't imagine what we have been through here – strikes, boycotts, demonstrations. Why, there were days when I couldn't walk out of my office onto the street. The parliamentary system is not suited to our needs.' J.P. was silenced and in jail, and the other most famous old Gandhian leader, Vinoba Bhave, reappeared out of his retirement to 'constructive' work to take Indira's side, declaring in benevolent Sanskrit that the 'era of self-discipline' had come. Placards plastered on buses and city walls heralded the value of hard work. Employees were forced to come to the office on time, policemen hammered into respectable queues the mobs trying to enter over-crowded buses. The Emergency began. The stock market soared.

'Indira is India, India is Indira,' said the Congress party leader Borooah. It was June, 1975, almost exactly the time of the United Nations International Women's Year Conference in Mexico City, which Indira Gandhi had been scheduled to attend but never made because she was too busy cleaning house at home. But in Mexico City, the representatives declared that the emancipation of women must be part of Third World countries' striving for economic development and self-reliance. The Indian delegates gave militant speeches in support of this. After all, wasn't their government trying to do just that?

12. 'Come on, unite!'

The Women's Liberation Conference

O Toiling Women

Chorus
O toiling women
Who labour in the house and out
— Come on, unite!

Gangu, you've worn yourself out
Working in the mill for twenty years.
Your hair has become white
While the boss has gotten rich.
Still the axe of unemployment
Is hanging over your head
And workless women everywhere
Sell vegetables in the streets —
Give us work! Come on, unite!

Where are you going, Miss Mary?
You're going to your factory?
Why is your face so pinched?
Why are you smiling just a little?
So — you've decided to marry
And your cheeks are blushing —
Then why is your face so sorrowful?
The boss will demand your resignation!
'Now the problem faces me . . .'
        Come on, unite!

Wearing a clean white sari
Who is walking so hurriedly?
This is our sister nurse
Who is the mother of the patient.
An eight hour shift in the day,
A twelve hour shift at night,
No hospital quarters for your family
So they tell you to live alone.
What to do, tell me? Come on, unite!

Here comes the teacher . . .
She lectures the whole day
But listen to the words in her mind:
'I teach one hundred children,
My children are left at home,
This is what is pinching me
Rooted deep in my mind.
What to say to anyone?' Come on, unite!

Bhagubai goes out each morning,
On her head a basket, on her back her baby,
For so many days she has searched for work.
If she's late the arrogant owner refuses.
Starvation work at a rupee a day,
Collecting kindling on the way home
With her hungry children before her eyes —
'Where can I borrow some grain?
So much worry . . . ' Come on, unite!

From the dawn, cooking grinding,
Cleaning the cowshed and the courtyard,
The peasant woman goes to the fields.
Weeding for the whole day,
Back in the evening for cooking,
Finally settling down to sleep
Harassed with fear for her daughter's marriage.
This goes on from year to year! Come on, unite!

In the fields and in the factories,
In the offices and schools,
In hospitals and in banks,
How many sisters are working!
Without a holiday, without rest,
Any day off is spent in housework,
Now after centuries of slavery
More exploitation in service.
Weariness is in my heart. Come on, unite!

Rise up, all you women,
Let us all unite together.

137

> Let us all go tell the government
> Now we are no longer helpless!
> Give in to our demands,
> See our army rising up —
> We will not retreat,
> We vow by our children. Come on, unite!

by Suman Katre 1975

18 October 1975: Women throng into the meeting hall. Students, nurses, bank clerks, agricultural labourers, Dalits, *adivasis,* Brahmans, the whole panorama. Some, professors from local colleges, women coolies from the railway yards, and of course the familiar municipal workers, are from Pune ('Welcome to our rural sisters!' says one of these expansively, sitting on the steps of the hall). Others have come from hundreds of miles away, travelling ten to twenty hours or more in jolting buses, and are tired but exhilarated as they register their names at the desk, pick up their conference badges (the famous brandished fist over the female symbol and, in Marathi, 'United Women's Liberation Struggle Conference') and glance at the literature table. 'Where is the women's liberation book?' ask some of the tribal women from Dhule, for these Shramik Sanghatana members have already been told of the new book written by Chhaya as an effort to give the history of women's oppression and struggles in Marathi, published just in time for the conference. These women are illiterate themselves, but they have been sent as delegates by the women of their villages, who raised an impressive 60 rupees for expenses, and they want evidence of their conference attendance, something real to bring back, something also that can be read to them by the educated children of their families. Then they search for a place to set their bedding and slump down against it, until volunteers come round with tea and, refreshed, they begin to roam the hall to examine the picture exhibition made by the Bombay group.

With student volunteers helping them to read the commentary, they can see graphics depicting the position of women in India and bold pictorial questions: a prostitute standing in self-conscious sexuality on a dirty street ('For what? – To fill the stomach!'), a harassed housewife examining an empty grain tin while her head whirls and crying children besiege her ('The second name of woman is sorrow!'), a woman construction worker ('Are women only fit for unskilled work?'), a new bride being carried to her marriage wrapped in gold and silk ('Who is a woman? A thing to be sold or an independent individual?'). And brief quotes from newspaper stories: a girl commits suicide because the dowry burden is too great for her parents; a wife throws herself and two children in a well because there is no more food. And, next to all this, the portrayal of the life of women in China, Russia, Vietnam, the US, driving tractors, sitting in cockpits of airplaines, fighting in liberation armies.

138

The meeting hall itself is simply arranged. Canvas mats are spread for people to sit on, the only chairs being those at the reception and literature tables and a few at the back. There is no platform for the 'leaders' as is common in most conferences and rallies, even those organized by socialists and communists. Instead, under a huge conference banner a microphone is placed and there is a cushion and a small note table for the chairwoman. Eating and sleeping arrangements will be common, again in contrast to the frequent custom in which middle class leaders troop off to the house of a well-to-do sympathizer while working class participants eat working class food. Pune local people will mostly go home to eat and sleep, but for the volunteers this is discouraged. And social integration is not a simple thing. It is not so much a matter of sleeping on a canvas mat on a hard floor — most Indians even of middle class background are used to this — but of food differences themselves. The first day's meal, provided by a Brahman establishment in the city, is simple but healthy food of the type the middle class volunteers are accustomed to. But the second day's meal, from a socialist-run food centre called *Kashtaci Bhakri* or 'Toilers' Bread', provides the radically different and much more heavily spiced food of the lower classes, and it is almost hotter than many of the upper middle class women can stand. But they eat it, nevertheless, and take turns serving. 'With my hands?' asks one professor who is used to serving spoons — but carries out her task cheerfully. The effort is to break down the class barriers between different groups of women, class barriers which are so vividly reflected in all aspects of daily life from speech to food habits and which are so frequently maintained by the distinction between 'leaders' and led even when a movement is being organized. But the women are out to fight all forms of cultural tradition and social inequality, they are waging the 'revolution in the revolution', and this kind of challenge is their speciality.

No men are allowed in the conference hall. This prohibition coexists, paradoxically, with the fact that the conference itself depends on men: many of the women from outside Pune are workers or agricultural labourers who have been contacted through their unions, and these do not come alone but in a group led by a male union organizer. Even these men must wait outside. The LNP party leaders, in Pune at the time for their own meeting and intensely curious about the conference they helped to initiate, come to see but halt fifty feet away until someone goes out to tell them what is going on; they too must wait. And this effort again, though it may seem limited, is new, for even when left organizations take up such things as 'women's issues' the male leaders and spokesmen simply assume their right to be present, to inaugurate the meeting, and to give it its direction in the form of the main speech of the day. If women are not yet fully self-reliant, at least they are fighting for the form.

The only men, in fact, who make it into the hall are the young fellow who plays the drum for the Bombay singing group and Madhav who, by this time, has written four women's liberation songs and included a part for himself in one of them:

> Hear us, O hear us . . . *(this is Madhav's line)*
> The age of oppression will be over now,
> Mother Ganga, mother Yamuna will not have to
>   meet the sea,
> No girl, no mother will have to fear any man.
> The age of oppression will be over now.
> On the earth the toilers will not be bound in chains
> And each woman will have the right to work
>   alongside men.
> Hear us, O hear us,
> The age of oppression will be over now.

('The rivers Ganga and Yamuna are considered female and the sea is supposed to be masculine,' says Madhav, explaining his symbolism; 'and it's always said that rivers have to flow into the sea. But in China,' he adds, for he is the main editor for a Marathi China friendship magazine, 'they even change the course of rivers.') In any case, the songs are a tremendous hit and my tape of them becomes one of the enduring organizational tools to be played again and again in meetings when there is no one to sing. We nearly miss having this tape, for American technology proves a disastrous failure at the conference — my camera turns out to be faulty and my tape recorder suddenly doesn't work (partly because I have not taken the time really to check either of them) and it is thanks to one of our two German visitors that we have any tapes at all.

Thus, with songs, a couple of afternoon talks on women's oppression and role in society, tea, more talks, food, a film in the evening and sleepy discussions as the women spread out their bedding and finally fall asleep to the sound of drizzling rain, the first day of the conference passes quickly. Volunteers, counting up the badges handed out and glancing through the registration book, estimate that nearly 750 women have come, and that about two-thirds of them are workers or agricultural labourers, though not all are present at one time since the Pune people in particular come and go. It is nearly four months after the declaration of Emergency. The Pune women's conference is beginning.

And from the beginning there have been weeks of uncertainty about whether the conference can be held at all. Returning from Kohapur after that fateful day, we find everyone in a state of shock. But reactions vary tremendously, partly because the working out of the impact of the Emergency is slow, arrests are extremely selective and the practical limits on activities are not clear. On the one hand, there is the young jouranlist I meet on the street and ask what the civil liberties organization is going to do now — 'What can you do under fascism?' is his despairing reply. And, in contrast, Leela, trotting off each week to the censors with the LNP publication material, is the embodiment of LNP wait-and-see attitude with her, 'Well, let's see, let's see what we can print.' This difference reflects varying political perceptions playing upon a still limited experience. Those who feel emotionally locked in battle with a terrorist state, who are hearing rumours, some confirmed, some not, of the arrest and torture of people whom they know or politically identify with, but who have up to now been living unwittingly in the security of lawyers, regulations and courts, are likely to feel that the ground is cut away from under them. On the other hand, those lacking this consciousness of rights and procedures, judging by immediate practical actions, take a different approach, like the workers who are won over for the moment simply by the simple stratagem of their pro-Emergency CPI leaders reading out to them, one by one, the names of people arrested, names all familiar to them as black marketeers, big merchants, and politicians (like Morarji Desai) with a long tradition of being on the other side. In spite of the shock, in fact, the wait-and-see attitude is most common. The few initial efforts to organize protest meetings to fight 'the destruction of democracy' meet with little response from either middle classes or working classes, and their organizers are simply whisked off to jail to add to the numbers already there.

The Conference Organizing Committee meets in a state of subdued tension. Everyone in it is involved enough with the left opposition to know some of those arrested, to have some image of being a possible prey for the state. But it is decided that the conference will go on. Clearly some changes will have to be made. There can be no concluding mass rally, no march through the streets, only an indoor 'delegates' meeting. Publicity material will have to be submitted to the censor, and in the process words like 'revolution' get changed to 'all-round social change'. No one, however, is ready to quit.

But these are new problems which deal the final blow to any hopes of left unity. The ranks of leading left-wing women have been decimated. Ahilya Rangnekar is one of the first to be arrested; she has given a speech at a hastily called oppositional rally in Bombay and spends the entire nineteen months of the Emergency in jail. Mrinal Gore goes underground and spends several months flitting from place to place organizing networks of propaganda and resistance before she is finally caught. Other socialist women are also totally caught up in their party's method of opposing the Emergency by organizing *satyagrahas* – non-violent demonstrations in which small groups of men and women go into the streets, shout 'down with the Emergency!' before the silently watching crowd, are arrested and spend some weeks or months in jail before they are turned loose. This type of underground activity and symbolic resistance leaves little scope for organizing women (whether 'underground' or openly) around their own problems. The CPI(M), for its part, wants to oppose the Emergency by organizing the masses but does not really know how to do this; its Pune woman activist goes around meetings of students and others connected with the women's group to talk about the party political line, but has no programme of action to give. Without Ahilya it seems that other CPI(M) women are unable to make a decision to join the Conference Organizing Committee. As for the activists who are sent underground, they are even more at a loss: 'We could do anything, walk around Bombay, ride on buses, go to cinemas, but we couldn't visit party offices, meet party people or go to our old areas of work,' recalls one later, disgusted, 'and there was no programme to organize. There was absolutely nothing to do.'

The Naxalites are even more under attack than the CPI(M) or the socialists. All their organizations are declared illegal and in many areas police repression is intensified. In most cases this is no qualitative difference — they were underground and facing repression of equal ferocity before. Naxalite-connected 'mass' organizations, though, find a difference, and the Emergency spells the end of the Hyderabad POW. Its president is arrested and beaten up in jail; it is said that she has been tortured and raped though it turns out later that the police themselves have deliberately exaggerated this to intimidate others in the organization. Another leader is locked up at home by badly frightened parents. A few go into hiding to do party work, but they are unable to maintain contact with the students of the organization and instead are sent to villages. In a later analysis, a POW founder exposes the underlying fragility of the organization: 'There was no time for consolidation . . . POW could not survive long enough to make a base among the working masses and to train cadres, since it invited state repression when the organization was still very young. Without taking into consideration the preparedness of the girls to participate in political struggle, it exposed itself to repression by regularly associating with Left student organizations . . . ' Disagreement over the policies of the particular Naxalite party the organization is connected with becomes another factor weakening POW, and shows its inability to maintain, in the end, its separate identity as a democratic women's group rather than just a 'party front'. Nevertheless, POW gets in one last blow with the publication of an English-language magazine, *Stri-Vimukti* (Women's Liberation) just after the Emergency is declared, though censorship makes it impossible to include a planned article on women political prisoners. The magazine is immensely popular; every copy that reaches Pune disappears within a week.

The Shramik Sanghatana also faces intensified attack. Many of its activists in Dhule and Bombay go underground but some are arrested first, and Chhaya becomes preoccupied in the early weeks of the Emergency with trying to meet liberal government officials or CPI leaders (who are thought to have some influence with the government) to help those in jail. The landowners step up their repression by bringing in north Indian mercenaries to 'guard the crops' and the new censorship makes impossible publicity of the sort they had before. The Sanghatana, however, manages to carry on some activities in spite of intensified pressure. The *adivasis* fight it out with the 'crop protectors' at times, and the literature and records of the organization are dispersed away from its known offices. One of those chosen to take care of the records is Bhuribai. 'The men may get caught or killed,' she says, 'but the Sanghatana should continue. These papers are necessary for future activists — ' and she makes a tour of the whole area on her own initiative to visit the tribal labourers and youth groups to maintain the morale of the members.

The CPI(M), Socialists, Naxalites and the *Magowa* Shramik Sanghatana are all, in their own way, standing clearly in opposition to the Emergency. Completely on the other side is the CPI, which leaps to support it as an 'anti-fascist' step, an effort to prevent a reactionary 'CIA-instigated coup' from 'destabilizing' the country. CPI activists are left untouched, except in a few areas where they are leading struggles too militantly, and since they are told to involve themselves in 'constructive' work, they ought to be part of the process of the progressive and undoubtedly constructive task of organizing women. But the CPI refuses to have anything to do with the conference. Supporting the government takes priority. 'What could we do?' Chhaya complains later at a CPI(M) women's conference. 'The CPI said they wouldn't come unless we passed a resolution in support of the 20 Point Programme. We weren't willing to do that. The socialists said they wouldn't come unless we passed a resolution opposing the Emergency. And we couldn't do that and still have an open conference! At least you' — addressing the CPI(M) leaders — 'should have helped in organizing!' But the CPI(M) does not help either, and so the LNP remains the main political backbone of the conference. The LNP, for its part, takes a wait-and-see attitude about the Emergency, partly because there is an unresolved political conflict among its leadership; but its general position is that the repressive, anti-democratic measures of the Emergency should be opposed by organizing the masses around their own problems. Other left women in the Organizing Committee find this position unsatisfactory and 'economistic' because it is unable to give any political direction to those being organized — but they really have no alternative, and within this framework it is at least possible to carry on some organization of women.

And the fact is that all the fragmentation of the left parties, all the arrests of militant and oppositional activists, all the fear of dictatorship pervading those conscious women who continue to work have almost no effect on ordinary women. The reality is that there is simply not much opposition to the Emergency among the vast majority of women. Some upper middle class women may feel, along with their men, a bitterness at the loss of civil liberties. Organized workers — from textile workers to unionized agricultural labourers to bank employees and teachers — feel an increased pressure on the job: they are forced to punch in on time whatever the hazards of commuting, speedup is imposed on a wide scale throughout the factories of India, workers are deprived of bonuses and pay rises, and in militant workplaces the pressure of government informers and the possibility of arrest is constantly felt. But there is little that can be done, with known leaders confronted by arrest, unable to pass out leaflets or hold meetings and rallies to organize strikes.

So workers begin to turn against the Emergency, and by the end of its nineteen months, in spite of the incapacity of union and party leaderships, strike movements and struggles organized from below are occurring on a wide scale. Many unorganized and underemployed workers in city slums also feel a new repression, as slum demolition campaigns to 'beautify' the cities go on and they see their homes destroyed and possessions scattered by the police. Slum demolition campaigns are not a new thing – but previously people could organize demostrations and resistance campaigns; now, as this proves impossible, they, too, experience the significance of the loss of democratic rights.

But in the countryside things are different. Where there has been no history of organized struggle – and this is still true for most of the rural poor – the loss of the right to organize makes little impact. Where people cannot read, censorship means nothing. 'Democracy' means little more than elections every few years – and the experience of these varies from the semi-feudal terror of simply being marshalled to vote by landlord thugs to a ruthless bargaining for a few rupees to the discovery that popular candidates from low caste backgrounds seem able to make little change. Cynicism runs deep. 'We have always lived under an Emergency,' writes one young Dalit journalist. 'The question is whether this Emergency will help in lifting that one.' And Indira is out to convince the rural poor that it will.

The fact is that the Emergency itself takes a different shape in the countryside. In the cities it is out front against the working class, but in the countryside it is putting pressure on landowners to 'shape up', to behave somewhat less like feudal barons and a bit more like sophisticated capitalist entrepreneurs. And it is throwing some crumbs to the poor, who have not yet learned to ask for the whole cake. Instead of demolishing huts as in the cities, the 20-Point Programme promises to build houses for the landless. And some houses do indeed go up. They seem miserably small, inadequate, windowless structures to people like me. 'They'll fall down with the first rains,' people say; 'Look how far outside the village they are – no challenging of caste discrimination here!' No, the 20-Point Programme does not challenge caste discrimination, or class exploitation, or attempt to halt the ongoing proletarianization and marginalization in the villages, but only seeks to sweeten this a bit. But for most of their recipients, these miserable huts are probably the first solid houses they have ever had. And for many, these clusters of huts continue to symbolize the Emergency long after the loss of the democracy they have never really known is forgotten. Even forced sterilization – the only Emergency programme with a really mass negative impact in the rural areas – seems more temporary, less widespread. And along with the houses are the promises of land, minimum wages, the offer of free bangles to women workers who had broken their own carrying loads of rocks, tiny little symbols of hope.

And everywhere, in all of these programmes, Indira's name is pronounced, with a propaganda barrage the left can never equal. In another telling incident, some Shramik Sanghatana women labourers one day hear the richest landowner in their area, an owner of 500 (illegal) acres, say to his foreman, 'Watch how you behave with the women, you might be arrested under MISA. It's Indirabai's raj now.' And hearing that their recognized class enemy is afraid of Indira makes them feel that she must be on their side, gives reality to the constant radio programmes extolling her, makes them feel that the arrest of Shramik Sanghatana activists must be somehow a local mistake.

If organized women workers are confused, unorganized women naturally tend to feel that something is happening in their favour. There is Laxmibai, the woman who washes dishes and clothes in the apartment complex where I live, working daily with her daughters for the professors of the Institute and living in a nearby one-room shed. When I ask her what she thinks of the Emergency, she says, 'Oh, she's going to stop the price-rise.' 'She' of course means Indira. But, I argue, the leaders of the Women's Anti-Price-Rise Committee are the very ones who have been jailed! But this means nothing, for Laxmibai has never heard of Ahilya Rangnekar or Mrinal Gore. It is a stark fact that, for all the impressive mobilization of the committee, they have actually reached only a small proportion of India's millions, while the name of Indira goes everywhere. Some weeks later Laxmibai asks me for a loan of 50 rupees. A relative in their village, she says, is getting some land under th 20-Point Programme and needs the money to pay a government official so that his name can be registered. Isn't it terrible, I say, that such corruption still goes on! But this fades before the prospect of getting land in a programme irrevocably identified with the name of Indira Gandhi. I give Laxmibai the money. After all, land is land.

The whole situation is a stark revelation of the weakness of the left. Take the question of the people's political consciousness. Left activists may know that all the government concessions do not really threaten the rural power structure and that they are indirectly a product of the people's own struggles, that they come not because of the innate goodness of the government but because a sophisticated political leadership has realized that some steps have to be taken to still the simmering discontent. But no one is going to understand this automatically. Those who have been criticizing the established parties for years for not giving political education, for not developing political cadres from among the very poor, begin to realize the enormity of the problem under a bourgeois state. 'We can give a two- or three-hour study class every week, or even hold some daily discussions. But every other hour of the day, in the marketplace, the home, the school, they're immersed in bourgeois and feudal ideology. How can we really make our movement touch every aspect of daily life?' is the way one Shramik Sanghatana activist puts it afterwards.

Or take the question of organization. In spite of the fact that the numerically largest left party, the CPI, is supporting the government, the rest still represent a major force. If they could act together on the basis of their numerical strength, their union base among workers and agricultural labourers, the result would be truly impressive. But it turns out that having the kind of party machinery geared to running for elections and carrying on a union movement characterized by top-down leadership — in which a leading party group makes decisions and then brings these to the workers, mobilizing the workers through speeches at gate meetings and mass rallies — does not mean that the workers or agricultural labourers under their leadership have much class political consciousness or that the parties are really rooted in the masses. To carry out strikes under Emergency conditions means that the leaders of the strike must be able to keep their identity hidden, which means in effect that leadership and decision-making must be collective and widely based, that workers themselves must be aware of the need to protect their leaders' identity and have the political understanding to take over if some are arrested. To organize a widespread mass upheaval — say, a general strike, a major street demonstration, events coordinated in several cities or throughout a major rural region — means having the kind of party machinery whose countless activists, down to the very base level, are not only accustomed to work in secret but also have the dedication to carry things through in the face of possible arrest or slaughter, the political understanding to take initiatives, and who are numerous and deeply based enough to be able to go to innumerable small village huts or city homes for meetings of small groups of people. But this degree of party machinery does not exist. Groups like the Naxalites or Shramik Sanghatana have mass influence only in small areas; and the parties with a relatively big 'mass base' like the CPI(M) or LNP prove to be lacking in the power to move it.

And so whatever resistance occurs is localized and generally spontaneous. Mass rioting over slum demolition in Delhi; continuing but subdued struggles in pockets of communist strength; a village schoolteacher rallying her fellow-workers to resist government pressure to bring names for sterilization; a strike against speedup bursting out violently and as violently repressed. Beyond this, there is no major mass resistance campaign. 'The Indian people are not used to working under dictatorship,' says a CPI(M) activist justifying his party's stand of putting all effort into the 'restoration of democracy', but what he means in fact is that Indian *parties* are not. And so hundreds are killed in Delhi at Turkman Gate opposing the levelling of their houses and the forced sterilization associated with it, but a dozen Marxist organizations working in an equally big slum in Bombay can do nothing to build resistance to similar onslaught. What is left, in effect, is the kind of policy LNP is following: organize the people on their own, primary-level economic demands, talk about 'implementation' of government promises as a tool for organizing, and leave large politics aside for the moment as far as any big open work is concerned.

And for organizing women, it turns out that the Emergency makes little difference. If the left parties have not touched the lives of the masses of women very much, neither after all has the state, and women continue to be ready to respond to basic issues. The women's movement itself is at such a primary level as to be not very threatening and is still far from organizing intense types of struggle. After all, talking about the burdens of housework and child care, the necessity of fighting reactionary cultural traditions, urging women to be a part of public life, to join together to resist rape and other atrocities, can hardly be viewed as subversive. The government itself has accepted legally the right to work for rural women and legislated a minimum wage for agricultural labourers, and women can be mobilized to demand that these be 'implemented'. 'Cultural programmes' can be held, and a lot of indirect propaganda, including most revolutionary songs, can be put out.

Such organizing efforts can at times even include the usual left speeches about the necessity of bringing in a toilers' state in order to achieve any of these basic reforms — perhaps because there is no clear evidence that such speeches make much difference in the absence of direct experience and concrete organizing towards such a goal. Of course, if women were to strike, to demonstrate in the streets without official permission, or to *gherao* a government official in order to win some of these minimal demands, things would be different. What the Emergency has done, in effect, is to raise the stakes for such forms of struggle, making arrest and indefinite detention of the most active leaders a likelihood. But the initial steps of organizing — coming together, raising consciousness, even talking about future struggles — is not looked on as threatening, particularly if those doing it are not 'politically identified' with a subversive organization.

Perhaps the government has too many other things to do at the moment to concern itself with women; perhaps they are taking note but no action at present. In any case, what presents itself is a kind of bland indifference. One day Sharda and I hold a meeting of textile workers in Bombay. The mill we go to is one in which there has been a huge free-for-all that very day, furious workers inside beating up the activists of the pro-government Congress-led union. Furniture is broken and slogans inscribed on the walls attack both the Congress and the CPI leaders for collaboration with the millowners. Tension is at a high level and there are numerous policemen around. But outside, when we call women of the mill to a discussion in a small local temple and four or five constables come by to check up, we tell them we're only discussing women's issues. They read through the conference leaflets. 'O.K., you're having a social meeting, not a political one.' It is clear that these policemen, anyway, see no connection between women's issues and the struggle inside the mill, however much Sharda and I and other women activists believe that such a connection exists. It is in a way humiliating to find that the women's movement is not automatically viewed as subversive, but it is also useful for the purpose of carrying on activity.

And so conference organizing takes place in an almost surrealistic atmosphere. The left-oriented women of the Organizing Committee feel the time to be one of deep but frustrating crisis, and experience the state as a dangerous and impending force. But this experiencing is embodied only minimally in concrete events — plainclothes police-women attending a meeting, someone on the bus asking our name, trips to a noncommittal censor, a few arrests here, stories distantly heard of jail atrocities elsewhere, occasional rumours of a protest riot and police massacre. Meanwhile little seems to happen in our direct presence and the working class and rural poor women we meet are very little touched by this. On the contrary, they continue to see Indira Gandhi as a benign figure. And as the organizing proceeds, with hardly a whisper of interest from police and government officials, it is natural to wonder: are they taking note of all our actions even though they are not ready to do something now, or are we genuinely being ignored? If we are being ignored, why? Is the force of women not something before which the exploiting classes should tremble? Or is it the unconscious chauvinism of most state officials that makes them feel that women's activity is something trivial? Or are our organizing methods so primitive, so far from really building up a women's liberation movement, that they see no reason to worry about us? With these questions in the background – but the last, in particular, hardly intruding at all on the fevered consciousness of activity – the Organizing Committee continues to meet, village programmes and factory gate discussions are held, posters and songs are prepared and we aim for the conference in October.

And so the October weekend comes, and with it the women, turning up in numbers beyond expectation. So many of the women I have met individually at different times and places have come together to meet each other, to take part in a collective process. Some familiar faces are missing, Kaminibai is not present because her village is simply too far away and because the movement has not reached it yet. Tanubai, the agricultural labourer ballad singer, is missing for a somewhat different reason: LNP activists have not brought her because relations are still somewhat strained, and the Organizing Committee women are not sufficiently organized to have independent contacts. But Bhagubai, from the Agricultural University, has come; agricultural labourers from Banage and other Kolhapur villages are there; and Bhuribai of the Shramik Sanghatana along with fifty-nine other tribal women has come the long way from Dhule in a specially rented bus. In spite of their scepticism about 'bourgeois feminism', the Shramik Sanghatana activists have supported the conference and the women have responded with enthusiasm, raising money locally to come as village representatives, and buying, if possible, new saris for the occasion. And another Shramik Sanghatana contingent of eight women have come from Kasegaon, a village to the south with a history of peasant militancy, led by Indumati, a woman veteran of the national movement struggle. With these and others, the representation of the rural poor at the conference is impressive.

So is that of workers. Tarabai and other municipal workers are there, Tarabai serving as one of the volunteers. From Pune, also, come another group of Dalit workers, the women coolies or load carriers of the railway yard who, in spite of their unionizing efforts, remain overworked and underpaid, carrying out their back-breaking labour daily in the hot sun and coal-choked atmosphere for 50 to 60 rupees a month. Because they are Dalits, their touch is still considered 'polluting' to foodstuffs and so they cannot get jobs in the more highly paid and better conditions of the grain market or vegetable market. Yet these women have also dug out their best saris and listen enthusiastically to all that goes on. From Bombay, Sharda and Chhaya come with a large delegation that includes textile workers and hospital workers as well as bank employees and other middle class workers.

College students are also well represented. Not the girls of Bimzani College, which is also really too far away, a day and a half's journey, but many others, idealistic and enthusiastic. The young organizers of the

Mahila Samta Sainik Dal are also missing, for their organization has more or less fallen into inaction. There is really no felt presence of young educated Dalit girls, though Dalit workers and farm labourers are plentiful. But Shantabai Dani, an older woman leader of the Dalits' Republican Party, a woman who is part of the long past history of Dalit struggles for their rights, is present.

And there are other 'new' women, new to me, that is. Above all, there is a representative of the Devadasis, women who symbolize at once the feudal backwardness of India and its capitalist transformation. For Devadasis were traditionally temple prostitutes (the name means 'servant of God'), girls vowed to the temple from childhood by illiterate and low caste parents, making the promise in return for some kind of divine help. In modern times, where the custom continues in the area south of Maharashtra, such girls serve a more commercial god: agents of the prostitution network in Bombay and other large cities recruit them, and they are brought into the profession in the cities. Such women have been organizing with the help of some socialist leaders (now in jail) and have held a conference of their own recently; their spokeswoman, Gorabai, has come to Pune.

And of course the political women are present. The chairperson of the conference, Nalini Pandit, is a socialist college professor. CPI(M) and socialist party workers turn up, after all, though their top leaders remain in jail. The socialist delegates from Barsi grumble about the lack of opposition to the Emergency, but the CPI(M) Bombay leader comes with two others to make an official gesture of a donation and support. One or two Pune CPI women also turn up, but they sit in the back observing the proceedings with critical eyes, just as does a local Congresswoman. In any event, including with these the LNP women, the wife of a leading Bombay Trotskyist, the unproclaimed Naxalite students and Shantabai Dani of the Republic Party, just about the full scale of 'left and progressive' parties is represented.

And they all — especially the 'non-political' workers and rural women — seem to be clamouring for a chance to speak! The second day of the conference includes a couple more educational talks plus discussion intervals of singing, and the passing of the conference resolutions (what this really means since, as in most conferences, the resolution has already been decided on, is speeches on the resolution by various of the political women). But it centres on giving scope to the participants themselves to address the conference, letting workers, agricultural labourers, students and employees talk about their own problems, their struggles, their hopes and their perceptions of 'women's liberation'. This 'mass speaking' has initially been the subject of fierce controversy within the Organizing Committee. Most of the student members in Pune and some of the *Magowa* women have been pushing for using the time for 'discussion groups', that is, breaking the women up into smaller groups to discuss the themes already presented in the conference educational talks, on the theory that such discussion rather than 'speeches and more speeches' is the best way to learn. This is one version of the struggle over whether the conference should be oriented to training activists or 'going to the masses'.

But Leela, fighting hard to keep the wide-open 'mass' character of the conference, prevails, and in the end turns out to have been closer to the mood of the women, at least at this time. For what the women coming to the meetings seem to want is not 'educative discussions' but a chance to speak out themselves, and not in a small group either but before the entire throng. Perhaps they too, hearing from so many others the same kinds of agonies and experiences that they themselves have faced, sense the power of a newly stirring force in so many women gathered together. Now they are demanding their chance to speak, so much so that trying to give everyone a chance proves impossible and the effort to make up an organized list falls into confusion; but very few in the end feel left out and as they speak a new voice does seem to be emerging, angry and questioning women, unexpectedly articulate, no longer mute and shy.

The themes that emerge are the familiar ones: the right of women to paid productive work; the burdens of housework; the bondages of a traditional culture; the torments of rape and the fear of rape and the subtler harassments of men on the streets; the wastages of alcoholism; rising prices and stagnant wages and the simplest necessities like water available only through long queues and arduous trips to a failing well, and the impossibility of home life under such conditions — all the familiar themes, but expressed with a new force in the language of illiterate women and in the songs that sweep the conference —

> This is the challenge of women's liberation
> Reaching to the sky

Students vow resistance to being bound to the home, and having marriages and dowry forced upon them. Workers tell of their unionizing efforts, of police beatings and employer victimization. Bhagubai tells of the Agricultural University struggle and says that she has been threatened with the loss of her job if she comes to the conference, 'But I wasn't afraid, I've come anyway — we must have unity!' Gorabai, the Devadasi representative, describes poignantly the workings of this most oppressive custom and says it should be reformed: 'If girls are going to get into this, at least they should be old enough to know what they're getting into, they mustn't be sold into slavery as children!' But this is a kind of anticlimax, and when volunteers later ask her why she didn't condemn the whole thing straight out, Gorabai is more frank and the underlying backbone of women's oppression stands out starkly: 'This is my occupation. If I really speak out, I'll lose all my customers. Already I'm in trouble for doing this much. If you can find me another job, then I can speak out . . . '

It is not always the most appropriate women who get a chance to speak. The Shramik Sanghatana spokesperson, for instance, is not a worker activist like Bhuribai, but rather the more middle class and slightly superior widow of the dead Bhil leader Ambarsingh, who has a tendency to treat the other tribal women as a part of a political retinue and implicitly claims the right to speak on the 'traditional' basis of her relationship with a man. But even she voices in her speech the force of the Dhule women's fight, the familiar themes of the struggle against work oppression and alcoholism and the newer themes of the customary independence of the tribal women. Nagubai, a tall and magnificently striking tribal woman from another area, also speaks, holding up an example of the roots people eat in the dry season as an illustration of their poverty; she has obviously been coached in this and has a tendency to refer to her meeting with a Bengali party leader as if he were a kind of visiting deity — but the struggle and the passion is real, people do have to eat roots, that is, they fall back on traditional methods of food gathering in an era when the forests are insufficient to support them in the old way and the food of the plains is beyond their reach; authenticity comes through at some point in every woman's speech. A nurse supervisor, in charge of the young nurses who go out to work in village clinics, actually breaks down in tears as she talks of the torments such unmarried and socially isolated women face from the village bosses who see them as an easy sexual prey. And with all these themes resounding in the hearts and minds of all present, by the end of the meeting, after all the speeches and discussions and the reading of the conference resolution, as everyone stands to sing again, and we come to the last verse of Suman Katre's song, sung in chorus repetitively and rhythmically to become a kind of chant —

> Rise up, all you women,
> Let us unite together,
> Let us go tell the government
> That we are no longer helpless!
> Give in to our demands
> See our army rising up,
> Give in to our demands,
> See our army rising up,
> Give in to our demands,
> See our army rising up —
> We will not retreat,
> We will not retreat,
> We vow by our children,
> We vow by our children —
> > Come on, unite
> > Come on, unite
> > Come on, unite

— all of us begin to feel that, whatever the faults and flaws of the conference, whatever the disorganization of the organizers, whatever the ambiguities and the hidden threads of bureaucratic dependence, whatever the inadequacies of any follow-up, that we have at least witnessed the beginning of something new, the mobilizing of the force of women fighting their oppression which really is a force potentially capable of shaking the foundations of society and the state itself.

See our army rising up . . . In the aftermath, though, so much of this is lost. Some women drift away, never to be contacted again at least by the Organizing Committee women. The registration papers, which the students had talked of using for 'survey' purposes to get data about working women, get lost in a dusty file somewhere in someone's office. The 'correspondence committee' which was as much as the factionalized organizers could agree on as an ongoing organizational medium withers away and dies. The newspapers write briefly and erratically about the conference ('Pune women demand men help with housework' is, unbelievably, the way the *Times of India* headlines its brief story, and a couple of snide editorial comments follow until Chhaya writes in to straighten things out and embarrassed progressives in the office — 'But you didn't allow our correspondents in!' 'Then why couldn't you send women reporters?' — agree to run another story) and then the subject is dropped. A socialist underground newsletter scolds us for not paying enough attention to the issue of caste, and the CPI woman writes a report characterizing the conference as a 'Maoist' effort. It is true that new contacts are made, that we have touched something deep, but no one seems able to follow through on these. An educated young married girl imprisoned in her village home writes an impassioned letter to Leela about her problems after reading about the conference. We are unable to contact her. A group of young unemployed high school graduates from a small town also read about it and decide to organize a 'women's liberation' conference of their own; they invite representatives from Pune and an amazingly enthusiastic local meeting of mainly agricultural labourers is held, a new band of militant activists seems to have been found, and then the contacts with them are broken also. The wife of one of the LNP activists, a man who had organized a big women's meeting in his own town and then brought nearly twenty women to the Pune conference, writes in to complain that her husband himself is an authoritarian in the home, that he won't let her go out of the house and 'for him to go to a woman's meeting is like a confirmed alcoholic going to a temperance meeting!' 'You're starting a cultural revolution in our party,' says A.D. Bhosle bemusedly one day as he sits with Leela and me, looking through Madhav's songs and planning a special women's issue of the Pune working class paper. But there is no revolution, neither in the party nor in Indian society, though many of us had seen the imposition of the Emergency in equally extravagant terms as the first sign of a final all-engulfing crisis.

We will not retreat . . . If the major failure remains an organizational one, the inability to build out of the conference an organization of trained and committed active workers who can maintain contacts with all the diverse women present, the inability to root that organization in the villages and slum neighbourhoods among the lowest classes of women themselves so that it can become a true medium for their own self-generating and continuing development, still some step forward has been taken. But what exactly is it? What really has the conference and all that mobilizing of International Women's Year accomplished?

Much later, Indumati, leader of the Kasegaon women's contingent to the conference and now my mother-in-law, reminisces about the organizing of women she was a part of during the period of the nationalist movement. 'What we had then was really a band of trained and dedicated women to go out and work on a nearly full-time basis throughout the villages and towns, during all the ups and downs of the movement. And you wouldn't believe it, we did so many of the things then that people are trying to do now. We had cheap marriages and marriages without dowry at all, and many of us said in those days that we would never marry, that we would devote ourselves to the work. That's what I said, and then after I got married I said that we shouldn't have children because they would take time away from the work — well you know what happened! But that was how we were in those days. We had long study camps, one three-week camp right here in this village with peasant women coming from all around. We had programmes of self-defence, and our leaders would say, "You can't depend on men to protect you, you have to learn to protect yourself!" There were even some women who fought themselves with guns during the time of the underground movement. And girls used to come every day, where there was a strong unit of the Rashtra Seva Dal, to our meeting ground and do exercizes and hear the daily national news and a short political speech. That's what built up a force, a band of organizers, full-time workers, and that kind of organization is what we don't have yet, that was what was lacking in the Pune conference, programmes and people to carry on.'

'Then, what do we have now?'

'Now . . . well, now times are different. Then all that was going on in the middle of the national movement which was sweeping the entire society. If something like that should happen again — but it would have to have a different kind of basis; now the time of the poor, of the working classes has come. Then we thought we were fighting for freedom for the poor but it turned out that the rich controlled things after all. The movement then was different. We didn't have so many working class women; there were peasant women, but not really agricultural labourers, and all the city women who came were middle class. What was really new about the Pune conference was that working class women and agricultural labourers and toiling women and all types of women should come from all over the state. And not only did they come, but they found a voice, a chance to speak out themselves, on their own, about their own feelings and problems. I think this was the first time that something like that happened. The conference was a *platform* for toiling women, and that was what was new, that was its speciality.' Then she falls silent.

'And . . . ?' I say.

'No, that's all. Now we have to begin . . . '

And I remember a meeting at the nearby village of Walwa before the conference, images flashing before my eyes of the local leader imperiously making arrangements and ordering people around, his harried and beaten-down wife, his ferocious mother, the 'old lady' who tyrannizes her daughter-in-law and everyone else and can get her way because there was a time when she too fought in the nationalist armed struggle; the late night cultural programme with the electricity periodically failing; and, in the afternoon the bright school yard, young girls shouting slogans of women's liberation, grinning and thrusting their arms forward, and behind them the gathering and still silent throng of women agricultural labourers.

This is the challenge of women's liberation reaching to the sky . . . But we have not been back to Walwa since that time. We still have to begin.

Afterword

Women reaching for the sky . . . In 1975 I was almost totally immersed in experiencing the force of the anger and aspirations of women among the most downtrodden sections of society. I was realizing that 'women's oppression' was not a Western defined abstraction but a concrete and resented reality to these toiling women and that, in the face of the necessity to struggle for even the bare minimals of survival, these women also aspired to the fullest participation in human existence – to what we call 'women's liberation'. The line, this time not from an Indian women's song but from a Western working class women's song still holds true: 'Oh, it is bread we fight for, but we fight for roses too!'

In 1975 we set out to organize a women's movement in the conviction that here was a force capable of shaking the foundations of society, an indispensable part of the people's revolutionary movement. For nearly nineteen months I was drawn into this effort, and this book is an attempt to recapture the turmoil and exhilaration of that period. It was written to bring to others something of the reality of Indian women's aspirations and struggles as I experienced them at the time. It was not intended to give a programme for those struggles or an analysis of the Indian women's movement. Hence the mood of involvement, and the style without commentary.

Invariably, however, people want to know, 'But what do you really think about what went on?' And inevitably it is necessary to pause and take stock of the situation in some way. After waves of singing 'See our army rising up' or reading of the Mahila Samta Sainik Dal saluting the 'women's liberation army', it is really necessary to ask just what is the evidence for the existence of *any* organized force of women aiming at their own liberation, much less an 'army'. After continuous calls for unity it is necessary to analyze exactly why factionalism, dissension and individualism continue to exist at the personal, political and every other level. After all the aspirations to have a different, democratic, self-expressive movement, it is crucial to examine why all the old bureaucratic practices continue to choke it to death. And after the thrill and exhaustion of a march, a demonstration, or a conference is over, it is time to ask as honestly as possible exactly what has been accomplished. Without this, the movement cannot go forward.

Is there really a women's movement in India?

At the time I thought that was what we were beginning. But the fact is that too many people now are saying 'No, not yet.'

On the positive side there is much going on. International Women's Day (March 8) has been celebrated by various left coalitions in at least fifteen towns and cities in Maharashtra (perhaps more than in all the rest of India combined), and separate conferences of working class women continue to be held. Two radical women's magazines are now in existence, and new left-feminist organizations have been started. General conferences of workers and agricultural labourers invariably now feature some themes of 'women's liberation', perhaps songs, perhaps speakers. There have been protest marches by slum women against rape and by middle class women against obscenity in films. In Delhi, recently, college students took a bold new step in organizing demonstrations against the continuing brutal harassment of women in buses and public places and vociferously chose to protest a university 'personality contest' that was a thinly disguised beauty contest sponsored by a multi-national soda pop company at the whim of a famous movie star. Some may recall that the first agitation of American radical women was against the 'Miss America' contest; the Delhi protest was in no way an attempt to imitate that, but arose out of the same outrage at being made objects of pleasure for a decadent imperialist culture. It can almost be said, with all this going on, that 'women's liberation' has become part of the national progressive consciousness in India more than ever before, and a good deal of this is an indirect outgrowth of the mobilizing efforts of 1975.

Yet still people are saying, 'There is no real women's movement,' or, as my mother-in-law puts it, 'Not even an ounce. Only in the cities, not in the villages, and only in a few towns and cities at that . . . '

How is this? And why? What is the cause of the current frustration many feel and what are the bases for moving ahead? First, to get some sense of the reality of the situation, it might be helpful to examine the current situation of the women described in the book.

I have written about many individual urban and rural working class women chosen partly because they themselves stood out in my memory and partly to illustrate the varying situations of such women: Kaminibai, Bhagubai, Tanubai, Tarabai, Gorabai, Bhuribai. Of these, **Kaminibai** was perhaps the most 'typical' of the majority of rural women in being uninvolved in any movement — militant, potentially a leader and ready for action, but unorganized. She remains so. Neither the organizing of agricultural labourers nor the women's liberation movement have really touched Yeotmal district let alone her village of Bori Arab.

Bhagubai and **Tanubai** of the tumultuous, movement-affected northern area of Ahmednagar district also remain in about the same situation they were four years ago. The union at Kathod Farm goes on and Tanubai with it remains involved in the movement (there was a women's day meeting in this area, in a nearby town) but only peripherally, without her singing talents being fully utilized. A new Lal Nishan drama troup has been formed, but without Tanubai — and while this in itself represents an important new thrust at cultural work in the rural areas and includes in its work the themes of caste and sexual oppression, it is the only one I know of in the entire state and could be compared with the twenty or so such groups I have records of from the 1920s when the peasant based non-Brahman movement was spreading to the villages its attack against casteism. Relative to the scope of the problem and even past efforts, in other words, such things seem strikingly weak. Bhagubai's union has also not recovered its previous strength; in fact the whole left movement in Ahmednagar appears stagnated, having proved incapable of consolidating the gains of famine period militancy and moving ahead. This is also true of many (perhaps most) areas of relatively strong agricultural labourer organizing, for instance Thanjavur (mentioned in Chapter 1) where the farm workers' union based on Dalits continues to be militant but has been unable to unite with non-Dalit labourers or poor peasants of various castes. Both in the case of Ahmednagar and Thanjavur, the rural unions proved incapable of effective action in the face of conditions under the Emergency or of moving ahead since.

Gorabai, the Devadasi who spoke at the final conference in Pune, is perhaps another example of a woman left 'hanging'. She was brought to a discussion conference held in Pune last February but for nearly half the time refused to talk at all about the problems of Devadasis on the grounds that nothing had been done to change the situation since the last time she had spoken before a mass of women. The girls of poor Dalit families of southern Maharashtra and Karnataka continue to be sacrificed in their tens of thousands to the goddess Yelamma and the god Capital, and if the fate of women in Ahmednagar illustrates the problems of stagnation in the class movement, the fate of these girls and Gorabai's disillusionment shows the weakness of the attack on religious superstition.

And the situation of all these women shows the root weakness of the organization of the rural poor. Some agricultural labour unions can be organized in enclaves and on big capitalist farms. The left parties are capable of mobilizing people for conferences or huge marches, with the CPI recently putting on a tremendous show by bringing some 500,000 farm labourers to Delhi for a 'March on Parliament' and LNP doing a small version with 3-4,000 labourers and workers in Bombay. But this is all. The unions themselves remain relatively weak at the local level, as the case of Bhagubai and the Agricultural University illustrates; they frequently continue to flounder on the rocks of caste discrimination and are often limited to one caste group of agricultural labourers, as in Thanjavur; and even when they exist it is only in enclaves, unable to reach the majority of the rural poor or halt the ongoing marginalization of the workers, and especially of the women, thus leaving people like Kaminibai unorganized and the parents of Gorabai, and all who sell their daughters into slavery, untouched by any alternatives. The poor peasants and landless labourers, among whom Dalits, *adivasis* and women are prominent workers, are the potential vanguard of the revolutionary movement in the rural areas. They are capable of leading a fight not simply for higher wages but against caste divisions, against the religious superstitions that ravage poor communities, against male oppression and habits like drink that ravage poor families. Ultimately, they could spearhead the struggle for revolutionary political power itself, taking up the challenge of the peasant revolt at Naxalbari. But so far this potential has hardly been felt, much less realized.

The result is that women such as Kaminibai, Tanubai, Bhagubai, Gorabai are all, in a crucial way, women who have been let down by the left. They are representative of a much larger number whom the 'women's movement' has touched, but only that − brought to a conference or a rally, contacted once or twice and then never met again, or met only intermittently and without any real ability to deal with their problems. What can one say about the effects of the 'women's movement' in such cases? Perhaps some spread of consciousness, perhaps the seeds of rebellion and hope sown among the listening crowds of women that will, with opportunity, flower into rebellion. But unless someone is around to organize that rebellion and give it support, it is hard to see where it can go. So many individual as well as collective rebellions have flowered in the past, only to be crushed. It has become almost a cliche to say that the fate of women is linked to the organization of the rural poor and the agrarian revolution, but so far no one has shown how this can go forward, and concretely how the organizing of women can help it go forward.

In contrast, **Bhuribai** and **Tarabai** represent highly organized workers' movements which are making some headway in dealing not only with wages (i.e. 'economistic') issues but also moving beyond this to political and cultural issues and attempts to unify different sections of the toiling people. Tarabai's municipal workers' union remains one of the most militant unions in Pune, with periodic strikes and study conferences and contributions to rural and women's organizing, and Tarabai is still involved in all of this. Women's Day is now celebrated regularly under the auspices of the union; and a local women's group, the Savitribai Phule Mandal (named after a woman social reformer), has been established in Tarabai's housing colony. But it still remains true that this is by and large a top-down effort in which the working women themselves do not yet take initiative and it has only a fragile link with the rest of the women's movement; efforts of other Pune women to be involved in intensive organizing in the municipal workers' colonies have floundered on the rocks of dissension.

The Shramik Sanghatana continues to do the most vital mass organizing in the rural or tribal areas of Maharashtra. In terms of organization, it is a relative success story not only on economic issues but also in bringing forward the leadership of the *adivasi* toiling masses on the social and cultural front in fights against male oppression and casteism. Its most recent initiative came after a ten-day long pogrom against Dalits in five districts of Maharashtra in August 1978, when a left alliance was formed to organize an 'Equality March' against caste oppression. The March was a seven-day mobilization in which nearly 1,500 *adivasis* and other supporters walked fifty to eighty miles in several groups from the villages of Shramik Sanghatana strength to the district town of Dhule, holding village meetings and cultural programmes along the way to propagandize against the evils of caste. In 1975 the Shramik Sanghatana activists had doubted the ability of women to walk long distances and so had not brought them to the huge march in Bombay in April. But, by 1979, women were vigorous participants and comprised nearly a third of the total number, including old women and young mothers with babies, marching along, singing, shouting slogans – 'Down with casteism!' 'Long live the unity of Dalits and toilers!' 'One blow! And another! Destroy the tyranny of the bosses!' Along with this, representatives of the Sanghatana, including women, have been invariable and vital participants in various united conferences of workers, agricultural labourers, and women.

Bhuribai has been a part of all this and is now a major Shramik Sanghatana representative and spokesperson for women's liberation. When the Sanghatana decided to contest the state assembly elections in February 1978 (hoping to do so without compromising its class character, without spending much money, and relying solely on its being rooted in local organizations of the masses), she was one of two candidates. But the election results illustrate a major dilemma of the Shramik Sanghatana's organizing, for they failed rather badly. The majority of the rural poor apparently took the position that, while the Sanghatana was clearly and irrevocably *their* organization for class struggle, for 'politics' they needed something different, a 'national' political representative. The Dhule experience shows clearly that, where there is a strong mass organization, one that takes up all issues of the life of the people and not just wage problems, women play an immense role. They emerge not merely as militants but also come forward as leaders and generate themes and movements on their own. At the same time, the problems are clear: How to move from being an inspiring 'example' of organizing in one corner of the state to being a real political force? How to go ahead from a powerful symbolic march against casteism to formulating a programme and organizing a mass force to break it down? How to move from participating in women's conferences and meetings and inspiring others to really giving leadership? And, finally the question raised but not solved by Naxalbari, how to organize in a way that may lead to the establishment of the armed power of the toiling masses?

Further questions are raised by looking at the 'party women' described in the book and at the current role of the established left parties in regard to women. Here there has also been no significant change. **Ahilya** and **Mrinal**, after coming out of jail at the end of the Emergency, were both elected to parliament, with Mrinal's Socialist Party becoming a constituent of the newly formed Janata (People's) party and Ahilya's CPI(M), its firm ally. The Janata government which came to power by defeating Indira Gandhi's Congress party is the final outcome of the united 'Opposition' described in Chapter 11. It has not changed the situation of women. For various reasons prices have not risen quite as much as before, and good weather and some technological progress have resulted in better harvests with no immediate famine. But unemployment and shortages of various essential goods continue to haunt the cities and villages of India. The new government is bringing in prohibition, but there is no sign that this is working any better than it did in the US or that it is making any impact on male drunkenness, wife-beating etc. It is also bringing in a ban on cow slaughter, which means depriving those groups who eat beef (including Muslims, Christians, Dalits, *adivasis*) of one important source of protein and driving up prices of the rest. Beyond this, strikes, revolts, demonstrations and police shootings continue on an even larger scale than before the Emergency. A certain section of rich land-owners have even taken the end of the Emergency as a kind of 'green light' to open up attacks on agricultural labourers continuing to fight for their rights. The attack on the workers of the Agricultural University at Rahuri described in Chapter 5 was repeated in 1978 on a horrifying scale at the huge Pantnagar Agricultural University in north India. Police there opened fire for forty-five minutes on a peaceful demonstration of some 6,000 agricultural labourers while horrified students barricaded in their hostels watched helplessly; they killed at least fifty and stopped only when some of the students managed to climb down drainpipes and intervene; even then, they went on to burn bodies in the sugar cane fields to destroy the evidence of the slaughter. Thus the 'restoration of democracy' has meant that the workers and agricultural labourers' assertion of their re-won right to organize has been met with an increasing ferocity of ruling class violence, and in this process low caste groups, Dalits, *adivasis* and women have as usual suffered the brunt of the assault.

The fact that the left remains as divided as before continues to affect the mobilization of women. The main difference is that, whereas before, it was the CPI which was allied with the ruling party and thus tending to remain apart from united oppositional movements, now it is the CPI(M) which is so allied and therefore remains separate and prone to compromise. Thus, Ahilya and Mrinal still tend to lead some agitations but only within the framework of trying to influence Janata party policies. The Women's Anti-Price-Rise Committee came to an end with the Emergency and has not been revived since.

This may not be the most important aspect of the work of party women, however. That they will subordinate the mobilizing of women to party policy (and thus to compromising alliances) is something everyone knows. They do continue to mobilize women; the more important question is *how* they do it.

In some ways the left parties are doing more work among women than before. They have been the main groups sponsoring the various women's day programmes recently, in particular the LNP. The CPI has a new women's newsletter in Marathi. The CPI(M) recently sponsored a 'Women's Worker-Employee Conference' in Bombay and held a national conference of working women in Madras prior to its national union meeting. This is all part of the spread of consciousness about the potential force women constitute.

But what has been done remains within the framework of bureaucratic politics. Rather than building up genuine locally rooted organizations of urban or rural working class or middle class women, involving them in action and decision-making and on this basis carrying out programmes and moving from there to higher level conferences and programmes, organization is from the top down. Conferences and rallies are called, women involved in unions controlled by the party or in electoral constituencies where the party is strong are brought together, decisions are made by party leaders and then 'approved' or 'passed', and then further activities are carried out on the basis of such programmes. Sometimes this is done by one party alone, sometimes by a coalition of several parties and some independent women's groups. On such a basis, impressive numbers of women can frequently be brought out, and this whole process is often described as organizing a women's movement. In reality, it is not. Realistically, this should be called a process of *mobilizing* women not of *organizing* them. If women's own initiative gets expressed in it, it is against the weight of the party leaderships.

The problem with bureaucratic politics is that it does not organize the force of women but simply taps it, to feed its own machine, and in the process sucks it out and leaves it stagnating. Does this sound too harsh? Then consider a conference where middle class party activists give hour long speeches one after another until the exhausted working women, who have travelled long distances in hot and crowded buses and sit listening on the hard ground with their suckling babies, fall asleep from weariness. Or a two day discussion forum where women sit in occupational groups to discuss in detail their particular problems and seek to evolve a programme of action — and then resolutions previously written by the coalition of party women who have been dominant in calling the conference are simply read out and passed by acclamation without any relationship to the experiences and conclusions of the participating groups. Or a left woman politician phoning up slum neighbourhood workers to 'provide' women for a demonstration — 'it's the "in" thing these days to have poor ragged women at demonstrations — the more ragged the clothes the better,' comment the activists sarcastically. And those carrying on such forms of organizing include some who from the beginning were taking part in the very women's meetings and mobilizations I was so immersed in. It is clear that whatever hopes many expressed originally of the women's movement being organized *in a new way* have proved futile — at least so far as the established parties are concerned.

But the critiques of these practices, the resentment of bureaucratic domination for the most part have little weight because the women making them — non-party, left, middle class women — have no alternatives to offer. The new women's groups that have sprung up among them, and that continue to emerge, remain fragile, fluctuating, unable to build ongoing live contacts with the masses as groups, and liable to individualism and bureaucracy themselves.

Again, to take concrete cases will help to illuminate this. The MSSD died fairly soon after my meeting its members. The POW died during the Emergency in its original form, with all but two of the initial activists leaving, but it has been revived since as a kind of 'party front' of one of the Naxalite organizations. Critics say that there is no longer any real energizing power of militant feminism in it. There is no doubt, however, that the old POW had its impact on the left movement, and this section of the CPI(ML) itself is sponsoring local women's organizations in several areas, including in some of the villages in Andhra where it is working. But the POW is no longer what it was at the beginning.

The Purogami Stri Sanghatana (Progressive Women's Organization) of Pune has been revived after about two years of inactivity. It has held a march against the exploitation of women's bodies in films; its members are and have been involved actively in publishing a Marathi women's magazine, *Bayja* (though officially *Bayja* is unconnected with the organization). Study groups and discussions are carried on and members take part in varied local activities of women as well as more general student, civil liberties and working class activities. But as an organization it remains middle class, and though members take part in programmes with working class women, this is invariably through the local parties and unions which continue to have the only ongoing organizational contacts with the masses of women.

There are two new women's organizations in Bombay, a Samajwadi Mahila Sangh (Socialist Women's League) which up to now has functioned primarily as a discussion group but which has begun bringing out a *Feminist Network* newsletter, and the Stri Mukti Sanghatana (Women's Liberation Organization) organized recently by Chhaya, and which has its main membership strength in women close to LNP. In both cases members are overwhelmingly working class, usually employees and housewives, and individuals are involved in working class and slum organizing, but not the organizations as such. In Delhi a Samta (Equality) organization was formed last year bringing together young left women (students and employees) from all over the city; it became involved in a number of demonstrations, decided to publish a journal, *Manushi,* and fairly quickly fell apart. *Manushi* is being carried on independently (with editions simultaneously in Hindi and English) and another new organization, Stri Sangarsha (Women's Struggle) has emerged with aspirations to 'coordinate' Delhi women's activity. There may well be similar examples elsewhere.

All these groups embody a significant trend among young educated women to fight the oppression that bears down on them and a desire to link this fight with the needs of the masses of toiling women. Most of them share some form of Marxist or at least socialist ideology. But they remain middle class. This in itself would not be an inherent flaw — for there must always be a petty bourgeois section of the women's movement — but for the fact that they aspire to become organizing 'centres' for the movement and nearly always have endless debates around the question, 'how will we organize women?' In fact they are much less than organizing centres. As groups they are almost incapable of organizing anything; the conferences, marches, mass rallies and other big programmes which occur nearly always depend on the party women, with the women's groups falling into the role of providing volunteers (i.e. the temporary activists which the parties lack) and various kinds of services including contacts with the media, cultural events such as slide shows, plays and poster exhibitions and so forth. Even where an event mainly involves the middle class itself and parties and unions are not involved in mobilizing for it, the new women's groups tend not to be very useful. For example, the recent agitation against the harassment of women in Delhi was carried out by some of the women who were involved in the Samta organization, but it was not organized through Samta but rather by an *ad hoc* committee based in a particular college.

And as long as the new women's activists are limited to working through established parties for their mass contacts, they feel tremendously restricted. The problems can be illustrated with a recent example from a small town where two young college teachers (a former leading member of the Pune women's group and a male colleague) tried to organize a march of women in protest against the rape of a woman tobacco roller by the sons of some of the rich merchants of the town. The two had been holding study groups for over a year among these women, one of the most oppressed but still union-ized sections of workers (see Chapter 10), working in conjunction with the union organizers, in this case CPI and LNP. But after the rape their protest efforts got no support, and even met with opposition from the CPI, out of a desire not to shake things up and with the argument that the woman had been a prostitute ('what was she doing walking the streets at night any-way?'). With the union leadership resisting, it proved impossible to mobilize more than a handful of tobacco workers for the march, though a large number of women from a 'nomadic tribe' community of casual labourers camped near the town came out.

The situation, then, can be summarized as follows. There is a significant spread of consciousness about the oppression of women. There is a fair amount of activity continuing in the form of marches, demonstrations, sit-ins, new magazines, conferences, programmes. Middle class women, students and young employees, come together on a spontaneous basis to fight various forms of oppression, but their organizations remain in flux, hampered by in-dividualism, lack of solidarity and the absence of a common perspective. Working class and rural women respond enthusiastically to calls to fight oppression but remain unable to organize spontaneously on their own; instead they are contacted and mobilized through parties and unions, usually from above and only rarely in the form of grass roots organizations linked to locally rooted class organizing.

All of this is, nevertheless, something. It may even be argued (as Chhaya did when we once discussed the nature of activity in 1975) that the primary step of the struggle is to spread a consciousness of oppression and libera-tion among the masses and that this is what is going on. But it is not enough. It is not a 'women's movement', and in 1975 most of us really thought that we were organizing a women's movement.

Why is this? Why is there the continuing gap between those moved by an ideology of women's liberation, whether party women or independent middle class women, and the masses of toiling women who may be inspired by its themes? Do objective conditions in India make a self-generated women's liberation movement impossible after all? Are the traditionalists who say 'Western women's liberation cannot apply to our ancient Indian culture' or the Marxists who say 'separatist bourgeois feminism is not relevant to the needs of the toiling masses' right after all? Or do Indian conditions only make organizing different and difficult, and if so what is the way forward?

It is clear that there are special features of the Indian situation. Whatever one may say about the 'uniqueness of Indian culture' or the 'hold of feudal values', it is certainly true that the continuing barring of women from productive employment — the ongoing and increasing 'marginalization' of women — makes it difficult for them to fight their dependence in the family. The old Marxist cliche about 'participation in productive labour' is true to the extent that such participation, while not leading to liberation by itself, gives women a base of strength from which to fight. The fact that now over 40% of all American workers are women has undeniably provided the objective basis for the radical women's movement which challenges male chauvinism at its roots — even though this movement has not yet found a leadership to give it a real thrust forward. In contrast, the fact that work opportunities are declining in India means that there is a whole middle level of society — the section between the toiling agricultural labourers on the one hand and the upper middle class employees on the other — where women are simply stuck in the home with little alternative to dependence.

Concretely this means that the sections from which the *activists* of movements are normally drawn (organized working class, educated sons of peasant failies, lower middle class) simply cannot provide them for the women's movement. In a village or slum, the young men who may be the core of a broader mass organization (call them what you like, Youth Federation, Dalit Panthers, Young Workers' League) are free to gather almost daily for that indispensable, educational and motivating discussion of issues and theory, i.e. for political work. In contrast, their sisters and wives of equivalent class background are almost unable to come out of the home, and are bound to a father's authority or a mother-in-law's whim or simply to household tasks. Consequently, it is that much more difficult to nurture the activist core of the movement. And consequently, we find in the militant but intermittent participation in mass action by poor women under the call and domination of the upper middle class women (and male) leaders, one of the roots of bureaucracy.

Even the work of poor women, 'productive' though it may be in the classic Marxist sense, is usually different in nature from that in an industrial capitalist society. Women quite often (as poor peasants, construction workers, sugar cane cutters, road workers, etc) work alongside the men of their family, as part of a family team and are sometimes not even paid separately. For such women the defence of the family remains crucial to economic survival, let alone as a value in itself. There should be no illusions here: the family thus defended remains still an oppressive family which binds women in crucial ways, and these women feel it. But the fact is that women will still defend the husbands who hold them down, who drink and beat them, simply because they need them.

The question is not one of the degree of women's oppression, or the consciousness of women about that oppression and their readiness to fight it — but of the *form* of oppression which is one that, in India, makes organization initially extremely difficult.

This constitutes a material base explaining the lack of a spontaneously self-generating women's movement. But it does not make a genuine movement impossible. There is still scope for forming organizations of women at the grass roots level, for developing from among them leading and conscious activists, for taking a step forward in self-determination. Coming out of the house once a week for a social or political meeting; fighting for cheaper marriages and acting for the protection of couples who want to make love marriages or inter-caste marriages; organizing a march to protest rape or other atrocities; coming out on the streets on a march for water or higher wages; taking collective action against cases of individual family oppression — all of these represent a step forward that is a step towards 'women's liberation' to the degree that these are collective actions arising out of discussions and decisions by the women themselves. The major challenge to women's subordination in the family and society may be only implicit in such activities — but the crucial point is that emerging out of the household is to claim the right of participation in 'public' activities, coming together as a collective force, and beginning the process of creative self-expression, decision-making and action.

The basis for this is the fact that women are oppressed, that they know it, that they are ready to fight. Their real organization can only occur in unity with a broader class movement (a slum organization, a local union or an agricultural labourers/poor peasants' committee), but it requires a class movement ready to fight on all aspects of people's oppression and a leadership committed to building up a women's movement as an independent, self-generating force aimed at women's liberation. In such a context and with such leadership, what might be called 'base-level women's committees' can be developed. Already the beginnings of them can be seen, in places like Dhule, elsewhere in many small pockets.

These base-level organizing efforts often look small at present, and the women's groups formed in this context may seem pitifully limited in the face of the parties' ability to mobilize tens and even hundreds of thousands of working men and women. Yet I feel that it is the 'base-level women's committees' which have the potential to carry forward the mobilization of women — which now is at the stage of *agitations,* i.e. marches, demonstrations, conferences and other special events — the point of developing a true women's *movement* which will not simply involve reactions to particular atrocities or oppression, or mobilization from above by bureaucratic means, but which will have a clear leadership of its own developed out of the movement on a democratic basis with a programme and a political presence capable of rallying women around it.

Why is this? Why is it that work in one slum or a few villages *does* have a

165

political impact often greater than that of the impressive looking conferences and marches organized by the parties? The fact is that much of the parties' organization is bogus in the sense that it is not real organization but a substitute for organization by using bureaucratic methods. It is the kind of mobilizing that is in a way fostered by the existence of bourgeois democracy and falls apart in the face of a dictatorship in which oppositional organizing must really be immersed in the sea of the people and part of and arising out of the needs of their everyday lives to be effective at all; this is the reason behind the organizational weakness of the established left parties so clearly exposed during the Emergency. Particularly in regard to women, the established left parties lack activists (as Ahilya Rangnekar described in my interview in Chapter 4) not only because they are unable to inspire young middle class women but also because their methods make it impossible to develop women activists from their union bases. So they are often desperately eager to recruit from the middle class women's groups, find it necessary to ally with such groups, and at the same time remain suspicious of the very existence of these groups as an alternative centre. In this situation, a developing alliance with a linked-up core of base-level committees can exercize a crucial influence in determining the character of the movement.

What role do the aspiring middle class but Marxist women's groups have in this process? An important one, as long as they do not attempt to become organizing 'centres' in and of themselves. First, their contacts with students and white collar employees can be developed as a kind of mass work itself — mass work among particular sections of exploited women. Students' groups among women, working in the general context of college or neighbourhood organizations, can function as 'base-level committees' similar to those in the slums or villages. Frequently, this kind of work at present is obstructed by the tendencies to dogmatism and exclusivism among the new women's groups and even by their guilt feelings at being middle class and their yielding to pressure that 'only working class women count', but it can be and in some areas is being developed.

Aside from this, such groups can function as informal link and communications (not 'coordinating') groups, for they will always include some members doing active and even full-time mass work. They can provide crucial 'service' functions for base-level work: helping with publicity and media contacts, rallying support when necessary for a particular case of repression or confrontation, providing resources, doing cultural work of all kinds from running magazines to organizing singing and drama troupes. And in fact this is the kind of activity they are most usefully doing at present.

All of this process, of course, requires a revolutionary left leadership (as does the problem of organizing the rural poor in general, mentioned earlier). So the question is how the revolutionary left views the issue of women's liberation. A good trend at present among the left is its openness to new analysis, rethinking, taking seriously such previously ignored issues as the oppression of lower castes and women, experimenting with new forms of practice and organization. But too often the revolutionary left in India as

166

well tends, like traditional Marxists elsewhere, to respond to women's issues with 'but women must be part of the general revolutionary movement', 'women's struggle must be linked to that of the oppressed masses', 'women should not be separatist, etc. But this is not at issue (and in any case those who say these kinds of things don't even really mean that 'the women's movement must be linked to the general movement' and so forth; what they are actually saying is that 'it must be linked to our party and proceed under the leadership of our party').

The question is not whether the women's movement will be 'linked' to the general movement. It *is* irrevocably linked to the revolutionary organizing of all the oppressed — to the extent that it is built as a movement at all. 'Women's liberation is a part of social revolution' does not mean that it *should* be a part. It *is,* and there should be no reason to fear and every reason to lead the building up of the 'autonomous' force of women fighting their oppression. The women's movement only becomes strong by organizing the force of the masses of toiling women. And in the lives of these women — whether peasants or factory workers or agricultural labourers, Brahmans or Marathas or Dalits or Adivasis, Whites or Blacks or Chicanos — *all* the issues of economic and social, racial and sexual, and caste and class (in the narrow sense) oppression are bound together, they cannot confront one without gathering strength to confront them all. 'Bourgeois feminism' is not to be criticized so much because it leads the women's movement in the wrong direction as because it cannot lead the women's movement at all — just as the left sectarianism of many Marxist groups fails to lead it. (Hence, in the US, the failure of women to halt the right-wing onslaught against the Equal Rights Amendment and abortion rights is the failure both of a 'bourgeois feminist' leadership that cannot take the movement to the working classes who alone can really give it strength, and of the left which has too little presence in this movement.) Bourgeois feminism cannot organize this force of women; neither can revisionism. Economism fails to take account of it at all; bureaucratism saps out its strength to give a glow to party machines; class collaborationism links what little movement there is to debilitating alliances with bourgeois political parties. Indeed, one test of the extent to which a revolutionary left can overcome all these evils is the degree to which women and the issues presented by women's oppression are really a part of the movement.

The process of moving towards a women's movement really is beginning, though only beginning. And the issues seem more urgent every day. This very day, as I write, has come a story in the *Times of India* of the horrifying custom of burning women. No, not traditional *sati*, modern commercialism. Young wives in wealthy industrialist and merchant families (Marwari or Gujarati by caste, i.e. the most 'traditional' of Hindus) who have come to their husbands' homes with dowries of 50,000 rupees or more, are deliberately killed by their husbands and in-laws because they cannot bring in continuing money; then the men can marry again and collect more money. And they are killed by having kerosene poured over them and being burned to death because this makes it most difficult to find evidence distinguishing it from accidental death. There were an estimated 350 such deaths in Delhi in 1975, International Women's Year. And when I tell this to my mother-in-law, a thousand miles to the south in the village of Kasegaon, she says, 'Yes, that happens. They burn women. It happened to one of my students, and it happened to Ramchand Shet's wife's sister's daughter . . . '

And in nearby Kolhapur, an amazingly energetic woman from a Dalit family – obviously upwardly mobile, the husband a tailor, one son an LL.B, eight children in all – tells us, half-weeping as she makes tea, about her daughter in hospital. The girl, educated to 'matric', had just been married with a relatively large dowry (new for this community) and had fallen sick with typhoid as a result, according to her mother, of the neglect and harassment of her in-laws. 'It cost us 500 rupees to go down and take her home. And such a fine girl. She could hardly even walk, hardly move, she was so sick. Now we're not going to give her back to them. We'll educate her, let her have employment, forget about marriage . . . '

The horrors remain. And the hope. But it is time for an organized women's movement.

Gail Omvedt
Kasegaon
22 April 1979

Appendices

Appendix 1: Draft Manifesto of the Progressive Organization of Women (POW)

The concept of the Indian woman as an equal partner of man and as an active participant in all walks of life has never been so clearly shattered as today. We have, on the one hand, our constitution mouthing pious platitudes about the equality of women, and a few women scattered here and there as leaders; and on the other hand, the terrible conditions of the majority of Indian women. To people who talk of Sita and Savitri, we talk of harsh, depressing reality.

Eighty seven out of every hundred women cannot read or write. The horrible practices of prostitution, child marriage, *purdah* and dowry have cut at the very root of the dignity of women. Feudal culture preaches to women seclusion at home and restriction from active participation in public life. Increasingly penetrating foreign culture, on the other hand, has reduced women to nothing more than decorative sex objects. Obscenity in art and literature is rampant. Aggressive male supremacy has led to the sickening practice of Eve-teasing, and one step further, rape. Some of us are not allowed to work for our own living, while others who work on a par with men are not treated on the basis of equal pay for equal work. The position of the housewife is no better. Confined to her home, working from morning to night at backbreaking chores, she has neither independence nor dignity.

These are just a few of the facts of the exploitation and domination of women. All of us know, through our day-to-day experience, what it is to be a woman — what it is to be regarded as something less than a human being. To achieve the objective of ending this age-old oppression, we must understand why we should support and unite with each other, what are the forces that can unite with us, what are the forces that oppose us, what is the line of action that we should take. What is it, then — the nature of this age-old oppression of women?

Nature of Oppression

What are the pillars on which the inferior status of women rests?

a) Economic dependence: About 72% of Indian women are not economi-

169

cally independent. Even if they work outside, it is only as a secondary source of income for the family. The centuries-old economic dependence on man is the base for all sexual, cultural and political domination. Even though women work at home, this labour is not paid for – this is private labour power, not social – and this gives rise to the low status of women in society.

b) Household drudgery (or the division of labour): Women have been, for centuries, isolated in the home, forced to carry out work that is considered unskilled. Because her work day is unending, because there is no one else to look after the children, to wash the clothes, to cook the meals, the woman is isolated from all public activities. Education and work, both are impossible for her, because of the back-breaking chores at home. Excluded from the world of productive labour giving rise to economically visible objects, the woman has become the invisible worker whose work cannot be valued. Thus the woman is practically a slave (slavery by the definition of modern economists = the power of disposing of the labour power of others).

c) Ideology of oppression: The concept of economic dependence and the division of labour is the economic base. But how do the oppressors justify these? Just as slavery, imperialism and fascism give rise to innumerable theories intended to demonstrate the inferiority of the oppressed peoples and justify genocide, an impressive number of theories have been designed and implemented to keep women 'in their place'.

The sex stereotype is not due to basic biological differences but due to the thousands of years in which the division of labour has prevailed, and men and women were conditioned to this ideology of male supremacy. Participating with others in the production of a car or an aeroplane (social production) is not the same thing as using, in isolation, the same broom in the same few square feet of kitchen (private production).

Confined to the narrow limits of the home, the girl child receives pots, pans, dolls, mirrors etc as toys. She is taught to imitate her mother, to learn the art of housekeeping, and to prepare for marriage. She is taught that clinging tendencies, meekness, decorativeness, and a pathological fear of independence are feminine, and she is further degraded. Little wonder today that women behave nearly always as they are expected to!

The oppression of women is universal, and the women of all classes face it. Take, for example, the young girls in school and college. Their education is either totally neglected or treated as secondary. Mostly from a middle class background, they are cloistered in the home and classroom. There is hardly any freedom of movement. Cafeterias, cinemas and walks are prohibited unless adequately chaperoned. For them, the day closes by 5.30 p.m. Even though education has opened new horizons for them, even these horizons are limited.

Take another example – working women. Though the Government of India has ratified the ILO Convention concerning 'equal pay for men and women workers for work of equal value' in 1958, it has not been implemented in most industries. Employers purposely use women as a source of cheap labour. Whenever their wages are brought on a par with men workers, they are thrown out of their jobs. Besides which, employers have to incur additional expenditure in the shape of maternity benefits and maintenance of creches, etc. This attitude towards women workers, their employment, their working conditions, and the social discrimination like unequal wages etc will continue so long as the present social system based on exploitation exists.

Reason for Oppression

One important and puzzling question is whether women have always been oppressed. If the oppression was not inborn in women, how did it arise at all?

History tells us that women were not always oppressed. In the stage of society called primitive communal, men hunted and fished, while women cared for the sprawling households and the handicrafts. At that time women had equal status, because all production was social. While men hunted together, women cooked together. Households were communal, and so were 'families'. When the mode of production slowly changed, when agriculture was discovered and man settled on land, the concept of private property (as distinct from communal property) slowly arose. With this, lands, animals and children came to be owned by men. This in short is the origin of the oppression of women.

Struggles of Women

After 27 years of independence, we have seen that the promises made by our rulers have been deceptive. Women, like Harijans, came out strongly in the struggle for independence. But just as 'freedom' has brought more discrimination, more torture and killings to the Harijans, it has brought more exploitation and suppression for the women. But this is only one side of the coin. On the other side, we see that women all over India are realizing the true nature of the system, and are breaking the chains of feudal exploitation. In the struggle for land, in the workers' just struggles for better living conditions, women have been in the forefront. More recently, we have seen the women of Gujarat, Bihar and Maharashtra participating actively in the movement against corruption, scarcity of essential commodities and sky-rocketing prices.

We are aware of the forms and nature of oppression of women. Since ages, women have been protesting, both individually and socially. What is the path to emancipation?

One thing we must remember is that any solution for the emancipation of an oppressed strata of society — say, women — must be radical and universal. Radical, because it must hit at the root cause of oppression, and cannot stop at reforms, and universal, because it must genuinely encompass the masses of women.

Way to the Emancipation of Women

a) Economic independence of women: For women to be economically independent, the precondition is that we should enter into social production. For the majority of women already in social production, the dignity of labour should be restored. But in these days of chronic unemployment, if women join the labour force the result will surely be the swelling of the ranks of the unemployed. Because a few people should gain immense profits, a vast army of unemployed is maintained to keep wages low. The answer to this problem is not that women should remain at home, but that both men and women should fight against exploitation and for socialism. It is clear that only in a socialist society, where the factories and the lands are in the hands of the people who plan production according to their needs, is the emancipation of women possible.

b) Removal of household drudgery: When women come out of their narrow, individualized spheres of labour and take part in social production, the work at home becomes a double burden. Household work should be shared by the couple, and cheap and efficient restaurants, creches, childcare centres and laundries should be created. But, in our society, restaurants and laundries are built not for the working people, but to satisfy the luxurious tastes of the upper classes. Maternity facilities are not provided in farms and factories, because employers care only for profits. Only in a socialist society, where industry and agriculture serve the toiling people and not private profiteers, where profits go not to fill the coffers of millionaires but to create cheap and efficient services for the people, can the emancipation of women be possible.

c) Ideology of equality: Along with the base of economic dependence and private work at home, the superstructure of male dominance should also be destroyed. Women should be encouraged to participate in all walks of life, and their potentialities in all spheres should be developed. Socialism, being the ideology of the oppressed classes, will also create the necessary and genuine climate for the equality of women.

The Role of Women
Women's struggle for emancipation is thus a very important component of the general struggles of the people for emancipation and towards socialism. Hence, the women have a direct, leading role to play in educating, organizing, and mobilizing women on their own demands, whether they be that of middle class women, college students, or working women. The majority of Indian women are slaves of slaves — they are slaves to the men who themselves are slaves to this exploitative economic system. It is thus necessary that we women take a direct, leading role in organizing the masses of women in their struggles for a better life and a changed system.

For this, it is of utmost importance that there be a broad-based genuine women's organization. The Progressive Organization of Women (POW) must and will fulfil this. Hence the POW shall:
1. Create a broad consciousness for upholding the dignity of women and fight for their emancipation.
2. Uphold and propagate scientific socialism.
3. Resolutely fight against feudal economy and culture that mainly oppresses women.

4. Support and unite with the toiling masses in their struggles against foreign domination and exploitation.
5. Support and unite with the toiling masses in their struggle against corruption and black marketeering and against the monopoly houses.
6. Support and unite with the students' demands for a scientific and production-oriented education system.
7. Resolutely fight against all forms of injustice, social oppression and repression.

As immediate demands, the POW:

1. Demands legislation against (a) prostitution, (b) obscene art depicting women as degrading sex objects.
2. Demands the enforcement of the legislation against (a) dowry and (b) child marriage.
3. Demands that daughters shall have an equal share of both earned and inherited property.
4. Demands implementation of the laws for equal pay, for equal work, maternity and creche facilities.
5. Demands better facilities for working women and students in the form of better and more hostels, cheap restaurants, etc.
6. Shall fight against corruption, black market hoarding, and for regular supply of essential commodities.

Conclusion

Let us not forget that we are all responsible citizens of India. So long as the wretchedness of a prostitute's life exists, so long as marriage remains a chattel auction, so long as children go to bed hungry, so long as an illiterate people grope for knowledge, so long as India remains in the grip of foreign domination, so long as poverty, hunger and famine stalk the land, so long as the dignity of women remains mere platform rhetoric, we women of India cannot afford to remain quiet. We women cannot afford to remain in our traditional passivity and feminine inactivity. Our duty is to rise, protest and struggle.

We proclaim solidarity with all women!
We proclaim solidarity with all oppressed classes!

Progressive Organization of Women
(Hyderabad-Secunderabad)
1974

Appendix 2: Manifesto of the Mahila Samta Sainik Dal

Many times tidal waves of equality have come to this country, but not a single one of them has reached the shore. The main reason is that half the population has remained isolated from this fight. While fighting for equality, the slaves who needed it did not feel the need as badly as they should have.

Unless women, who are enslaved by the social structure and are the support of the social structure, change, the fight for equality will not be complete. Such is our opinion. So we are proclaiming the fight for equality and we are determined to become soldiers in the fight.

The social structure of India has been based from the beginning on inequality. In this country society is divided into *jati* and *varna*; because of this, distinctions of superior and inferior are made among human beings. Many castes and groups exist here in different forms and carry on marriage and social interaction within the caste only. Human desires and hopes, ideals and actions are limited by this ideology. People are labelled by their caste and crippled and enslaved. Therefore, until the caste system is torn up from the roots, the caste ideology which discriminates among people will not die. Complete equality will not be established; this is our firm opinion. The caste system has been constructed by a handful of selfish people for their own interest. We have become soldiers to destroy it.

It is the custom here to nourish this slavery under the name of religion. It is this religion which has enslaved women. The holy books have carried through this way of thinking. These holy books, which made women and *shudras* inferior and deprived us of education, knowledge and independence, are selfish. We are sure that they were written to profit by the exploitation of others. All these books were written by men and have enslaved women. Therefore, we don't take Rama, who made his pregnant wife Sita leave his house, as our ideal. 'Your ideal father' who gave birth to and promulgated the custom of veiling, is not our ideal.

Buddha, the great one, was the first to free women from slavery. Women's fight for liberation begins from here; Lord Buddha is the commander of this fight. We are the heirs of Mahatma Phule. One hundred and twenty five years ago he began the fight for emancipation, making education available to women and asking the question of equality to the entire patriarchal culture: if your wife dies, will you become a *sati*? Savitribai is our ideal mother. She sacrificed her life in establishing the right of women to education and in fighting against the atrocities of society and the phony religious men and so-called leaders of foolish thought. We honour as our ideal Babasaheb Ambedkar, who presented the historic Hindu Code Bill to the Parliament and resigned his ministerial post when there was opposition to it, who gave us full public equality with men and gave legal form to our rights. Ramamata, Karve and Shinde, who gave education to child widows even when religious frauds opposed women's freedom, are the warriors of liberation. Taking these as our model, we are starting our journey.

It is evident that men decide everything about how women should act, how they should live, and what fashions they should wear. The selfish trick behind this is the idea that women should sacrifice everything for men. We do not accept the traditional belief that women have no intelligence of their own. A woman is not simply a female. The idea of *pativrata* [devotion to the husband] is based on the purity of a single organ. Here also no importance is given to the woman's mind. It is our opinion that women, like men, should also be evaluated by their intelligence. The idea of family purity is decided not on the basis of the purity of a special organ of men but only on the basis of the purity of a special organ of women and so she is locked up inside the house. The male caste has done a gross injustice to women by this mistrust. It is our firm opinion that men have kept women deprived of freedom and apart from knowledge and have made them slaves only for sexual pleasure. Up to now we haven't even been given the right to choose our own life-partners. Education is given only up to marriage. Marriage is held up as our only aim. If love is expressed, bullets are shot as if we were animals. All this is pure hypocrisy.

No matter what the reason for any conflict, women become victims in the end. We condemn the tendency to commit atrocities on women for satisfaction of revenge in wars, conflicts, hatred, malice. It is not necessary to treat women as inferior because they have accepted the responsibility of bearing children. The stripping naked of women in Sirasgaon, the public humiliation of Pushpa Nikam, the atrocities against women in Brahmangaon and Nilanga are all like a man assaulting his own mother, so we feel. We defy the selfish religious books and organizations which spread the perverted belief that woman is a thing for 'enjoyment' by men who are superior in religion, caste, race and country.

Men who shout that 'freedom does not mean free sex' are phony. This discrimination of intelligence is made to keep women dependent on men. Behind it is the assumption that women have no mind of their own. This is an indication of mistrust in womankind. The dowry custom is a trade in women done by men. The bride's party and the groom's party are the dealers in this marriage market. Young men who ask for dowries show bourgeois behaviour. This is an effort to squeeze the bride's side for revenge. We condemn the parents of the bride and the young men who have no faith in their own ability for not recognizing the existence of women, and we hail the young men who have declared a revolt against this custom.

Prostitution is an insult to women. The social structure which forces a woman to sell her body in order to feed her stomach is to blame. It is the woman's misfortune that she is sacrificed to the social order. Our frank opinion is that this option has been held open to women by society and the patriarchal culture only for economic reasons. When specific castes are made penniless and their women are made prostitutes, it is pure hypocrisy to say that prostitution is a necessity of society. We pity those sisters who prove sociology in following this path. That is why we think it is of the utmost necessity to change the entire social structure.

This hypocritical society has made us worship the men who have made us slaves. The strange custom exists that the slaves themselves are given the job of protecting slavery. We have to fight against the thoughts of Manu which treat women and *shudras* as inferior, against the caste system which sticks the label of *karma* on everything, against god who puts woman among the untouchables, and against the ideology of natural inequality. But while we are burning up all these thoughts, some slaves (sisters) are fighting to protect them. This is our mental slavery. We are eagerly getting equipped in this fight for equality. We are moving forward with knowledge, condemning caste, religion, race, superstition. Unless we change, turmoil and inequality will not end in this country. Two hundred and eighty million women should lead the fight for equality. There is one trend of thinking that if women change, the whole family structure will collapse. The relation between men and women is a natural one: both should take this into consideration and strive to reach this goal. These goals and institutions will have meaning only when the patriarchal culture accepts women's rights. It is not necessary to mourn if this social structure dies which deprives 280 million women of education, wealth, knowledge, freedom and rights.

Positions have been given to women only in some particular fields of employment such as secretaries, typists, salesgirls and air hostesses. Otherwise, their helplessness has been taken advantage of many times. We are ready to stand against this. Science has proved that women can work equally with men. It is our opinion that there should be no limits to their education and employment. Likewise there should be no books in the curriculum which treat women as inferior and give rationales for inequality. Those writers who try to picture the ideal woman and show old men walking down the aisle with a girl their daughter's age and recommend polygamy are all bourgeois. Against all this we hope that youth will stand up and give us help in this fight.

Indian women have to struggle to gain the rights which are given them in the Constitution. It should not be thought that women's education is progressing just because the girls of one caste are being educated. What can we say about the women in those communities where even the men are not educated? In Maharashtra at least, you don't see a non-Brahman woman in any field. That is why it is necessary to speed up women's education by campaigning and propagandizing. It is necessary to make efforts in this direction to change the situation. Today 80% of women are illiterate. Is this equality?

Whether a country is democratic or not is said to depend on the degree of personal freedom. We are 280 million slaves and along with Dalits and *adivasis* we make up 70 to 80% of the people. How then can 25% show the freedom of the country? Those who rebel against slavery, the Dalits who aim for freedom, the *adivasis* and toilers are our brothers. We are battling for equality along with men in the liberation war for human liberation called for by Dr Ambedkar. This is history. And so we wish every success to the workers in the American women's liberation movement and to Angela Davis and to the women's liberation army.

Sisters, understand these principles and become members of the Mahila Samta Sainik Dal.

Mahila Samta Sainik Dal
(League of Women Soldiers for Equality)
Aurangabad, April 1975
(Translated from Marathi)

Appendix 3: 'So that my mother may be convinced . . . '

by Namdev Dhasal

A body broken down for seven generations,
Gentle mother, your feet haven't travelled through
    ten continents,
You never, never, never could leave your village world.

Throughout life you carried, with your eyes shut, the
    burden of Devout Wife.
With no other way, you read again and again the stones
    and boulders.
Without speaking, you took the heirloom mantle of
    Chaste Wife.
You wore the long, long robes of the Married Woman.
All your life, you have put patches on your heart,
                on your pride in living,
                on the clothes on your body,
                on your home.
In your prime, you became weak, naive,
                a tethered cow.

Mother, you never understood:
This land does not value the woman, the Shudra, the worker,
    the landless.
Today your son, in his twenties, stumble-shuffling,
Of whom you made an elephant from a grain of sand,
Enduring the hot winds of poverty and hard times,
Whom you fed grains of rice while your own stomach pinched,
Whom you nurtured, making a lamp of your eyes and a cradle
    of your arms,
Whom you protected in the stress of life as one protects
    a sore on the palm of the hand,
Mother, he, your favourite, has rebelled against this
    culture, this tradition, this custom, this thought and
    these justifiers of the status quo.
Now, you are exhausted, shaken.
You cry, instead of placing a helmet on my head.
Mother, all that is unnecessary.
Mother, your son is not a child.
He is the son of this age's rebellion.
He can see clearly the injustice, himself as victim.
Governmental machinery, means of living, power of toil,
    mines of coal and iron, warehouses, factories –
    there: protection, guarantee of food and money.
My face, lying in the dust, separated from all of this.

Mother, as your ancestors have not given you anything,
So you have not given me anything.

You haven't taught me the wise ways of history.
Father has drunk the liquor of this system and is intoxicated.
Mother, you have drunk the water of ignorance and are
    finished.
Like an ordinary woman, you dream of a son's married life.
In your mind you have a grandson, plump as the child on
    the Amul milk tin,
        a one-in-a-million daughter-in-law,
        a little bird's house, with you
        looking after everything with your old eyes.
In your pitty-petty mind, resounded kisses and overflowing
    love.
In the end, a peaceful death, while you still wear *kum kum*
    in never-ending bliss.

Mother, remember your troubled life.
The start of your life —
That day you were a new bride, anointed with turmeric,
Coming ceremoniously to your father-in-law's house.
How many wishes, how many hopes were in your mind?
From then to now — dragged through life.
Mother, doesn't it gnaw you?
How can you so easily drop a curtain over the atrocities
    of those long years?
Can you tell me the purpose, the reasons for these atrocities?
All your life you were sucked dry and even now you bow before
    the system.
Your natural fearlessness, your willing toil, your
    ability to make decisions,
Your wanting to learn new techniques of production,
Your prominent place in individual development, public
    development,
Your faith in freedom, your part in national defence,
Your accomplishments in all of this,
All of this vanished when man came to know the use of land.
The male dominated culture kept you bound to kitchen
    and children,
Gave you secondary status.
You were seen as machinery for the production of worms.
Your natural being, your gift of giving colour to masculinity,
    fell into slavery.

Mother, your woman's life story lives in a house in my heart.
It makes me see you clearly.
That's why I don't kill you, don't rip out your innards.
Because — just as I have been stripped bare, so have you.
Both of us have been stripped bare by the same one.
I want to rip out his innards.

At this moment, mother, I need you.

Please understand me.
Mother, we are separated from our origins,
And all people like us have lost our identity.
The circumstances which brought these times to you, my
    father, all of us,
Mother, I want control over these circumstances.
Long before we can effectively confront our enemy
You must trust me.
I am going through all this for happiness and a high
    standard of living.
O mother of poverty, don't think my hardship is trivial.
Look, poverty is at the door.
Don't come in my way with love and affection.
Don't forecast defeat for the weapon which the 20th century
    has put into your son's hands.
A weapon increases respectability!
We had no history. A weapon will create history!
Mother, I don't need your love and barren affection.
I need your faith, I need your sacrifice.
Mother, we don't have any right to even this petty,
    simple life.
I need the payment money to get those rights.
Mother, today, tell me the stories of that payment.

In the 18th century the whole human race was turned upside
    down,
But even today you haven't heard of it.
You don't know the chronology of the buying and selling of
    human beings,
You don't know the nations and the John Hawkinses who
    traded in slaves,
You don't know that on 21 January 1793 the guillotine was
    raised and before thousands of people Louis XVI was
    beheaded,
You don't know the terrible massacre in history
        don't know the revolutionary year of 1848
        don't know Baboeuf who brought the torch of liberty.

Mother, the day that you cut my umbilical cord, why didn't
    you slash my throat with your fingernails?
Today you are terrified just thinking of my torment,
                terrified of my imprisonment, the future noose.
Mother, I can't tolerate this cool death.
Please understand all this.
The 20th century has given eyes to your son;
He will lead you on the path of plenty.
Even if he falls on the battlefield, say with pride,
    'He was mine.'
He will create wise economists,
He will re-shape the land,

He will produce the things that the people need.
You yourself used to say, 'O Lord, give me a strong son who
    will put his banner on top of the three worlds.'
Mother, think of me like that.
Mother, you have been sucked dry all your life.
You didn't moo even once from the depths,
You didn't stir the sky with a shrill cry,
The earth did not crack.
How easily you lived, wrapped in rhinoceros hide.
Mother, I cannot put on the hide of a rhinoceros.
I have become aware of exploitation and I have lost myself.
The bliss of life in blinkers!
I have become Satan.
When I see women selling their bodies or begging in the
    bazaar,
Mother, I think of you.
Mother, what has this country given to you, this country
    which teaches begging and incest?
Mother, be the support for my weapon.
O mother of poverty, make me free for the new world.

You have become bent thinking of my execution.
If you crumble to dust at this crucial moment
Then I'll have to walk over your inert body.
Mother, please don't make me master of that deed.

Translated from Marathi by
Jayant Karve, Vidyut Bhagwat,
Eleanor Zelliot.

Glossary

adivasi: Literally, 'original inhabitant', the term used for themselves by tribal people, that is, those communities who have been on the whole outside the orthodox caste system, living in the hilly and moutainous areas and practising hunting and gathering or shifting cultivation in pre-British times.

a-ga: 'Say, you' (familiar form for women), a way of hailing someone.

a-ho: 'Say, you' (polite form for both men and women).

anna: One-sixteenth of a rupee in the old coinage, but still common in peasant speech.

a-re: 'Say, you' (familiar form for men).

bai: 'Woman'; lower class term, used as a polite form of reference and added as a suffix to the personal names of adult women.

bhakri: The unleavened bread, made from a kind of millet, that is the staple food of Maharashtrian peasants. *Jawari bhakri* is made from *jawar,* a particular kind of millet; *lal bhakri* from American-provided *milo* or sorghum.

Bhil: The largest tribal group of Maharashtra.

Brahman: The highest of the four *varnas,* traditionally priests, intellectuals, administrators or landlords. There are many separate castes of Brahmans in India.

caste: A group of people who have a traditional profession and are supposed to inter-marry and eat only with each other. Castes are ranked, within traditional Hinduism, in a hierarchy according to the degree to which they and their traditional duties are considered pure or polluting. Caste identity continues to be hereditary even though people leave their traditional profession.

Congress Party: Formerly known as the Indian National Congress, the main party which led the independence movement in India and afterwards became the governing party.

CPI: Communist Party of India. Name for the original united party which was, after a 1964 split, kept by the pro-Moscow section. Still the largest party (550,000 members).

CPI(M): Communist Party of India (Marxist). After the 1964 split, the more pro-China group took the name of CPI(M). Second largest communist party (about 100,000 members) and dominates in the traditional com-

181

munist stronghold of West Bengal, where it currently (1979) forms the government. At present it considers both China and Russia to be 'revisionist' but generally follows the Russian line in foreign affairs; it condemns the theory of 'peaceful transition' but remains absorbed in parliamentarism.

CPI(ML): Communist Party of India (Marxist-Leninist). Formed in April 1969 as a pro-Chinese party after the Naxalbari armed revolt, mainly by cadres who had come out of the CPI(M). At present it is split into many sections, some of which call themselves CPI(ML), others of which use different names ('Organizing Committee for CPI(ML)' etc). It is impossible to estimate membership since it has been primarily illegal and most sections still function underground.

Dalit: Literally, 'downtrodden', the term now preferred by militant untouchables (particularly in Maharashtra) for themselves.

Dalit Panthers: Militant organization of Dalit youth formed in 1970, mainly based on the Buddhist-Mahars but with some influence elsewhere. It has, like almost all Indian political organizations, experienced splits.

daru: Alcohol or country liquor, in Maharashtra made from sugar cane.

dharma: Religious duty; as defined by traditional orthodox Hinduism, a man's *dharma* centres on following his father's caste profession and a woman's *dharma* is to obey her husband within the context of the same.

devadasi: Literally, 'slave of god', used for girls vowed to temples as temple servants; in modern times these mainly become commercial prostitutes.

gherao: Literally, 'to surround'. A technique of class struggle used by workers, peasants and women in which an individual enemy is pinpointed and surrounded by the people and held as a kind of captive until he or she (but nearly always the officials, managers and industrialists are men) gives in to demands, or until the police break up the *gherao.*

Green Revolution: Term used for the effort to raise agricultural production through the use of new seed varieties, fertilizers and other technologies.

Jan Sangh: Right-wing party emphasizing the glories of Hindu culture and the necessity of creating strength and solidarity among Hindus. Its main social base is among merchants and upper castes and in north India.

Janata Party: Literally 'People's Party', formed by the coming together of the Jan Sangh, Socialists, some rich peasant-based parties, some ex-Congress Party members and many smaller parties after the ending of the Emergency in 1977; it is now the governing party in India.

jati: The Indian term for 'caste'.

ksatriya: The second highest of the four *varnas,* traditionally warriors and rulers.

kum kum: Red powder used to mark a woman's forehead, considered a sign of beauty and good fortune.

left: A term loosely used in this book to refer to all organizations and individuals with some link with the working class and professing some form of Marxist or socialist ideology.

LNP: Lal Nishan or 'Red Flag' Party, a communist party existing only in

Maharashtra, formed in 1965 from a group that had existed as a separate communist organization from the 1940s; has a strong union base among urban and rural workers and inclines to be pro-China in its international line, though it differs from the Naxalites in its analysis of Indian society and on the question of armed struggle.

Magowa: Name of a political organization of young people which formed around a Marxist magazine, *Magowa,* after 1970 and which brought together those inclined towards communism but critical of the established parties and disillusioned with the Naxalites. Has contained various trends; dissolved in 1975 two months before the proclamation of Emergency. Its members organized loose coalitions of young people *(Magowa mandals)* throughout Maharashtra, and worked in the Shramik Sanghatana of Dhule and in certain sections of the working class in Bombay.

Maharashtra: A state of over 50 million people in western India.

Mahar: The largest (perhaps 10 to 12% of the total population) untouchable caste in Maharashtra and the most militant; now mainly converted to Buddhism and so known also as Buddhists or Neo-Buddhists.

mahila: Middle class term for 'women'.

mangalsutra: The traditional gold wedding necklace worn by Maharashtrian women after marriage.

Manu: The mythical Hindu lawgiver (the term means 'man') who propagated the hierarchy of castes and the subordination of women; according to Manu a woman was supposed to be under the control of her father when a child, of her husband when adult, and of her son when old.

Maratha: The largest caste in Maharashtra (about 30%), mainly peasants but including also traditional landlords and rulers. Their lower sections are called Kunbis. The Marathas were traditionally classed as *shudras* though the aristocratic families claimed *ksatriya* status.

Marathi: The language spoken in Maharashtra, Indo-European and derived from Sanskrit.

Marwari: The wealthiest merchant caste of India, originating in the north but now spread all over the country and controlling about one-third of the big business houses.

Matang: The second largest untouchable caste in Maharashtra.

mul: 'Child'; *mul ani cul* or 'child and hearth' symbolized the traditional place and duty of women.

Naxalite: Term applied to the pro-China revolutionary communists who reject the parliamentarism of the established parties and emphasize underground work and armed struggle. They take their name from Naxalbari region in northern Bengal where there was a peasant revolt in 1967; many but not all joined the CPI(ML) in 1969. The term is also used more loosely for all Marxists to the left of the established parliamentary parties.

PDSU: Progressive Democratic Students' Union, a student organization formed in Hyderabad in 1971 by activists loyal to one of the Naxalite groups.

POW: Progressive Organization of Women, formed in 1974 by women students in Hyderabad who had been connected to the PDSU.

Rashtra Seva Dal: 'National Service League', a nationalist volunteer organization led by Socialists within the Congress party from the 1930s.

Republican Party: Political party formed by followers of the Dalit leader Dr B. R. Ambedkar in 1956; with aspirations to be a general radical-democratic, socialist party but limited mainly to Dalits, especially the Mahars of Maharashtra.

samajwadi: Marathi word for 'socialist'.

Samajwadi Mahila Sabha: 'Socialist Women's Group', the women's organization of the Socialist Party.

Samajwadi Mahila Sanghatana: 'Socialist Women's Organization', formed in 1977 by independent young Marxists in Bombay.

Sarvodaya: Organization for the uplift of the poor founded by followers of Gandhi, based on principles of nonviolence, constructive work and harmony between classes and castes.

sati: Traditional Hindu custom of women burning themselves to death on their husbands' funeral pyre; practised usually only by the high castes.

shramik: 'Toiler' or 'labourer', used for all who do manual work as contrasted to *kamgar* or 'industrial worker'.

Shramik Mahila Sabha: 'Toiling Women's Group', women's organization of the CPI in Maharashtra. Their All-India organization is the National Federation of Indian Women.

Shramik Mahila Sangh: 'Toiling Women's Organization', CPI(M) women's organization in Maharashtra.

Shramik Sanghatana: 'Toiler's Union', organization of landless labourers and poor peasants in Dhule district; most members are Bhils.

shudra: Lowest of the four *varnas*, traditionally thought to be toilers and servants of the higher *varnas*.

Sita and Savriti: Mythological Hindu heroines symbolizing the devotion of women to their husbands.

Socialist Party: The main party of Indian Socialists, who have now with few exceptions joined the Janata Party. Socialists distinguish themselves from Communists by a belief in parliamentarism, a rejection of the 'dictatorship of the proletariat' and a large admixture of Gandhism in their ideology.

stri: Upper class word for 'woman'.

stri-mukti: 'Women's liberation'.

Stri-Mukti Sanghatana: 'Women's Liberation Organization', formed in 1978 by young left women in Bombay.

Teli: A caste in Maharashtra, traditionally oil-pressers.

untouchable: Term for the lowest castes or *jatis* who traditionally lived outside the villages and performed the most polluting tasks of the society (working with leather or cleaning away dirt and manure) as well as basic manual labour in the fields and for feudal overlords. They are called 'Scheduled Castes' in official documents, but often now prefer the term Dalit for themselves.

varna: One of the four *varnas* or caste categories in the Hindu ideological system, ranked in the order of *brahmans* or priests and intellectuals, *ksatriyas* or warriors, *vasiyas* or merchants and *shudras* or manual workers. Untouchables are considered outside of and lower than all four. The existing castes, of which there are thousands (all with vague and shifting social 'boundaries') try to fit themselves within this ideological system, if they do not reject it altogether, but claiming as high a *varna* status as possible.

wada: Special section of a village, e.g. Maharwada, Mangwada.

Wadars: A low caste whose traditional duty was stonebreaking and other heavy labour.

Bibliographical Notes

There is a large and growing volume of literature on women in India, but very little of it deals with the lives of lower class women and their experiences and perceptions. The most comprehensive report on women as a whole is still that of the Status of Women Committee, *Towards Equality* (New Delhi: Government of India, 1974). Another useful and inexpensive collection is the special issue on women of *Social Scientist,* November-December, 1975, available for Rs 10 from the Indian School of Social Sciences, Trivandrum, India. Karen Leonard, 'Women and Social Change in Modern India', *Feminist Studies* 3 (Spring-Summer 1976) is a useful survey; Padmini Sengupta, *Women Workers of India* (New York: Asia Publishing House, 1970), is an early study republished; and Harshad R. Trivedi, *Schedule Caste Women: Studies in Exploitation* (Delhi: Concept Publishing Company, 1976) gives material, though in a somewhat confused presentation, on both the Uttarkashi prostitution mentioned in Chapter 1 and the Devadasis mentioned in Chapter 12, as well as some general discussion of Dalit women. The special issue on Women in Asia of the *Bulletin of Concerned Asian Scholars* (now unfortunately out of print) Vol. 6 (Spring, 1974) contains translations of songs and three articles on India — Maria Mies, 'Indian Women and Leadership' dealing with the Dhule movement and women; Gail Omvedt, 'Class, Caste and Women's Liberation', an early survey statement of mine; and Susan Mody and Sharayu Mhatre, 'Slum Women of Bombay', a sensitively presented depiction of the fate of three very different low class women. Other articles of mine are 'Women and Rural Revolt in India', *Journal of Peasant Studies,* Vol. 5, No. 3, April 1978, and 'On the Participant Study of Women's Movements' in Gerrit Huizer, (ed.), *The Politics of Anthropology* (The Hague: Mouton, 1979).

Beyond this, the journal, *Economic and Political Weekly* (published from Skylark Building, 284 Frere Road, Bombay) provides a remarkable range of academic and journalistic discussion on every issue from a general left perspective, and if a reader wants to get beyond the Western-biased academic material and into some of the best Indian thinking on the subject of women (or other issues) perhaps the best way is to delve through its pages for articles and debates on women agricultural labourers, the women's movement, women workers, book reviews and general background material.

Information is also available from some of the new women's groups and journals. *Manushi,* a bimonthly published in English or Hindi, is available from Madhu Kishwar, A-5, Nizamuddin East, New Delhi; subscription rates including airmail postage are (as of mid 1979), for individuals $11/£6.40 and, for institutions, $14/£8.20. *Feminist Network* comes out as an occasional newsletter and also makes available a collection of mimeographed articles on women; no foreign subscription price is cited but donations are welcome and necessary. Its address is Gayatri Singh, c/o Shukla, Bhavna Apartments (1st Floor), S. V. Road, Ville Parle (West), Bombay 400 056. Ongoing Indian research on women motivated at least to some degree by a Marxist and/or feminist perspective is being carried on under the auspices of the Indian Council of Social Science Research (write to Veena Mazumdar, Indraprastha Estate, IIPA Hostel, New Delhi 1); the National Institute for Bank Management (Govind Kelkar, 85, Nepean Sea Road, Bombay 400 006); the SNDT Women's University (Neera Desai, Bombay); and the Shankar Brahme Research Institute (Sulabha Brahme, 1259/2 J. M. Road, Pune 411 004). Those interested can write for information.

On Dalits, mentioned in many chapters of this book, Dilip Hiro, *'The Untouchables of India,* Minority Rights Group Report No. 26 gives a brief but useful survey, and J. Michael Mahar, (ed), *The Untouchables in Contemporary India* (Tucson, Arizona: University of Arizona Press, 1972), is a good but somewhat outdated collection. Eleanor Zelliot's article, 'Gandhi and Ambedkar', in the latter book contains a brief survey of the work of the most famous Dalit leader of India and the hero to most of those whom I encountered. A collection of Dalit poetry in translation is available in *Bulletin of Concerned Asian Scholars,* Vol. 10, No. 3 (1978), and by far the most comprehensive set of articles on the whole caste-class issue is to be found in the 1979 Special Number of *Economic and Political Weekly,* including contributions by some of India's leading Communists. For the Dalit point of view itself, readers should go to Ambedkar's own writings, particularly *What Congress and Gandhi Have Done to the Untouchables, Annihilation of Caste, Emancipation of the Untouchables, States and Minorities,* and *The Rise and Fall of Hindu Women.*

On the Naxalite Movement, the best academic discussion is probably Manoranjan Mohanty, *Revolutionary Violence: A Study of the Maoist Movement in India* (Delhi: Sterling Publications, 1977), but readers should also go the documents of and on the movement published in *Naxalbari and After: A Frontier Anthology,* 2 volumes (Calcutta: Kathashilpa, 1978) and for the peasant revolt in Naxalbari itself (with material on the role of women), to Partha Mukherji, 'Naxalbari Movement and the Peasant Revolt in North Bengal' in M. S. A. Rao, (ed.), *Social Movements in India,* Volume 1 (New Delhi: Manohar, 1978). Needless to say all of this material remains controversial, as do all the books on the Indian communist movement generally.

On *adivasis* there is a fascinating interpretation of the role of tribals in regard to Indian culture as a whole in F. G. Lannoy, *The Speaking Tree* (Oxford University Press, 1975). The biggest tribal groups within India are the related Santals, Mundas and Hos living in the area now known as Jharkhand. W. G. Archer, *The Hill of Flutes* (Pittsburgh University Press, 1974) gives a good deal of material on Santal culture particularly with reference to love and marriage customs. Martin Orans, *The Santals* (Detroit: Michigan State University Press, 1960) is a standard anthropological interpretation. And there is various material on the Jharkhand movement itself in the *Economic and Political Weekly*. Neville Maxwell, *India and the Nagas*, Minority Rights Group Report No. 17, is one study of the turbulent revolts in the northeast. For Maharashtra itself, Godutai Parulekar, *Adivasis in Revolt* (details not available at time of going to press) describes an early communist-led movement, and Maria Mies, 'A Peasant Movement in Maharashtra', *Journal of Peasant Studies* (1975) is a study of the Shramik Sanghatana of Dhule.

On the general political economy of India there are numerous Marxist interpretations, including the useful collection of articles in Kathleen Gough and Hari Sharma, *Imperialism and Revolution in South Asia* (New York: Monthly Review Press, 1974); Dilip Hiro, *Inside India Today* (London: Routledge and Kegan Paul, 1976) and David Selbourne, *An Eye to India* (London: Penguin, 1977) which focuses on the Emergency. For those who are interested in the theoretical framework behind my interpretation in Chapter 11, see Gail Omvedt and Bharat Patankar, 'The Bourgeois State in Post-Colonial Social Formations', *Economic and Political Weekly*, 31 December 1977.

Specific chapter references are as follows:

Introduction: The quotation is from David Mandelbaum, *Society in India, Volume I: Continuity and Change* (Berkeley: University of California Press, 1970), p. 82.

Chapter 1: The discussion with Kaminibai is taken from an interview taped on 15 February 1975 and is published in a different form as 'The Downtrodden Among the Downtrodden: An Interview with a Dalit Agricultural Labourer' in *Signs* Vol. 4, No. 4 (Summer 1979). Mary Tyler's stories of Bihar Women are told in *My Years in an Indian Prison* (London: Penguin Books, 1978). The Uttarkashi story is given by Trivedi as mentioned above. The Kilvenmani (Thanjavur) story is told by Mythily Shivaraman in Kathleen Gough and Hari Sharma, (ed.), *Imperialism and Revolution in South Asia* (New York: Monthly Review Press, 1974) and Kathleen's own article in the book deals with the social background of the affair in that district; her 'Green Revolution in South India and North Vietnam' in *Bulletin of Concerned Asian Scholars*, Vol. 10, No. 1 (1978), brings the Thanjavur story up to date a bit.

Chapter 2: The discussion with the Pune municipal workers was on January 19, 1975, and was written up by Leela Bhosle in the union paper, *Mazdur Morcha*, March-April 1975. Tarabai's account of her life is from an interview taped on 10 April, 1975.

Chapter 3: The Bimzani College discussion on 11 February 1975, was taped, and the discussion with Milind students on 18 April 1975 is from my notes.

Chapter 4: The discussions with Leela took place over several months. Her account of her childhood was taped for German radio in February, 1976. Rukmini's discussion of the POW in January 1975 is from my notes.

Chapter 5: Interviews at Rahuri, Mula Dam and Mula Canal were taped on 7 and 8 April 1975.

Chapter 6: The discussion at Kathod Farm was taped on 9 April 1975.

Chapter 7: The discussions with Ahilya Rangnekar and Mrinal Gore were on 9 January and 5 February 1975 and are from my notes. The quotation at the end of the chapter is from Sharayu Mhatre and Susan Mody, 'Slum Women of Bombay', cited above.

Chapter 8: See the articles on *adivasis* cited above.

Chapter 9: The tape of the study camp at Nandurkheda was made on 9 May, 1975.

Chapter 10: The book referred to is *Days and Nights in Calcutta.* Written by an author called Mukherjee, it gives a vivid description of upper class life in Calcutta and Bombay, including the state of nervous tension among the elite at the time.

Chapter 11: Quotations cited are from the *Vogue* interview, published in the January, 1977 issue; Henry Hart, 'Indira Gandhi: Determined not to be Hurt', in Hart, ed. *Indira Gandhi's India* (Colorado: Westview Press, 1976). Oriana Fallaci, 'Indira's Coup', in *New York Review of Books,* 18 September 1975; and Kuldip Nayar, *India: The Critical Years* (Delhi: Vikas, 1974). None of this journalism needs to be taken too seriously, but it often makes fascinating reading.